Forging the American Character

Readings in United States History to 1877

Volume I

Second Edition

John R. M. Wilson, Editor

Southern California College

Prentice Hall, Upper Saddle River, New Jersey 07458

Library of Congress Cataloging-in-Publication Data

Forging the American character / John R. M. Wilson, editor — 2nd ed.
   p. cm.
   Contents: v. 1. Readings in United States History to 1877 —
  ISBN 0-13-576653-2
   1. United States—Civilization. I. Wilson, John R. M.
  E169.1.F745 1997
  973—dc20   96-23386
                                        CIP

Acquisitions editor: *Sally Constable*
Production editor: *Jean Lapidus*
Copy editor: *Maria Caruso*
Manufacturing buyer: *Lynn Pearlman*
Cover design: *Bruce Kenselaar*

This book was set in 10.5/12.5 Palatino by The Composing Room of Michigan, Inc.
and was printed and bound by Courier Companies, Inc.
The cover was printed by Phoenix Color Corp.

© 1997, 1991, by Prentice-Hall, Inc.
Simon & Schuster/A Viacom Company
Upper Saddle River, New Jersey 07458

Printed in the United States of America
10 9 8 7 6 5 4 3 2 1

ISBN 0-13-576653-2

PRENTICE-HALL INTERNATIONAL (UK) LIMITED, *LONDON*
PRENTICE-HALL OF AUSTRALIA PTY. LIMITED, *SYDNEY*
PRENTICE-HALL CANADA, INC., *TORONTO*
PRENTICE-HALL HISPANOAMERICANA, S.A., *MEXICO*
PRENTICE-HALL OF INDIA PRIVATE LIMITED, *NEW DELHI*
PRENTICE-HALL OF JAPAN, INC., *TOKYO*
SIMON & SCHUSTER ASIA PTE. LTD., *SINGAPORE*
EDITORA PRENTICE-HALL DO BRASIL, LTDA., *RIO DE JANEIRO*

Contents

Preface

A long United States history textbook may run to 1,000 pages. Although that length may seem intimidating to students, it does not allow extended treatment of a wide variety of fascinating topics. A book of readings does. The theme of this reader is the American character. I trust that the concept will illuminate American history without being overly restrictive.

A reader like this enables students to explore subjects ranging from the moral aspects of the American "invasion" of 1492 to the debate over multiculturalism in the 1990s, from the horrors of life and death in the Civil War to the national obsession with the Kennedy assassination. The nature of the selections varies. Some offer new interpretations of the past; others introduce readers to new findings; while still others synthesize the writings in a historical subfield. The readings do not pretend to cover every possible topic; rather, they explore various areas that shed light on the American character yet suffer comparative neglect in many textbooks.

Trying to define the American character can be very frustrating. No one has been able to develop a widely accepted definition of the concept. Authors often use different meanings in the same piece of writing—for instance, referring interchangeably to the character of the individual American and to the character of the mass of Americans. National character, especially in a country as big and heterogeneous as the United States, can be useful only as a large-scale generalization to cover the most prominent characteristics of the national culture. Some scholars have criticized efforts to capture the national character, suggesting that in many cases they may be merely intellectually sophisticated forms of racial stereotyping.

Yet the practice persists, perhaps because it is so convenient to group people and thus make them more manageable. Perhaps the most useful definition would be that national character means generalizations about a nation or nationality developed to elucidate the ways in which it is distinctive.

A national character suggests tendencies on the part of a people, not fixed positions held by everyone. It means that, all things being equal, the people of a given nation are more likely to believe or behave a certain way than those of another nation. There is an inherent comparison implied in suggesting a national character, although studies of the American character generally tend not to explicitly explore other nationalities.

The genre began very early in the history of the United States with the publication in 1782 of J. Hector St. John de Crévecoeur's *Letters from an American Farmer;* the immigrant asked the famous question, "What then is this American, this new man?" Crévecoeur's pioneering inquiry into the American character ran up against geographical and cultural heterogeneity, which has become a vastly greater obstacle in the succeeding two centuries. The most famous inquiry came in the 1830s when Alexis de Tocqueville wrote *Democracy in America* and provided penetrating French insight into the nature of the conforming, religious, liberty-loving joiners he observed. Over the years, historians and other social observers have sought to explain American distinctiveness through such characteristics as abundance, exposure to the frontier, pragmatism, belief in progress, and mobility. They have debated the relative influence of mother England and the wilderness, and in so doing have illuminated American self-understanding—without providing any final answers. The quest continues, as the popularity of *Habits of the Heart* (1985) attests.

This collection suggests that Americans have defined themselves not only by what they are, but by what they are not, and the latter negative definition is an important component of Americanism. By and large, Native Americans have not been allowed to share their heritage with Europeans. For other nationalities, conformity to the English cultural model was long required for acceptance in the United States, although a more pluralistic, open society seems to be emerging in the late twentieth century. Yet over the past half century, the increasingly diverse American population has frequently defined itself less by what it is than by what it is not—as antifascist and, especially, anticommunist.

This book should help to clarify some of the various forces, ideologies, people, and experiences that have helped forge today's distinctive American character. If, as Socrates said, the unexamined life is not worth living, then this excursion into the life of a people should help make it more worth living.

In closing, I'd like to thank the reviewers of my book, John Powell, Pennsylvania State University at Erie, and Anthony N. Stranges, Texas A&M University.

John R. M. Wilson
Costa Mesa, California

1

The Moral Dimensions of 1492[*]

James Axtell

The five hundredth anniversary of Columbus's discovery of America stimulated a large outpouring of writing on the meaning of the cultural clash that ensued. The idea that someone could "discover" and self-righteously stake claims to a land where as many as a hundred million people lived seemed terribly Eurocentric. More critically, whatever the population when Columbus arrived, within a couple of generations much of it had been almost entirely wiped out. The advanced Aztec and Inca empires had been looted and destroyed and the Spanish had established a new colonial empire in their place.

The "European invasion" combined disease (especially smallpox, measles, and influenza), brought into the new continent unknowingly by somewhat immune Europeans, and brutal slaughter and subjugation, deliberately imposed on the Indians. The impact of both deliberate and inadvertent factors was devastation. The combination of a sense of divine mission with a hunger for land and riches that had inspired the Spanish led Americans in later centuries to mistreat Indians, slaves, Mexicans, Filipinos, and whoever else got in the way of the "manifest destiny" of the United States to expand.

Defenders of the quincentennial celebration pointed out that

*Reprinted from the Autumn 1993 issue of *The Historian,* journal of Phi Alpha Theta, the international history honor society, by permission.

peoples, including Indians, had been conquering their neighbors since the beginning of history. The invasion of America was hardly on a different moral plane than those of the Mongols or the Arabs or Romans, or even of the Inca or Aztecs. Further, it is difficult to blame Europeans for spreading diseases that they didn't understand themselves.

James Axtell, Kenan Professor of Humanities at the College of William and Mary, chaired the American Historical Association's Columbus Quincentenary Committee. His own reflections, some of which are summarized in this article, are explored at length in his 1992 book *Beyond 1492: Encounters in Colonial North America*. In short, he calls upon students of history to exercise care in making sweeping judgments about the past. Though they are emotionally satisfying, they do not advance the cause of truth unless handled very carefully. His cautionary voice merits serious consideration.

The chair of the American Historical Association's Columbus Quincentenary Committee tried to keep track of all the Columbian and encounter scholarship that has been pouring forth since 1986. This material included a large number of articles, newsletters, and manifestoes by Native Americans and by people and groups—usually on the political left—who wished to protest or forestall the celebratory nature of the quincentenary.

Many scholars who have endeavored to put native peoples on America's historical map and to get them a fair hearing at the bar of both justice and history have been struck by the frequency of the use of the word "genocide" to characterize European treatment of the natives in the colonial period. In the counter-Columbus, counter-celebratory literature, genocide has become the dominant abbreviation or code word to describe Columbus and his successors' relations with the Indians.

For example, an ad hoc group of "progressive" educators, ecologists, and community activists who formed "The Columbus in Context Clearinghouse," proposed to "celebrate the resistance of Native Americans to 500 years of genocide."

Jan Elliott, the editor of *Indigenous Thought,* a Florida-based anti-Columbus newspaper, described the loss of American Indian life as "the biggest holocaust in history" and called Columbus a "mass murderer." Elliott wrote in the first issue that "Celebrating Columbus's 'discovery' of America is analogous to celebrating Hitler's holocaust." Indian activist Russell Means further raised the moral ante. When he protested an exhibition on Spanish-Indian encounters at the Florida State Museum, he told the press that "Columbus makes Hitler look like a juvenile delinquent." The governing board of the National Council of Churches of Christ declared that after Columbus, America was the scene of "invasion, genocide, slavery, 'ecocide,'" and the "rape of mineral as well as natural resources." Genocide appeared nine times in their five-page statement.

How should historians, teachers, and students of history respond to this characterization? We should ask five rather standard questions about it: How is genocide defined by its users? What historical evidence do they adduce to support their indictment? What counterfactual evidence have they explored? In their indictment, who, *specifically*, is judged guilty? Why is the word so widely used?

First, in the protest literature, "genocide" is never defined, perhaps on the assumption that we all know what it means. But do we? The word was coined in 1944 to describe the infamous Nazi attempts to annihilate the Jews, a group they chose to characterize as a biological subspecies or race. Webster's definition of genocide is not much help: the use "of deliberate, systematic measures toward the extermination of a racial, political, or cultural group." One of the best and most comprehensive definitions in the large literature of genocide is that of Frank Chalk and Kurt Jonassohn: "Genocide is a form of one-sided *mass* killing in which a *state* or other authority *intends* to destroy a group, as that group and membership in it are defined by the *perpetrator*." Such a definition excludes from consideration victims—civilian or military—of two-sided war, of any natural or unintended disaster, and of any individuals or "loose cannons" acting outside the orders of the state or political authority. The last are, more precisely, homicidal maniacs or mass murderers who massacre innocent people.

The examples most frequently adduced to support the charge of genocide are the Spaniards' wanton killing of Taínos in the gold-bearing interior of Hispaniola during Columbus's inept governorship in 1494–95, the high body counts of Indian warriors during the conquests of Peru and Mexico, and the precipitous decline of native populations in subsequent decades. These examples do not amount to relevant or unambiguous evidence of genocide. The conquest phases of the various European invasions of the Americas were dedicated to the achievement of military, political, economic, and religious hegemony over the native peoples, not their mass destruction, and they were aimed at temporary and numerically superior political and military opponents. In Central and South America, resistant native armies were targeted for defeat or destruction, but native populations per se were largely protected by Spanish law and colonial self-interest so as later to provide labor or tribute to the *encomenderos*. Crown officials were entrusted with their spiritual and, to some extent, physical well-being. In North America, native populations were equally vital to the military and economic needs of the European colonies, as allies against colonial rivals, as fur trappers and hunters, and as food producers.

The evidence for genocide from Indian population decline is ambiguous because newly imported epidemic diseases killed the vast majority of Native Americans after contact. Gross demographical statistics—conjured from fragmentary figures and social-scientific assumptions and often inflated for moral or political reasons rather than historical necessity—are impossible to interpret clearly because they include the victims of intertribal warfare, migration and dislocation, and uncontrollable natural disasters, as well as overwork and other forms of colonial oppression.

Even enslavement and forced relocation of the natives of the Bahamas and other Caribbean islands do not constitute genocide because the intent of the Spanish slavers was not to annihilate the natives physically; on the contrary, it was to ensure their physical viability so they could provide free labor wherever they were needed by colonial entrepreneurs. There is no need to resort willy-nilly to inflated indictments of genocide when man-stealing, kidnapping, enslavement, and other accurate terms are available. If genocide is to retain any meaning or moral impact at all, it must not be applied wholesale to every Indian death in the colonial period. To do so is to dilute the meaning of the word to insipidity and to squander its intellectual and moral force.

This is not to say that bona fide cases of genocide cannot be found in colonial America. Although no European colonial government ever tried to exterminate all of the Indians as a race, there are at least five authorized colonial attempts to annihilate single tribes—men, women, and children. The Puritans of Massachusetts and Connecticut tried unsuccessfully to obliterate the Pequots of Connecticut in 1636–37. The French, who in Canada come off smelling like a moral rose in the textbooks, had better success in exterminating the Mississippi River Natchez and the Wisconsin Foxes in the 1730s. The English assaults on the Powhatan chiefdom in Virginia might be included, but these took place only after the sudden native uprising of 1622, which then gave the outnumbered settlers reason to believe they were repulsing a military attack and acting in justifiable self-defense.

Perhaps the most heinous act of genocide—from the vantage point of the "Age of AIDS"—was the calculated use of germ warfare, which was not resorted to, we should emphasize, for more than two-and-a-half centuries after Columbus's landing and then by only one European power that we know of. In 1752 the acting governor of Canada told his French superior in Paris that "twere desirable that [smallpox] should break out and spread, generally, through the localities inhabited by our rebels." By this he meant the Ohio Valley and Great Lakes tribesmen who were asserting their independence or switching their allegiance to the English. "It would be fully as good as an army," he concluded, with callous disregard for native women and children.

The French governor was only indulging in wishful thinking. The English commander for the same area put the thought into action eleven years later, during Pontiac's (so-called) Rebellion. In June 1763 Sir Jeffrey Amherst conspired with his field commander, Colonel Henry Bouquet, to send two blankets and two handkerchiefs from a smallpox hospital among the "rebellious" Delawares, Shawnees, and Ohio Senecas. By the following autumn it was reported that "The poor Rascals are Dieing very fast with the small pox; they can make but Lettle Resistance and when Routed from their settlements must parish in great Numbers by the Disorders."

Have the protestors explored any evidence that would undermine their ascription of widespread colonial genocide? They have not, except for disease. Yet, Jan Elliott's reaction to the disease panel of the Florida State Museum's exhibit may be typical. She accused exhibit designers of cowardly apologetics and trying to slip off the skewer of moral responsibility. One purpose of their carefully worded labels, she said, was to "deflect the focus from murder and genocide and the reparations which these acts would demand to disease as an unintended consequence." Another purpose was to deflect attention "away from the social problems that . . . Indian peoples face today by emphasizing that most . . . Indians died out by the 1600s."

In addition to minimizing the lethal legacy of disease and ignoring the Spanish *hidalgos'* self-interest in preserving the lives and labor of their Indian subjects, the protestors fail to understand that some native populations actually managed to reproduce themselves and even to grow modestly once the initial onslaught of epidemics had passed and the survivors acquired lifesaving immunities. The protestors have also failed to realize that native populations were partially lost through nonmortal miscegenation with black Africans and white Europeans. Nor have they recognized the irony of yelling genocide in a national theater that seats almost two million self-declared Indians, nearly as many as watched the opening scenes of the Columbian Encounter in 1492.

Granting that at least some Indian groups were the victims of colonial genocide, who is, or was, to blame specifically? The protestors blackwash with a broad brush. Sometimes Columbus is the archfiend. At other times, conquistadors, the Spanish, Europeans, white males, capitalists, and Christians, as well as a generalized, modern "we" are condemned to share the admiral's guilt. Such charges are neither responsible history nor acceptable morality. The major problem with genocide as a description of, or even analogy to, the post-Columbian loss of life is that the moral onus it tries to place on the European colonists—equating them with Heinrich Himmler and the Nazi S.S.—is misdirected and inappropriate. As Edmund Burke warned in the late eighteenth century and as we have come to realize in the twentieth, "you cannot"—or rather, *should* not—"indict a whole nation" for the misdeeds and crimes of a few. The colonists were personally and directly guilty for only a small fraction of the Indians who died in the three centuries after contact. Disease, not the Spanish, was responsible for most of the native deaths in Latin America. Genocide, as distinguished from other forms of cruelty, oppression, and death, played a very small role in the European conquest of the New World.

Why do protestors use genocide so frequently? Most of the time they offer no clue. But Jan Elliott, the Cherokee director of *Indigenous Thought*, shed some light on her motives when she spoke of the "reparations" which the "murder and genocide" of Indian people in the past "would demand" if the truth were known and acknowledged. We may also assume another motive on the part of native protestors: moral leverage in current fights for justice and equity. Making a white judge, juror, or congressman feel guilty for the genocidal behavior of his racial or national ancestors may lead to better results in the political or judicial process today or tomorrow.

Who can blame them for resorting to such tactics, given the odds they face? Yet we must distinguish between history as a truth-seeking discipline and the selective use of historical truths or half-truths for unapologetically political ends. When political maneuvers are passed off as historical truth, historians have an obligation to subject their claims to careful scrutiny. Otherwise, we risk turning our profession into an agency for the dissemination of propaganda, which can easily turn against us with the slightest shift of ideological winds.

What should the historian's response be to those, especially native people, who use genocide freely to characterize the 500-year Columbian Encounter? First, we should acknowledge the legitimate emotional source of their need to use genocide to describe what happened to their ancestors as recently as our own century. Genocide—as a shorthand for a long legacy of injustice, pain, and loss—feels right to the survivors and descendants, many of whom experience on a daily basis what they regard as distressingly similar assaults on their lives, dignity, and livelihood. Yet, after fully acknowledging the emotional justice of the natives' cause, historians should limit the use of the word to historically verifiable occurrences, rather than encouraging an indiscriminate scattershot assault on the past. We owe all the people of the past equal and impartial understanding, not just its victims or the fashionable favorites of the media and textbook publishers. At the end of the twentieth century, we should feel an obligation to protect the innocent of whatever era, group, or action from injustice and defamation.

Second, historians should also counsel against the use of any kind of moral blackmail and resist any collective guilt-trips. Blackmail is always blackmail, whether it be emotional or intellectual, and is always illegitimate. Furthermore, if important and even long-overdue gains can be made through the use of moral blackmail, those same gains can be retracted when susceptible hearts and soft heads turn hard in new ideological climates. Social and moral gains are much more secure when they are the products of good history, free conscience, and consistent, durable principles of justice.

Having addressed the issue of genocide and one moral extreme of the quincentenary, historians should not pat themselves on the back for their moral moderation and professional probity. Such congratulations would be premature and perhaps hypocritical because we have jumped to judgment—a few to the right but most to the left—like lemmings, without much study or benefit of forethought. Like our predecessors, we have found it easier to judge than to understand. We have conveniently forgotten that understanding in some depth usually undermines the seemingly firm ground of rectitude, often obviates the need for judgment, and sometimes even leads to forgiveness, that most unfashionable virtue. Our all-too-human propensity to jump on moral bandwagons and to make snap judgments about human behavior in other times and places cause a lot of mischief in our classrooms and publications because we commit too many elementary sins against straight moral thinking.

We hang simplistic, abstract labels when we should unpack and examine fully the complexity of past events, social conditions, and human motivations. To declare the Columbian legacy as nothing more than "Imperialism & Colonialism, Racism and Oppression," as the New York "progressives" have done ins capital letters, is to close discussion, not to open it. Labeling is a form of name-calling, with few benefits, even if it fulfills some atavistic need for visceral vocalization. It does no justice to the object of reproach and leads to no reforms.

Another mistake we make is stereotyping people on the basis of one or a few characteristics (usually the only ones we have bothered to learn about), when we should search for their full and individual humanity, withholding judgment until we know much more about them. We are experts at lumping people into racial, national, political, and other cultural categories, particularly people with whom we have no personal acquaintance. We should work much harder at splitting the human race into its individual components, and at recognizing many more human faces in our mental crowds, just as we would like to be recognized by others.

We are also impeded in our moral thinking by our sloppy handling of moral vocabulary, which is nearly as large as the language itself and for the most part unspecialized. Most of the words we use in history and everyday speech are like mental depth charges. When heard or read, these words quickly sink into our consciousness and explode, sending off cognitive shrapnel in all directions. On the surface they may look harmless or benign, but as they descend and detonate, their resonant power is unleashed, showering our understanding with fragments of accumulated meaning and association. Therefore we should use words—not just the moral-sounding ones, but all of them—with extreme care because they are powerful instruments of judgment and can maim heedless handlers. Those who brandish genocide at every opportunity are particularly prone to accidents, but so are the careless wielders of other sharp words.

None of these criticisms should be construed as an argument against the legitimacy and utility of judging the past. Historians do it all the time, we are incapable of not doing it, and we should do it. But we should do it well and we should do it for valid reasons, not because our knees or trigger fingers twitch every time we open a history book.

We judge the past for at least three important reasons. The first is to appraise action, an intrinsic part of historical thinking. Not to make such judgments is to abandon the past to itself, rendering it unintelligible and untranslatable to the present. The second reason is to do justice to it, although making judgment is not the same as passing sentence. As historians, we are too involved in both the prosecution and the defense since the words and reputations of the dead on all sides are in our hands. History's goal is not to punish or rehabilitate historical malefactors, who are morally incorrigible in any event, but to set the record straight for future appeals to precedent. The third reason for judging the past is to advance our own moral education, to learn from and, in effect, to be judged by the past. Since we think and speak historically for our own generation, we can have judgmental effect only on ourselves. Consequently, history becomes, in Lord Bolingbroke's famous phrase, "philosophy teaching by example," a "preceptor of prudence, not of principles." After bearing witness to the past with all the disinterestedness and human empathy we can muster, we should let ourselves be judged by the past as much as, or more than, we judge it. The past is filled with the lives and struggles of countless "others," from whom we may learn to extend the possibilities of our own limited humanity. As we learn about what it is like to be other than ourselves, we are better able to do justice to the past.

The relationship between the past and the present is always troubled and troubling. Historians cannot help but draw on the past for materials, methods, and models. Our self-images and social foundations are fabricated from historical elements, all inherited but reshaped by our current needs and biases, and then rewoven by our flawed and fluid memories. We need the past to give us bearings, but we often construct pasts that are merely useful and undemanding, more wishful than true. This leads to serious problems for historians because we cannot cure inherited social ills or make moral amends for past wrongs unless we know how the past actually was. It is perhaps the profession's most important task to ensure that our image of the past is as nearly full, complex, and true as the past itself was, lest we lose our bearings in fantasy and waste our resources and moral energies on false trails.

What responsibility should the present feel toward the past? Are we, the living, obliged to redress the mistakes, injustices, and crimes of the past? If we are so obliged, how should we go about it? Who should be the beneficiaries? If we discover through the assiduous study of the past that our ancestors did wrong to people in the past and that we have benefitted—directly or indirectly—from those transgressions, what should our personal and collective response be? What is the range of alternatives?

The first and perhaps toughest questions to be answered revolve around identity: who are we who feel morally responsible? How closely related—biologically or socially or politically—are we to our perpetrating ancestors? Who were the victims? To whom should redress be made? It makes some difference whether the present we and the past ancestors consist of a national, ethnic, racial, religious, or gender group, and how great the temporal and lineal distance is between "them" and "us." Before moral responsibility can be fairly laid, it is also important to determine what proportions of the offenders were directly and indirectly responsible for the acknowledged misdeeds, and what proportions of the victims directly and indirectly suffered them. We must know the latter to be able to designate the beneficiaries of our tardy justice once we have decided what form it will take.

There are essentially three types of moral responsibility assigned by historical critics of the quincentenary. The first attributes past social wrongs to systemic rather than personal or even collective agents. Adherents of various forms of Marxism and other universalizing ideologies tend to blame history's ills and crimes on large, reified abstractions such as Western civilization, imperialism, racism, capitalism, or "phallocentrism." Systems and historical processes present easy targets for blame, but they are virtually impossible to apprehend and bring to trial; they are notoriously immune to short-term reform, particularly when the prosecutors are largely their heirs and social products. Systemic indictments seem to work much better for political ideologues and activists than for moral reformers since they allow the former to assert their moral superiority and political rightmindedness without actually doing anything to change what was or is wrong, much less to redress the historical grievances of the wronged.

The second type of moral responsibility is attributed to groups, although not all groups are equally good candidates. How can any groups other than nation-states effectively redress past injustices in material ways? It is hard to imagine, for example, all men compensating women for millennia of lower status and pay, or Christians for past spates of antisemitism other than by regretting the past, acknowledging their complicity in it, and promising full and quick reform. One hundred thirty years after the Emancipation Proclamation, it is difficult to see how even the descendants of slaveholders, if they were moved and able, could materially indemnify the scattered descendants of their ancestors' black slaves.

The national government can do something for the victims of legal injustice who are still living or their descendants, provided those victims were treated unjustly according to laws under which we still live. The Japanese-Americans whose civil and property rights were violated during World War II have received reparations, however tardily and inadequately, from Congress. Many Indian peoples whose ancestors lived in what became the United States have obtained retrospective justice, monetary awards, and even the return of land through the Indian Claims Commission, the federal courts, and the provisions of the Trade and Intercourse Act of 1790, which prohibited any sales of Indian land without federal authorization. Certain standards of evidence must be met by tribes wishing to prove lineal descent from the victims, the tribal ownership of the land in question, and the economic value of the land at the time of loss, but these have proven superable in nearly 300 cases in which native groups received belated justice.

But what about American Indians who were wronged between 1492 and 1790? Should Queen Elizabeth II and the British Parliament own up to and pay reparations for lands taken, traders cheated, murders unpunished, and religions subverted under the British colonial regime? Or were the innocent Indians simply taken advantage of by disingenuous sharpers from the sophisticated Old World? Are their losses cause for reparation or simply a regrettable object lesson for the future? Might we not legitimately feel just as sorry for the other victims of British colonialism? Why do we select for belated justice groups that were mistreated only after 1492 and in the Americas? As denizens of the all-encompassing world made possible by Columbus, should we not extend our moral sympathy and indignation to the victims—black, brown, or white—of the Aztecs, Incas, Cahokia mound-builders, Iroquois, Muslim invaders of the Iberian peninsula, Mongols, Ottomans, Persians, Greeks, and Romans? While there is no statute of limitations for historical judgment, there must be one for retrospective legal justice. Over the long haul of history the human skein simply gets too tangled for administrative purposes and the moral connection between "them" and "us" becomes too attenuated.

The present generation carries all the weight it can bear from its own dilemmas and conflicts and does not need any excess baggage from the colonial period. Despite the resort to universalizing labels such as imperialism and colonialism, most of the battles of the sixteenth and seventeenth centuries are behind us. As a nation of law and order (however imperfect) and increasingly refined sensibilities, we are not guilty of murdering Indian women and children, of branding slaves on the forehead, or of claiming and confiscating any real estate in the world we happen to fancy. We have a related but quite different set of moral problems: personal and institutional racism toward people of all colors; poverty and disease on Indian reservations and in inner cities; leveraged buyouts and junk bonds; disproportionally large black and Indian prison populations; military intervention in Latin America and the Middle East; immigration quotas; abortion policies; and campus intolerance, to name just a few.

The third and fundamental basis for moral responsibility is personal. As individuals of conscience, we are capable of a wide variety of responses to past injustice. One response that will probably not find much favor is to deed over some or all of our property to descendants of its last aboriginal owners or to the slaves who worked our ancestors' plantations, although there might well be a conflict over which group takes moral precedence. If we have similarly benefitted from past injustice but in a less direct and documentable way, we might choose to share our partially ill-gotten gains by contributing liberally to the Native American Rights Fund or the United Negro College Fund. With or without money, we could support actions designed to give all Americans a fair shot at realizing their human and economic potential.

Historians are particularly well qualified to take additional steps to prevent present and future generations from perpetuating unthinkingly attitudes and actions that have damaged people in the past. We can inspire and teach students to read enough history to realize that our current fortunes and misfortunes are the product of complicated, interlocking, ongoing human stories whose next chapters do not have to be written the same way. We can work to include slighted peoples in the mainstream, not the mere eddies, of our national or continental history. In the process, of course, we must strive to fashion a new synthesis that does justice to our checkered and polychromatic past, with narratives that resemble intelligible mosaics rather than jumbled grab-bags of shreds and tatters. Finally, we can work conscientiously to destroy maleficent myths without erecting politically correct or convenient new myths in their place. Myths of any kind commit the most basic kind of injustice against the past and hobble us and our successors. Only by learning and teaching history that is palpably real, scrupulously fair, and recognizable to all the participants of the past, not merely their interested descendants in the present, will we fulfill our most important social obligation and render the past the highest form of justice.

QUESTIONS TO CONSIDER

1. What word do "progressives" use to characterize European treatment of American natives in the colonial period? To what infamous atrocity do some compare the experience?
2. What does Axtell suggest as a definition of the word?
3. What motivation does Axtell attribute to those who morally indict the European colonists?
4. What are problems with moral blackmail? What alternatives does Axtell suggest?
5. What three reasons does Axtell advance for judging the past?
6. What are three types of moral responsibility assigned by historical critics of the quincentenary? What is Axtell's appraisal of each?

2

The Spain Among Us*

Henry Wiencek

As we approach the end of the twentieth century, Hispanics are poised to overtake blacks as the largest minority group in the United States. In the sun belt, from Florida to California, their contribution to American life is particularly substantial. Yet when most Americans think of the growth of the nation, they reflexively see English civilization moving from east to west, the famous westward movement, as the basic thrust of development. One of the most intriguing "what ifs" of American history has to do with a possible alternative pattern of growth. If Spain had triumphed over England in the struggle for European supremacy, with colonial spoils accompanying the mother country's victory, would we not date our history from Cortez's 1519 landing in Mexico and see a natural development from south to north into the present United States? Would not the sixteenth century be rich with stories of our forbears as they conquered a continent and brought into it European patterns of life? Consider the different perspective such a history would offer—and note that the events did, in fact, occur. We have simply neglected them.

Henry Wiencek has traced some of the elements of the Spanish heritage that shaped the American past and provide a significant part of our present. In doing so he suggests that Spanish seekers like Coronado embody the American character because the very

*Reprinted from *American Heritage* Magazine, April 1993, by permission of the author.

act of seeking is a crucial element of our national makeup. So ponder the what-might-have-beens, and recognize the actuality of "the Spain among us."

In 1883 Walt Whitman received an invitation to visit Santa Fe and deliver a poem at a celebration of the city's founding. The ailing sixty-four-year-old poet wrote back from his home in Camden, New Jersey, that he couldn't make the trip or write a poem for the occasion, but he sent along some remarks "off hand": "We Americans have yet to really learn our own antecedents, and sort them, to unify them. They will be found ampler than has been supposed, and in widely different sources. Thus far, impress'd by New England writers and schoolmasters, we tacitly abandon ourselves to the notion that our United States have been fashion'd from the British Islands only, and essentially form a second England only—which is a very great mistake."

Whitman was concerned less with rearranging a view of the past than with creating a vision of the future. Although the United States was enjoying immense prosperity, the poet said that the country did not possess "a society worthy the name." The national character was yet to be established, he thought, but he knew that it would be a "composite" and that "Spanish character will supply some of the most needed parts": "No stock shows a grander historic retrospect—grander in religiousness and loyalty, or for patriotism, courage, decorum, gravity, and honor. . . . As to the Spanish stock of our Southwest, it is certain to me that we do not begin to appreciate [its] splendor and sterling value. Who knows but that element, like the course of some subterranean river, dipping invisibly for a hundred or two years, is now to emerge in broadest flow and permanent action?"

But in fact, the Spanish achievement was far from subterranean. It merely seemed so from the Northeast. A great part of the West, from Texas to California, was profuse with the landmarks of Spanish achievement—towns and villages, ranches and churches, places where the Spanish language and culture were defining. The town where he was asked to speak, Santa Fe, was then and is now the oldest political capital in the United States, having been founded in 1609. And the city where Whitman had lived for many years, New York, had been home to a community of Sephardic Jews as early as 1654. Yet Whitman was correct in saying that the Spanish role in America's past was not fully appreciated and that the Spanish role in America's future would be critical. These points are being raised more forcefully as the Americas mark the five hundredth anniversary of their discovery by Columbus, on behalf of Spain.

What exactly is the Spanish legacy? What is the Spanish imprint on the United States? For most Americans the word *Spanish* immediately summons up the word *mission* and an image of whitewashed walls and ornate towers gleaming in the California sun. The missions are indeed the best-known Spanish legacy. In their time they influenced the spiritual and cultural life of millions, and they exert a broad influence on American architecture to this day. The oldest surviving documents written in the United States by Europeans are Spanish—parish registers from St. Augustine, Florida, which is the oldest surviving European settlement in the country. Millions of Americans live in places founded by the Spaniards, places such as San Antonio, El Paso, Santa Fe, San Diego, Los Angeles (actually founded by a party of blacks and Indians under Spanish auspices), and San Francisco. Many of these cities and towns continue to be largely Hispanic in population, culture, and language. The West was explored and settled by Spaniards. Ranching, which is regarded as a peculiarly American way of life, was invented by the Spaniards, and without the efforts of a man named Bernardo de Gálvez we might have lost the Revolutionary War.

But the Spanish legacy runs far deeper and influences us more today than a list of buildings and place names and heroes would suggest. We are still on a path that the Spaniards began to blaze five hundred years ago. They were the first pupils of the New World, the first to learn the lesson that these continents are the land of dreams. In their books we read the first descriptions of the sequoia, of hailstones that dent helmets, and the inextinguishable hope that the place of utter happiness is just over the horizon. The words *más allá* (farther on) appear like an incantation in their chronicles. *Not here? Very well. Más allá!*

From the twentieth-century perspective the wanderings of the first Spanish explorers have a comical element—who would look for gold in Kansas? In some books you will find Francisco Vásquez de Coronado written down as a fool for doing exactly that (one prominent writer speaks of the "Coronado fiasco"). Then why, we might ask, have scores, even hundreds, of modern Americans, professionals and amateurs, expended fortunes in time, money, laborious study, and physical effort in trying to trace the exact path of this fool and find the merest scrap of material evidence of him? The answer is that we have learned, in large part from the efforts of the Spaniards, that the very act of seeking lies at the heart of the American character. We look for Coronado's path because he was a great, original American seeker. He went in search of wealth and found something better instead; he found the American West. Wallace Stegner writes, "America was discovered by accident and explored to a considerable extent by people trying to find a way to somewhere else": to India; to a Northwest Passage; to the land of El Dorado; to the fabled land of Queen

Califía, for whom the Spaniards named California; or to the Seven Cities of Cíbola—Coronado's personal dream. With some three hundred men he searched through Arizona, New Mexico, Texas, Oklahoma, and into Kansas.

Do we still laugh that Coronado found Kansas instead of gold? In one of our own modern myths, Dorothy returns, transformed, to that very place, unburdened by the emeralds of Oz, but having learned about courage, love, and wisdom. The Spaniards were the first to learn about the transforming power of the New World, that this is a place of mirage and miracle and that the two are forever getting mixed up; that the land that refuses to yield up silver or gold dispenses, *más allá*, a Grand Canyon, maize, buffalo, and an Eden in the Rio Grande Valley—and, in time, the richest nation in history.

The Grand Canyon was discovered when Coronado sent a detachment under García López de Cárdenas to find the passes to the South Sea (the Pacific) that the Indians had told of. López went off, did not find the South Sea, but did find himself at the edge of a precipice the likes of which he had never seen before. He sent men down to the river at the bottom. It did not seem that far, judging by some rocks below that appeared to be a man's height. The scouts came back in a few hours; too far to the river— those rocks are higher than the tallest tower in Seville!

In Texas the chronicler Pedro de Castañeda found himself in the field of dreams; the earth there was so flat it seemed round "in the shape of a ball"; it was like standing at the top of the world: "wherever a man stands . . . he is surrounded by the sky at the distance of a crossbow shot." Farther on they found America's inland sea, the ocean of grass. Walking across it was like sailing in a boat with no rudder. It could swallow an army. In amazement Castañeda watched the grass spring up again after the column had passed. "Who could believe," he marveled, ". . . they left no more traces when they got through than if no one had passed over?" One man strolled into the grass and was never seen again; the search party itself was lost for days.

At home in Mexico Castañeda pondered the worth of the enterprise: "For although they did not obtain the riches of which they had been told, they found the means to discover them and the beginning of a good land to settle in and from which to proceed onward." *¡Más allá!*

Charles F. Lummis, the great collector and savior of Southwestern art and architecture, called the Spanish the "world-finders." A tremendous outpouring of Spanish exploration culminated in 1542, the year Coronado's expedition ended. Hernando de Soto's party was on its way to Mexico, having landed in Florida in 1539 and explored Georgia, the Carolinas, Tennessee, and Alabama, crossed the Mississippi (the first Europeans to do so), and pressed up the Arkansas River into Oklahoma. At sea Juan Rodríguez Cabrillo sailed from Mexico along the Baja Californian coast and discovered San Diego Bay and the Channel Islands. After Cabrillo's death his second-in-command continued up the Pacific coast to make the first European sighting of Oregon. Ruy López de Villalobos sailed across the Pacific to a group of islands he named the Philippines. Francisco de Orellana, having ascended and descended the Andes to reach the headwaters of the Amazon, emerged at the mouth of that river after two years.

It is interesting to compare this record with that of English wanderlust. Nearly two centuries later William Byrd, upon his return from a surveying trip along the Virginia-Carolina border, wrote that "our country has now been inhabited more than 130 years by the English, and still we hardly knew anything of the Appalachian Mountains, that are no where above 250 miles from the sea."

The period from Columbus's first landfall in 1492 to 1607, when the English made their settlement at Jamestown, has traditionally been a blank spot in American history books. Some texts state quite plainly that the history of the United States begins in 1607, making only the most cursory mention of the sixteenth century—the century when, in the words of the historian Bernard Bailyn, Spain created "the largest and most populous empire the western world had seen since the fall of Rome." The historian Howard Mumford Jones also compared Spain's sixteenth-century achievements to those of antiquity: "The Spaniards invented a system of colonial administration unparalleled since the days of ancient Rome; in religion they launched the most sweeping missionary movement since the Germanic tribes accepted Christianity. . . . As for culture, the Spaniards transplanted dynamic forms of Renaissance art, thought, and institutions to the Americas with amazing quickness." The Spanish established a college for the sons of Indian chiefs, in Mexico in 1536, a university in Santo Domingo in 1538, the University of Mexico in 1553. Spaniards set up the first printing press in the New World in 1539, and, as Jones observed, "When in 1585 a forlorn little band of Englishmen were trying to stick it out on Roanoke Island, three hundred poets were competing for a prize in Mexico City."

The earliest naturalist of the New World was probably Gonzalo Fernández de Oviedo y Valdés, who first visited the Americas in 1514 and published a multivolume general and natural history between 1535 and 1557. Two centuries later Capt. Alejandro Malaspina led one of the most important West Coast explorations. In the early 1790s Malaspina's ships made their first landfall in Mulgrave Sound in Alaska, where Malaspina and his staff studied a glacier that was later named for the captain, traded with the Tlingits for artifacts (the Spaniards carefully noted the Tlingit names for the objects they collected), and carried out experiments with a pendulum, seeking to measure the intensity of gravity at that latitude as a way of computing the exact size of the earth. Heading south, a member of the expedition became the first botanist to discover and describe the sequoia. The paintings of birds and landscapes made on this visit are today the oldest surviving works of art made in California.

In California Malaspina received valuable assistance from Father Fermín Francisco de Lasuén, the founder of nine missions, who provided native guides to take the scientists into the field. The first European settlement in California had been established in 1769 at San Diego by Gaspar de Portolá, who blazed El Camino Real, today's Highway 101; discovered the La Brea tar pits (the Indians had long used their pitch to caulk their boats); and experienced an earthquake that knocked his men from their feet. With Portolá came Father Junípero Serra, who founded nine missions. Fathers Serra, Lasuén, and their successors established a total of twenty-one missions and baptized about 88,000 Indians in the course of nearly seven decades of evangelical work. The two great mission founders are buried at the jewel of the California missions, San Carlos Borromeo del Río Carmelo, in Carmel. The high architectural aspirations of the Franciscans there were carried out by Indian workers inexperienced at making such things as a Moorish dome. The result, with its irregular walls and heartfelt but misshapen dome, is a handmade frontier masterpiece of poignant beauty. When it was crumbling in the 1870s, Robert Louis Stevenson helped raise funds for a restoration with an angry article, saying, "The United States Mint can coin many millions more dollar pieces, but . . . when the Carmel church is in the dust, not all the wealth of the states and territories can replace what has been lost."

The greatest Spanish landmark on the East Coast is at St. Augustine, Florida: the Castillo de San Marcos. This fortress is the oldest in the United States, begun in 1672. But even before that, nine previous Spanish fortresses, made of wood, had stood on the site; the first one was put up more than half a century before the Pilgrims landed. But the fortress is only the most visible evidence of Florida's Spanish heritage. It is not widely known that Florida was once the site of a flourishing system of missions comparable to those in the Southwest and California. In the mid-1600s 70 Franciscans were ministering to 25,000 Indians at 38 missions in the Southeast.

Florida has been a part of the United States only since 1821; it was Spanish for three centuries. It is one of those parts of the country that were fought and argued over, quite bloodily, by Americans, Spanish, French, and English. The standard schoolbook texts dutifully explain the swaps, treaties, and overseas diplomatic maneuverings that ushered into our borders such places as Florida, the Northwest Territory, the Oregon Territory, and that peculiar strip known as the Gadsden Purchase. In the American mind it all tends to have been inevitable, and the rest is just details. But after the Revolution, when this country was at its most vulnerable, the United States might not have had the breathing space—not elbowroom, but vital territory—that it needed to survive had it not been for the masterful military and naval campaign led by Bernardo de Gálvez. As governor of Louisiana, which France had transferred to Spain in 1762, Gálvez opened the port of New Orleans to American privateers and clandestinely funneled thousands of dollars in cash—"very secret service money," it was called—to the American agent in New Orleans. This money went directly to George Rogers Clark to pay for his campaign against the British in the Northwest Territory. When Spain declared war on England in 1779, Gálvez personally led a column north, captured British forts at Manchac and Baton Rouge, and successfully demanded the surrender of all the British forts on the Mississippi. In March 1780 he bombarded the British fort at Mobile into surrender. His greatest feat took place the following year, when he besieged and captured the formidable British stronghold at Pensacola. At the start of the assault, Gálvez led a small fleet past the guns of the fort, while a larger Spanish fleet tarried fearfully out of range. Gálvez sent the reluctant admiral in charge a note: "Whoever has valor and honor will follow me." The admiral followed.

The naval world is a small one, and it is not unlikely that Gálvez's stinging note was much talked about. His words had an echo more than eighty years later in the famous utterance of a Union commander exhorting his officers to enter a minefield in Mobile Bay: "Damn the torpedoes! Full speed ahead!" Admiral David Glasgow Farragut might have heard of the Spanish commander's exploits from his father, a Minorcan of Spanish blood who served for a time in the Continental Navy and whose name was Jorge Ferragut. After the Revolution Gálvez was made viceroy of Mexico. In 1785 he ordered a survey of the Texas coast, and the leader of the expedition honored his superior by putting the name Galvestown on his map. Anglo settlers changed the spelling to Galveston.

It is commonly known that much of the peculiar lingo of the American cowboy was derived from Spanish. *Bronco, rodeo, lariat, cinch, mustang,* and *chaps* all are based on Spanish words. From *vaquero* came "buckaroo," and from *juzgado* came "hoosegow." What is less well known is that the very concept of the ranch—lock, stock, and barrel—was Spanish. From the Old World to the New the Spaniards brought horses, cattle, sheep, goats, burros, and swine. The semiarid plains of the West were similar to the lands in central Spain, where Spaniards had centuries of experience raising cattle. Branding had been practiced in Iberia since the tenth century. The stock that the Spaniards brought with them became the trade-mark of the Western cattle baron. Known popularly as the Texas longhorn, they had been bred on the semiarid Spanish plain and were perfectly suited for a rugged life in the New World. For one thing they were virtually wild; they fended for themselves, needing no man's help to find food.

Cattle raising had been carried on all over Europe, but Iberians were the only Europeans to practice large-scale cattle ranching. From the Iberian Peninsula, Spaniards transferred their knowledge to the Caribbean, Mexico, Panama, South America, and the North American West. The cattle drive was not invented in Texas; it was an established custom in Iberia, where herds were moved to different pastures with changing seasons. Other Europeans managed their small herds on foot, using dogs. Only the Spaniards herded on horseback. They developed the distinctive saddle that we now identify with the West, with its stirrups that let the cowboy's legs stay fully extended during a long day on the range, large flat footrests for stability during gallops, and, perhaps most important, the big pommel to which the vaquero, with his lightning-fast hands, would tie his lariat (*la reata*) after he had roped a cow. Vaqueros were the acknowledged masters of this tricky maneuver, one that cost many an Anglo cowpoke a finger or two in trying to learn it. The timid preferred to tie the rope to the pommel first and then lasso the animal. From observing the success of the Spanish, Anglos learned that the West was suitable for ranching and that ranching was a way up the economic ladder for a man or woman with small capital.

Spaniards began to settle in the West about sixty years after Coronado's expedition had passed through, when Juan de Oñate led a group of three hundred people, nearly half of them soldiers, to the Rio Grande Valley in 1598. Santa Fe was founded in 1609 by Pedro de Peralta. Despite the best efforts of the government to persuade settlers to live together in walled towns for their own protection, the Spaniards set themselves up in scattered isolation, each family close to its fields. Nonetheless, by 1800 Santa Fe had a population of about 2500. In 1807 the United States government sent Lt. Zebulon Pike to look around and size up the region. When Pike built a small fort and ran up the Stars and Stripes, the alarmed Spanish arrested him and escorted him out through the Rio Grande Valley, which impressed the spy with its beauty and fertility. Pike's published description of the region excited great interest in the East. When Mexico attained its independence in 1821, its government opened the borders to trade with the United States, with the result that a brisk and profitable commerce sprang up along the Santa Fe Trail.

One of the premier artists and mythmakers of the West, Frederic Remington, spent a great deal of time in the old Spanish section and was impressed by what he saw, or more accurately, by what he didn't see: "The Americans have gashed [the rest of the] country up so horribly with their axes, hammers, scrapers and plows that I always like to see a place which they have overlooked; some place before they arrive with their heavy-handed God of Progress."

In New Mexico some Indians managed to retain their old ways of life partly because their Hispanic neighbors had left them alone, to a degree. Charles Lummis gave credit to the Spanish for what they had done and not done, in comparison with the acts of the United States: "It is due to the generous and manly laws made by Spain three hundred years ago, that . . . the Pueblos enjoy today full security in their lands, while nearly all others (who never came under Spanish dominion) have been time after time ousted from lands our government had solemnly given to them."

Attracted by the unspoiled landscape and by the chance to see the Indian cultures of the time, many artists began to head to the Southwest in the early 1900s. Expecting to concentrate solely on the Indians, the newcomers were fascinated by New Mexico's Spanish legacy, preserved in Taos, in Santa Fe, and in remote valleys. They painted portraits, adobe churches and houses, and religious and folk festivals. They found themselves openly accepted by the Indians and Spanish and were enchanted by the old carved woodwork they discovered in Spanish houses and churches, by the metalwork wrought in local smithies, and, most of all, by the religious images called *santos*, which they avidly collected, causing an unfortunate boom in scavenging by curio dealers.

A 1907 literary history states: "It is curious what an attraction Spain and Spanish history have always had for the best Americans. It is, as Hawthorne once said, as if America wished to pay the debt she owed to her discovery." America's literary fascination with Spain and Spanish America began with Washington Irving, who wrote a biography of Columbus and a highly popular collection of sketches, *The Alhambra*, recounting old Spanish and Moorish tales. James Fenimore Cooper wrote a novel about Columbus; William Dean Howells introduced American readers to the works of Spanish realists; Herman Melville brooded upon the character of a Spanish captain, Benito Cereno, and scribbled notes in the margins of his copy of *Don Quixote*. Probably the deepest and most significant Spanish literary imprint of this era was on the quintessentially America writer Mark Twain. The characters in *Huckleberry Finn* are New World versions of Quixote and Sancho Panza, and one critic went so far as to say, "Mark Twain is not fully understood without Cervantes."

There was another, darker element in American writing and thinking about Spain—the so-called Black Legend, a durable mélange of anti-Hispanic and anti-Catholic propaganda that presented the Spanish as uniquely cruel and barbarous, interested only in gold and not in planting permanent colonies. The legend had its origins in the brutal and widespread mistreatment of the Indians in the first decades of the Spanish exploration, when the Spaniards killed tens of thousands of Native Americans and enslaved hundreds of thousands. Hundreds of thousands more died of European diseases—smallpox, measles, diphtheria, cholera—to which the inhabitants of the New World had no immunity.

Many Spanish priests were appalled at the treatment of the Indians and protested to the crown. The most prominent was Father Bartolomé de las Casas, who was himself a plantation owner and slave-holder on Hispaniola until 1514. While preparing a sermon, he came across a verse in Ecclesiastes that sparked a conversion: "He that sacrificeth of a thing wrongfully gotten, his offering is ridiculous, and the gifts of unjust men are not accepted." It became clear to him "that everything done to the Indians thus far was unjust and tyrannical." He immediately freed his own slaves and preached that the Spaniards were sinners for exploiting the Indians. Thus began the remarkable career of the man who would be the chief voice crying in the wilderness against the conquest. One would assume that the royal apparatus, delighted at the gold that poured into its coffers from the efforts of the conquistadors, would brush aside criticism from whistle-blowing clerics, but that was not the case.

In a debate in 1519 conducted at Barcelona before nineteen-year-old King Charles I, Las Casas declared, in words that would have a secular echo in Thomas Jefferson's declaration of liberty and equality for all, that "our Christian religion is suitable for and may be adapted to all the nations of the world, and all alike may receive it; and no one may be deprived of his liberty, nor may he be enslaved on the excuse that he is a natural slave."

Although the king made it plain that mistreatment of the Indians would not be tolerated and promulgated laws to protect them, the abuses continued. In 1550 the royal Council of the Indies suggested to the king that "it would be fitting for Your Majesty to order a meeting of learned men, theologians, and jurists . . . to . . . consider the manner in which these conquests should be carried on . . . justly and with security of conscience." And amazingly, Charles ordered that the conquest of the New World be held in suspension until such a convention could discuss the morality of the enterprise. As the historian Lewis Hanke has observed, "Probably never before had such a mighty sovereign ordered his conquests to cease until it should be decided if they were just." Las Casas spoke before the convention for five days, describing atrocities that Spaniards had committed and begging for an end to them.

The conquest stopped dead for sixteen years while a new legal policy was worked out. The "New Laws" of 1573, published during the reign of Philip II, placed strict limits on the use of force. Slavery was forbidden, although it continued to exist in secret. The taking of land or homes was forbidden. However, Indians were still expected to render tribute to the government and provide labor.

In reviewing the record of Spain's colonization of the Southwest, the historian Elizabeth John wrote, "Contrary to the Black Legend, and notwithstanding the flagrant violations of Indian rights, it is on the Spanish frontier that one finds the earliest commitment to due process for Indians and the only consistent efforts to foster self-governance of Indian communities." Hanke regarded Spanish reforms as the first social experiments in the New World and remarked, "No European nation . . . took her Christian duty toward native peoples so seriously as did Spain."

The reforms failed to kill the Black Legend. Las Casas's accusations against the conquistadors were published in Spain. During the Protestant Reformation these books became a weapon against Spain, the primary defender of Catholicism. The Black Legend infected the political debates of three centuries in Europe and America and seeped into the writings of historians, including some of the premier American historians of the nineteenth century—George Bancroft, John Lothrop Motley, and Francis Parkman. Parkman described Spain as "a tyranny of monks and inquisitors, with their swarms of spies and informers, their racks, their dungeons and their fagots [crushing] all freedom of thought and speech"—a view that fails to account for the fact that Las Casas and other reformers published their unpopular views, gained the ear of the king, and influenced imperial policy.

The Black Legend reared up mightily in the United States during the Spanish-American War and was enshrined in textbooks, one of which condemned the Spanish for a custom that was actually enlightened: "Their morals were lax, and their treatment of the savages was cruel, despite the tendency of the colonists to amalgamate with the latter, and thus to descend in the scale of civilization." Indeed, many historians have taken note of the rapidity with which Spaniards intermarried with Native Americans. The historian Michael Kammen describes "a socio-racial pluralism institutionalized and stabilized by law and custom" in the Spanish colonies, which contrasted markedly with the "tribalism" of the "exclusive and withdrawn" Puritan, Quaker, and German colonies. Of all the Europeans who settled in America, it might be said that the Spaniards were the least racist in this regard, although intermarriages followed class lines; members of the Spanish colonial nobility married into what they perceived to be the Native American upper class. The children of these New World unions were welcomed into upper-class society in Spain itself.

The Spanish were the first to confront the questions posed by colonization: What is the proper, just, and moral relationship between Europeans and Native Americans? To what extent should Europeans, in an effort to "civilize" and "improve" Native Americans, impose European culture, technology, and religious beliefs upon Native Americans? Is it acceptable for European, African, and Native American peoples to become intermingled to create a new race of mixed blood? If Europeans can use American land more productively than Native Americans, can the land simply be taken? The only ideal response would have been the impossible one: to "repeal" the discovery and leave the Americans to their original inhabitants.

Más allá. When the Mexican writer Carlos Fuentes received the Cervantes Prize for Literature in 1987, he gave an address saying, "The quixotic adventure has not yet ended in the New World." He spoke about the "debate with others, debate with ourselves" over the meaning of the five-hundredth anniversary "of a disquieting date—1492" and asked: "Who is the author of the New World? Columbus, who first set foot on it, or Vespucio, who first named it? The gods who fled or the gods who arrived? . . . What does America mean? To whom does this name belong? What does New World mean? . . . How does one baptize the river, mountain, jungle, seen for the first time? And, most importantly, what name do you give to the anonymous vast humanity—Indian and Creole, mestizo and Black—of the multiracial culture of the Americas? . . . Who is the author of the New World? All of us are, all of us who incessantly imagine it because we know that without our imagination, America, the generic name of new worlds, would cease to exist."

QUESTIONS TO CONSIDER

1. How does Wiencek relate Coronado's "fiasco" to the American character? How was the discovery of much of America the result of mistakes?
2. How did Spain dominate the sixteenth century in America? How much more impressive than the English record, even by the mid-eighteenth century, was the Spanish?
3. Who was Bernardo de Gálvez and why was he significant in American history? How is his name best known today?
4. What was the relationship of the Spanish to ranching? What did they contribute to American ranching practices?
5. What was the Black Legend? What does Wiencek suggest as an alternative interpretation of Spanish behavior? Why has the Black Legend lived on?
6. How did Spain's record on race relations differ from England's?

3

Were the Puritans "Puritanical"?*

Carl Degler

Carl N. Degler (1921–   ), president of the Organization of American Historians in 1979–80, enjoyed a long and fruitful career. After earning his Ph.D. at Columbia in 1952, he taught fourteen years at Vassar and then at Stanford after 1968. His primary research interests were the history of the American South and American social history, particularly women and the family, as exemplified by his splendid book *At Odds: Women and the Family in America from the Revolution to the Present* (1980). He won several awards for his penetrating comparative study *Neither Black Nor White: Slavery and Race Relations in Brazil and the United States* (1971). The article that follows is taken from *Out of Our Past* (1959), a stimulating social and intellectual history of the United States.

In the pleasure-oriented 1920s, satirist H. L. Mencken defined a Puritan as a person who was desperately afraid "that someone, somewhere, may be happy," a theme used as a counterpoint for Hugh Hefner's "playboy philosophy" in the 1960s and 1970s. In this article, Degler takes issue with the Mencken image and sets the record straight in a responsible historical reevaluation. He refutes the "puritanical" nature of the Puritans in the areas of drinking, dress, music, art, and sex. Tempered by such twentieth-century horrors as two world wars, Stalin, Hitler, and a nuclear arms race,

Degler finds the negative Puritan view of human nature more realistic than did earlier, more optimistic historians.

The Puritans played a disproportionately large part in forging the
American character. Their Calvinistic view of humans as inherently
sinful has been a powerful force in the nation's history and has contributed to Americans being among the most morality conscious
in the world. Their emphasis on the importance of education, given
secular support by Thomas Jefferson, reflects a continuing fundamental American attitude. All-in-all, Degler demonstrates that the
American character has not changed as much over the centuries
as many people believe.

To most Americans—and to most Europeans, for that matter—the core of
the Puritan social heritage has been summed up in Macaulay's well-
known witticism that the Puritans prohibited bearbaiting not because of
torture to the bear, but because of the pleasure it afforded the spectators.
And as late as 1925, H. L. Mencken defined Puritanism as "the haunting
fear that someone, somewhere, may be happy." Before this chapter is out,
much will be said about the somber and even grim nature of the Puritan
view of life, but quips like those of Macaulay and Mencken distort rather
than illumine the essential character of the Puritans. Simply because the
word "Puritan" has become encrusted with a good many barnacles, it is
worth while to try to scrape them off if we wish to gain an understanding
of the Puritan heritage. Though this process is essentially a negative one,
sometimes it is clarifying to set forth what an influence is *not* as well as
what it is.

Fundamental to any appreciation of the Puritan mind on matters of
pleasure must be the recognition that the typical, godly Puritan was a
worker in the world. Puritanism, like Protestantism in general, resolutely
and definitely rejected the ascetic and monastic ideals of medieval Catholicism. Pleasures of the body were not to be eschewed by the Puritan, for,
as Calvin reasoned, God "intended to provide not only for our necessity,
but likewise for our pleasure and delight." It is obvious, he wrote in his
famous *Institutes*, that "the Lord have endowed flowers with such beauty
. . . with such sweetness of smell" in order to impress our senses; therefore, to enjoy them is not contrary to God's intentions. "In a word," he concluded, "hath He not made many things worthy of our estimation independent of any necessary use?"

It was against excess of enjoyment that the Puritans cautioned and
legislated. "The wine is from God," Increase Mather warned, "but the
Drunkard is from the Devil." The Cambridge Platform of the Church of
1680 prohibited games of cards or dice because of the amount of time they
consumed and the encouragement they offered to idleness, but the ministers of Boston in 1699 found no difficulty in condoning public lotteries.

They were like a public tax, the ministers said, since they took only what the "government might have demanded, with a more *general imposition* . . . and it employes for the welfare of the public, all that is raised by the *lottery.*" Though Cotton Mather at the end of the century condemned mixed dancing, he did not object to dancing as such; and his grandfather, John Cotton, at the beginning saw little to object to in dancing between the sexes so long as it did not become lascivious. It was this same John Cotton, incidentally, who successfully contended against Roger Williams' argument that women should wear veils in church.

In matters of dress, it is true that the Massachusetts colony endeavored to restrict the wearing of "some new and immodest fashions" that were coming in from England, but often these efforts were frustrated by the pillars of the church themselves. Winthrop reported in his *History*, for example, that though the General Court instructed the elders of the various churches to reduce the ostentation in dress by "urging it upon the consciences of their people," little changes was effected, "for divers of the elders' wives, etc., were in some measure partners in this general disorder."

We also know now that Puritan dress—not that made "historical" by Saint-Gaudens' celebrated statue—was the opposite of severe, being rather in the English Renaissance style. Most restrictions on dress which were imposed were for purposes of class differentiation rather than for ascetic reasons. Thus long hair was acceptable on an upper-class Puritan like Cromwell or Winthrop, but it was a sign of vanity on the head of a person of lower social status. In 1651 the legislature of Massachusetts called attention to that "excess in Apparell" which has "crept in upon us, and especially amongst people of mean condition, to the dishonor of God, the scandall of our profession, the consumption of Estates, and altogether unsuitable to our poverty." The law declared "our utter detestation and dislike, that men or women of mean condition, should take upon them the garb of Gentlemen, by wearing Gold or Silver Lace, or Buttons, or Points at their knees, or to walk in great Boots; or Women of the same rank to wear Silk or Tiffany hoods, or Scarfes, which tho allowable to persons of greater Estates, or more liberal education, is intolerable in people of low condition." By implication, this law affords a clear description of what the well-dressed Puritan of good estate would wear.

If the Puritans are to be saved from the canard of severity of dress, it is also worth while to soften the charge that they were opposed to music and art. It is perfectly true that the Puritans insisted that organs be removed from the churches and that in England some church organs were smashed by zealots. But it was not music organs as such which they opposed, only music in the meetinghouse. Well-known American and English Puritans, like Samuel Sewell, John Milton, and Cromwell, were sincere lovers of music. Moreover, it should be remembered that it was under Puritan rule that opera was introduced into England—and without protest, either. The first English dramatic production entirely in music—*The Siege of Rhodes*—was presented in 1656, four years before the Restoration. Just before the end of Puritan rule, John Evelyn noted in his diary that he went "to see a new opera, after the Italian way, in recitative music and scenes. . . . " Furthermore, as Percy Scholes points out, in all the voluminous contemporary literature attacking the Puritans for every conceivable narrow-mindedness, none asserts that they opposed music, so long as it was performed outside the church.

The weight of the evidence is much the same in the realm of art. Though King Charles's art collection was dispersed by the incoming Commonwealth, it is significant that Cromwell and other Puritans bought several of the items. We also know that the Protector's garden at Hampton Court was beautified by nude statues. Furthermore, it is now possible to say that the Puritan closing of the theaters was as much a matter of objection to their degenerate lewdness by the 1640s as an objection to the drama as such. As far as American Puritans are concerned, it is not possible to say very much about their interest in art since there was so little in the seventeenth century. At least it can be said that the Puritans, unlike the Quakers, had not objection to portrait painting.

Some modern writers have professed to find in Puritanism, particularly the New England brand, evidence of sexual repression and inhibition. Though it would certainly be false to suggest that the Puritans did not subscribe to the canon of simple chastity, it is equally erroneous to think that their sexual lives were crabbed or that sex was abhorrent to them. Marriage to the Puritan was something more than alternative to "burning," as the Pauline doctrine of the Catholic Church would have it. Marriage was enjoined upon the righteous Christian; celibacy was not a sign of merit. With unconcealed disapprobation, John Cotton told a recently married couple the story of a pair "who immediately upon marriage, without ever approaching the *Nuptial Bed*," agreed to live apart from the rest of the world, "afterwards from one another, too. . . . " But, Cotton advised, such behavior was "no other than an effort of blind zeal, for they are the dictates of a blind mind they follow therein and not of the Holy Spirit which saith, *It is not good that man should be alone.*" Cotton set himself against not only Catholic asceticism but also the view that women were the "unclean vessel," the tempters of men. Women, rather than being "a necessary Evil are a necessary Good," he wrote. "Without them there is no comfortable Living for Man. . . . "

Because, as another divine said, "the Use of the Marriage Bed" is "founded in man's Nature" the realistic Puritans required that married men unaccompanied by wives should leave the colony or bring their wives over forthwith. The Puritan settlements encouraged marriages satisfactory to the participants by permitting divorces for those whose spouses were impotent, too long absent, or cruel. Indeed, the divorce laws of New England were the easiest in Christendom at a time when the eloquence of a Milton was unable to loosen the bonds of matrimony in England.

Samuel Eliot Morison in his history of Harvard has collected a number of examples of the healthy interest of Puritan boys in the opposite sex. Commonplace books, for example, indicate that Herrick's poem beginning "Gather ye rosebuds while ye may" and amorous lines from Shakespeare, as well as more erotic and even scatological verse, were esteemed by young Puritan men. For a gentleman to present his affiance with a pair of garters, one letter of a Harvard graduate tells us, was considered neither immoral nor improper.

It is also difficult to reconcile the usual view of the stuffiness of Puritans with literally hundreds of confessions of premarital sexual relations in the extant church records. It should be understood, moreover, that these confessions were made by the saints or saints-to-be, not by the unregenerate. That the common practice of the congregation was to accept such sinners into church membership without further punishment is in itself revealing. The civil law, it is true, punished such transgressions when detected among the regenerate or among the nonchurch members, but this was also true of contemporary non-Puritan Virginia. "It will be seen," writes historian Philip A. Bruce regarding Virginia, "from the various instances given relating to the profanation of Sunday, drunkenness, swearing, defamation, and sexual immorality, that, not only were the grand juries and vestries extremely vigilant in reporting these offenses, but the courts were equally prompt in inflicting punishment; and that the penalty ranged from a heavy fine to a shameful exposure in the stocks . . . and from such an exposure to a very severe flogging at the county whipping post." In short, strict moral surveillance by the public authorities was a seventeenth century rather than a Puritan attitude.

Relations between the sexes in Puritan society were often much more loving and tender than the mythmakers would have us believe. Since it was the Puritan view that marriage was eminently desirable in the sight of God and man, it is not difficult to find evidence of deep and abiding love between a husband and wife. John Cotton, it is true, sometimes used the Biblical phrase "comfortable yoke mate" in addressing his wife, but other Puritan husbands come closer to our romantic conventions. Certainly John Winthrop's letters to his beloved Margaret indicate the depth of attachment of which the good Puritan was capable. "My good wife . . . My sweet wife," he called her. Anticipating his return home, he writes,

"So . . . we shall now enjoy each other again, as we desire. . . . It is now bed time; but I must lie alone; therefore I make less haste. Yet I must kiss my sweet wife; and so, with my blessing to our children . . . I commend thee to the grace and blessing of the lord, and rest. . . . "

Anne Bradstreet wrote a number of poems devoted to her love for her husband in which the sentiments and figures are distinctly romantic.

> *To my Dear and loving Husband*
> *I prize thy love more than whole Mines of gold*
> *Or all the riches that the East doth hold.*
> *My love is such that Rivers cannot quench,*
> *Nor aught but love from thee give recompense.*

In another poem her spouse is apostrophized as

> *My head, my heart, mine Eyes, my life, nay more*
> *My joy, my Magazine of earthly store*

and she asks:

> *If two be one, as surely thou and I,*
> *How stayest thou there, whilst I at Ipswich lye?*

Addressing John as "my most sweet Husband," Margaret Winthrop perhaps epitomized the Puritan marital ideal when she wrote, "I have many reasons to make me love thee, whereof I will name two: First, because thou lovest God and, secondly, because thou lovest me. If these two were wanting," she added, "all the rest would be eclipsed."

It would be a mistake, however, to try to make these serious, dedicated men and women into rakes of the Renaissance. They were sober if human folk, deeply concerned about their ultimate salvation and intent upon living up to God's commands as they understood them, despite their acknowledgement of complete depravity and unworthiness. "God sent you not into this world as Play-House, but a Work-House," one minister told his congregation. To the Puritan this was a world drenched in evil, and, because it truly is, they were essentially realistic in their judgments. Because the Puritan expected nothing, Perry Miller has remarked, a disillusioned one was almost impossible to find. This is probably an exaggeration, for they were also human beings; when the Commonwealth fell, it was a Puritan, after all, who said, "God has spit in our faces." But

Professor Miller's generalization has much truth in it. Only a man convinced of the inevitable and eternal character of evil could fight it so hard and so unceasingly.

The Puritan at his best, Ralph Barton Perry has said, was a "moral athlete." More than most men, the Puritan strove with himself and with his fellow man to attain a moral standard higher than was rightfully to be expected of so depraved a creature. Hence, the diaries and autobiographies of Puritans are filled with the most torturous probing of the soul and inward seeking. Convinced of the utter desirability of salvation on the one hand, and equally cognizant of the total depravity of man's nature on the other, the Puritan was caught in an impossible dilemma which permitted him no rest short of the grave. Yet with such a spring coiled within him, the Puritan drove himself and his society to tremendous heights of achievement both material and spiritual.

Such intense concern for the actualization of the will of God had a less pleasant side to it, also. If the belief that "I am my brother's keeper" is the breeding ground of heightened social conscience and expresses itself in the reform movements so indigenous to Boston and its environs, it also could and did lead to self-righteousness, intolerance and narrow-mindedness, as exemplified in another product of Boston: Anthony Comstock. But this fruit of the loins of Puritanism is less typical of the earthy seventeenth-century New Englander than H. L. Mencken would have us think. The Sabbatarian, antiliquor, and antisex attitudes usually attributed to the Puritans are a nineteenth-century addition to the much more moderate and essentially wholesome view of life's evils held by the early settlers of New England.

To realize how different Puritans could be, one needs only to contrast Roger Williams and his unwearying opponent John Cotton. But despite the range of differences among Puritans, they all were linked by at least one characteristic. That was their belief in themselves, in their morality and in their mission to the world. For this reason, Puritanism was intellectual and social dynamite in the seventeenth century; its power could behead kings, overthrow governments, defy tyrants, and disrupt churches.

The Reformation laid an awesome burden on the souls of those who broke with the Roman Church. Proclaiming the priesthood of all believers, Protestantism made each man's relationship with God his own terrifying responsibility. No one else could save him; therefore no one must presume to try. More concerned about his salvation than about any mundane matter, the Puritan was compelled, for the sake of his immortal soul, to be a fearless individualist.

It was the force of this conviction which produced the Great Migration of 1630–40 and made Massachusetts a flourishing colony in the span of a decade. It was also, ironically, the force which impelled Roger Williams to threaten the very legal and social foundations of the Puritan Commonwealth in Massachusetts because he thought the oligarchy wrong and himself right. And so it would always be. For try as the rulers of Massachusetts might to make men conform to their dogma, their own rebellious example always stood as a guide to those who felt the truth was being denied. Such individualism, we would call it today, was flesh and bone of the religion which the Puritans passed on. Though the theocracy soon withered and died, its harsh voice softened down to the balmy breath of Unitarianism, the belief in self and the dogged resistance to suppression or untruth which Puritanism taught never died. Insofar as Americans today can be said to be individualistic, it is to the Puritan heritage that we must look for one of the principal sources.

In his ceaseless striving for signs of salvation and knowledge of God's intentions for man, the Puritan placed great reliance upon the human intellect, even though for him, as for all Christians, faith was the bedrock of his belief. "Faith doth not relinquish or cast out reason," wrote the American Puritan Samuel Willard, "for there is nothing in Religion contrary to it, tho' there are many things that do transcend and must captivate it." Richard Baxter, the English Puritan, insisted that "the *most Religious*, are the *most* truly, and *nobly rational*." Religion and reason were complementary to the Puritan, not antithetical as they were to many evangelical sects of the time.

Always the mere emotion of religion was to be controlled by reason. Because of this, the university-trained Puritan clergy prided themselves on the lucidity and rationality of their sermons. Almost rigorously their sermons followed the logical sequence of "doctrine," "reasons," and "uses." Conscientiously they shunned the meandering and rhetorical flourishes so beloved by Laudian preachers like John Donne, and in the process facilitated the taking of notes by their eager listeners. One of the unforgivable crimes of Mistress Anne Hutchinson was her assertion that one could "feel" one's salvation, that one was "filled with God" after conversion, that it was unnecessary, in order to be saved, to be learned in the Bible or in the Puritan writers. It was not that the Puritans were cold to the Word—far from it. A saint was required to testify to an intense religious experience—almost by definition emotional in character—before he could attain full membership in the Church. But it was always important to the Puritans that mere emotion—whether it be the anarchistic activities of the Anabaptists or the quaking of the Friends—should not be mistaken for righteousness or proper religious conduct. Here, as in so many things, the Puritans attempted to walk the middle path—in this instance, between the excessive legalism and formalism of the Catholics and Episcopalians and the flaming, intuitive evangelism of the Baptists and Quakers.

Convinced of reason's great worth, it was natural that the Puritans should also value education. "Ignorance is the mother (not of Devotion but) of Heresy," one Puritan divine declared. And a remarkably well-educated ministry testified to the Puritan belief that learning and scholarship were necessary for a proper understanding of the Word of God. More than a hundred graduates of Cambridge and Oxford Universities settled in New England before 1640, most of them ministers. At the same date not five men in all of Virginia could lay claim to such an educational background. Since Cambridge University, situated on the edge of Puritan East Anglia, supplied most of the graduates in America, it was natural that Newtown, the site of New England's own college, would soon be renamed in honor of the Alma Mater. "After God had carried us safe to New-England," said a well-known tract, some of its words now immortalized in metal in Harvard Yard, "one of the next things we longed and looked after, was to advance learning, and perpetuate it to posterity; dreading to leave an illiterate ministry to the churches, when the present ministers shall lie in the dust." "The College," founded in 1636, soon to be named Harvard, was destined to remain the only institution of higher learning in America during almost all the years of the seventeenth century. Though it attracted students from as far away as Virginia, it remained, as it began, the fountainhead of Puritan learning in the New World.

Doubt as one may Samuel Eliot Morison's claims for the secular origins of Harvard, his evidence of the typically Renaissance secular education which was available at the Puritan college in New England is both impressive and convincing. The Latin and Greek secular writers of antiquity dominated the curriculum, for this was a liberal arts training such as the leaders had received at Cambridge in England. To the Puritans the education of ministers could be nothing less than the best learning of the day. So important did education at Harvard seem to the New Haven colony in 1644 that the legislature ordered each town to appoint two men to be responsible for the collection of contributions from each family for "the mayntenaunce of scolars at Cambridge. . . . "

If there was to be a college, preparatory schools had to be provided for the training of those who were expected to enter the university. Furthermore, in a society dedicated to the reading of the Bible, elementary education was indispensable. "It being one chief project of that old deluder Satan to keep men from the knowledge of the Scriptures" began the first school laws of Massachusetts (1647) and Connecticut (1650). But the

Puritans supported education for secular as well as religious reasons. The Massachusetts Code of 1648, for instance, required children to be taught to read inasmuch "as the good education of children is of singular behoof and benefit to any Commonwealth."

The early New England school laws provided that each town of fifty families or more was to hire a teacher for the instruction of its young; towns of one hundred families or more were also directed to provide grammar schools, "the master thereof being able to instruct youths so far as they may be fitted for the University." Though parents were not obliged to send their children to these schools, if they did not they were required to teach their children to read. From the evidence of court cases and the high level of literacy in seventeenth-century New England, it would appear that these first attempts at public-supported and public-controlled education were both enforced and fruitful.

No other colony in the seventeenth century imposed such a high educational standard upon its simple farming people as the Puritans did. It is true, of course, that Old England in this period could boast of grammar schools, some of which were free. But primary schools were almost nonexistent there, and toward the end of the seventeenth century the free schools in England became increasingly tuition schools. Moreover, it was not until well into the nineteenth century that the English government did anything to support schools. Primary and secondary education in England, in contrast with the New England example, was a private or church affair.

Unlike the Puritans, the Quakers exhibited little impulse toward popular education in the seventeenth and early eighteenth centuries. Because of their accent on the Inner Light and the doctrine of universal salvation, the religious motivation of the Puritans for learning was wanting. Furthermore, the Quakers did not look to education, as such, with the same reverence as the Puritans. William Penn, for example, advised his children that "reading many books is but a taking off the mind too much from meditation." No Puritan would have said that.

Virginia in the seventeenth century, it should be said, was also interested in education. Several times in the course of the century, plans were well advanced for establishing a university in the colony. Free schools also existed in Virginia during the seventeenth century, though the lack of village communities made them inaccessible for any great numbers of children. But, in contrast with New England, there were no publicly supported schools in Virginia; the funds for the field schools of Virginia, like those for free schools in contemporary England, came from private or ecclesiastical endowment. Nor was Virginia able to bring its several plans for a college into reality until William and Mary was founded at the very end of the century.

Though the line which runs from the early New England schools to the distinctly American system of free public schools today is not always progressively upward or uniformly clear, the connection is undeniable. The Puritan innovation of public support and control on a local level was the American prototype of a proper system of population education.

American higher education in particular owes much to religion, for out of the various churches' concern for their faiths sprang a number of colleges, after the example of the Puritans' founding of Harvard. At the time of the Revolution, there were eight colleges besides Harvard in the English colonies, of which all but one were founded under the auspices of a church. William and Mary (1693) and King's College, later Columbia (1754), were the work of the Episcopalians; Yale (1701) and Dartmouth (1769) were set up by Congregationalists not comforted by Harvard; the College of New Jersey, later Princeton (1747), was founded by the Presbyterians; Queens College, later Rutgers (1766), by the Dutch Reformed Church; the College of Rhode Island, later Brown (1764), by the Baptists. Only the Academy of Philadelphia, later the University of Pennsylvania (1749), was secular in origin.

The overwhelming importance of the churches in the expansion of American higher education during the colonial period set a pattern which continued well into the nineteenth century and to a limited extent is still followed. Well-known colleges like Oberlin, Wesleyan, Haverford, Wittenberg, Moravian, Muhlenberg, and Notre Dame were all founded by churches in the years before the Civil War. By providing a large number of colleges (recall that England did not enjoy a third university until the nineteenth century), the religious impulses and diversity of the American people very early encouraged that peculiarly American faith in the efficacy and desirability of education for all.

When dwelling on the seminal qualities of the seventeenth century, it is tempting to locate the source of the later American doctrine of the separation of Church and State and religious freedom in the writings of Roger Williams and in the practices of provinces like New York, Maryland, and Pennsylvania. Actually, however, such a line of development is illusory. At the time of the Revolution all the colonies, including Rhode Island, imposed restrictions and disabilities upon some sects, thus practicing at best only a limited form of toleration, not freedom of religion—much less separation of Church and State. Moreover, Roger Williams' cogent and prophetic arguments in behalf of religious freedom were forgotten in the eighteenth century; they could not exert any influence on those who finally worked out the doctrine of religious freedom enshrined in the national Constitution. In any case, it would have been exceedingly difficult for Williams to have spoken to Jefferson and the other Virginians who fought for religious freedom. To Williams the Puritan, the great justification for freedom of religion was the preservation of the purity of the Church; to the deistic Virginians, the important goal was the removal of a religious threat to the purity and freedom of the State.

QUESTIONS TO CONSIDER

1. Against what did Puritans caution and legislate in the area of enjoyment? Why?
2. What was the purpose of most Puritan restrictions on dress?
3. What was the Puritan attitude toward sex?
4. What was the Puritan view on human nature? How did that affect them?
5. Were Puritans conformists or individualists? Why? What did this imply for them?
6. What was the Puritan attitude toward reason? How did that attitude influence education in Massachusetts?
7. What lessons did you learn from the article that you will be able to share when Puritanism comes up in future discussions?

4

The Quest for the National Character*

David M. Potter

After earning his Ph.D. at Yale in 1940, David Potter (1910–1971) spent his career teaching at Yale and Stanford. His major interests were his native South, particularly the Civil War period (see his *Lincoln and His Party in the Secession Crisis* and *The South and the Secession Crisis*), and, later in his career, social history. His *People of Plenty* (1954), a landmark in the analysis of American society, suggested that abundance, rather than democracy, was the determining factor in forming the American character. The implications of his thesis are profound, for American efforts to remake the world in the image of the United States have reflected a far greater ability and willingness to export democracy than to export the abundance that Potter feels is necessary to make it work.

This 1962 essay goes right to the heart of the forging of the American character. Potter holds that almost all theories of the American character fit into one of two molds, both set forth in the early nineteenth century. The first, initially proclaimed by Thomas Jefferson, describes the American as an idealistic individualist. The second, articulated by France's Alexis de Tocqueville, calls the American a materialistic conformist. Potter seeks to reconcile the contradictions between these two theories by focusing on their common commitment to equality. This resolution may not answer all ques-

*Reprinted from *The Reconstruction of American History,* John Higham, ed., © 1962, by permission of Unwin Hyman, Ltd.

tions raised by the conflict, but it does afford a means of harmonizing two dissonant views of the American character.

Unlike most nationality groups in the world today, the people of the United States are not ethnically rooted in the land where they live. The French have remote Gallic antecedents; the Germans, Teutonic; the English, Anglo-Saxon; the Italians, Roman; the Irish, Celtic; but the only people in America who can claim ancient American origins are a remnant of Red Indians. In any deep dimension of time, all other Americans are immigrants. They began as Europeans (or in the case of 10 percent of the population, as Africans), and if they became Americans it was only, somehow, after a relatively recent passage westbound across the Atlantic.

It is, perhaps, this recency of arrival which has given to Americans a somewhat compulsive preoccupation with the question of their Americanism. No people can really qualify as a nation in the true sense unless they are united by important qualities or values in common. If they share the same ethnic, or linguistic, or religious, or political heritage, the foundations of nationality can hardly be questioned. But when their ethnic, religious, linguistic, and political heritage is mixed, as in the case of the American people, nationality can hardly exist at all unless it takes the form of a common adjustment to conditions of a new land, a common commitment to shared values, a common esteem for certain qualities of character, or a common set of adaptive traits and attitudes. It is partly for this reason that Americans, although committed to the principle of freedom of thought, have nevertheless placed such emphasis upon the obligation to accept certain undefined tenets of "Americanism." It is for this same reason, also, that Americans have insisted upon their distinctiveness from the Old World from which they are derived. More than two centuries ago Hector St. John de Crevecoeur asked a famous question, "What then is the American, this new man?" He simply assumed, without arguing the point, that the American is a new man, and he only inquired wherein the American is different. A countless array of writers, including not only careful historians and social scientists but also professional patriots, hit-and-run travelers, itinerant lecturers, intuitive-minded amateurs of all sorts, have been repeating Crevecoeur's question and seeking to answer it ever since.

A thick volume would hardly suffice even to summarize the diverse interpretations which these various writers have advanced in describing or explaining the American character. Almost every trait, good or bad, has been attributed to the American people by someone, and almost every explanation, from Darwinian selection to toilet-training, has been advanced to account for the attributed qualities. But it is probably safe to say that at bottom there have been only two primary ways of explaining the American, and that almost all of the innumerable interpretations which have been formulated can be grouped around or at least oriented to these two basic explanations, which serve as polar points for all the literature.

The most disconcerting fact about these two composite images of the American is that they are strikingly dissimilar and seemingly about as inconsistent with one another as two interpretations of the same phenomenon could possibly be. One depicts the American primarily as an individualist and an idealist, while the other makes him out as a conformist and a materialist. Both images have been developed with great detail and elaborate explanation in extensive bodies of literature, and both are worth a close scrutiny.

For those who have seen the American primarily as an individualist, the story of his evolution as a distinctive type dates back possibly to the actual moment of his decision to migrate from Europe to the New World, for this was a process in which the daring and venturesome were more prone to risk life in a new country while the timid and the conventional were more disposed to remain at home. If the selective factors in the migration had the effect of screening out men of low initiative, the conditions of life in the North American wilderness, it is argued, must have further heightened the exercise of individual resourcefulness, for they constantly confronted the settler with circumstances in which he could rely upon no one but himself, and where the capacity to improvise a solution for a problem was not infrequently necessary to survival.

In many ways the colonial American exemplified attitudes that were individualistic. Although he made his first settlements by the removal of whole communities which were transplanted bodily—complete with all their ecclesiastical and legal institutions—he turned increasingly, in the later process of settlement, to a more and more individualistic mode of pioneering, in which one separate family would take up title to a separate, perhaps an isolated, tract of land, and would move to this land long in advance of any general settlement, leaving churches and courts and schools far behind. His religion, whether Calvinistic Puritanism or emotional revivalism, made him individually responsible for his own salvation, without the intervention of ecclesiastical intermediaries between himself and his God. His economy, which was based very heavily upon subsistence farming, with very little division of labor, also impelled him to cope with a diversity of problems and to depend upon no one but himself.

With all of these conditions at work, the tendency to place a premium upon individual self-reliance was no doubt well developed long before the cult of the American as an individualist crystallized in a conceptual form. But it did crystallize, and it took on almost its classic formulation in the thought of Thomas Jefferson.

It may seem paradoxical to regard Jefferson as a delineator of American national character, for in direct terms he did not attempt to describe the American character at all. But he did conceive that one particular kind of society was necessary to the fulfillment of American ideals, and further that one particular kind of person, namely the independent farmer, was a necessary component in the optimum society. He believed that the principles of liberty and equality, which he cherished so deeply, could not exist in a hierarchical society, such as that of Europe, nor, indeed, in any society where economic and social circumstances enabled one set of men to dominate and exploit the rest. An urban society or a commercial society, with its concentration of financial power into a few hands and its imposition of dependence through a wage system, scarcely lent itself better than an aristocracy to his basic values. In fact, only a society of small husbandmen who tilled their own soil and found sustenance in their own produce could achieve the combination of independence and equalitarianism which he envisioned for the ideal society. Thus, although Jefferson did not write a description of the national character, he erected a model for it, and the model ultimately had more influence than a description could ever have exercised. The model American was a plain, straightforward agrarian democrat, an individualist in his desire for freedom for himself, and an idealist in his desire for equality for all men.

Jefferson's image of the American as a man of independence, both in his values and in his mode of life, has had immense appeal to Americans ever since. They found this image best exemplified in the man of the frontier, for he, as a pioneer, seemed to illustrate the qualities of independence and self-reliance in their most pronounced and most dramatic form. Thus, in a tradition of something like folklore, half-legendary figures like Davy Crockett have symbolized America as well as symbolizing the frontier. In literature, ever since J. Fenimore Cooper's Leatherstocking tales, the frontier scout, at home under the open sky, free from the trammels of an organized and stratified society, has been cherished as an incarnation of American qualities. In American politics the voters showed such a marked preference for men who had been born in log cabins that many an ambitious candidate pretended to pioneer origins which were in fact fictitious.

The pioneer is, of course, not necessarily an agrarian (he may be a hunter, a trapper, a cowboy, a prospector for gold), and the agrarian is not necessarily a pioneer (he may be a European peasant tilling his ancestral acres), but the American frontier was basically an agricultural frontier, and the pioneer was usually a farmer. Thus it was possible to make an equation between the pioneer and the agrarian, and since the pioneer evinced the agrarian traits in their most picturesque and most appealing form there was a strong psychological impulse to concentrate the diffused agrarian ideal into a sharp frontier focus. This is, in part, what Frederick Jackson Turner did in 1893 when he wrote *The Significance of the Frontier in American History*. In this famous essay Turner offered an explanation of what has been distinctive in American history, but it is not as widely realized as it might be that he also penned a major contribution to the literature of national character. Thus Turner affirmed categorically that:

> The American intellect owes its striking characteristics to the frontier. That coarseness and strength, combined with acuteness and acquisitiveness; that practical inventive turn of mind, quick to find expedients; that masterful grasp of material things, lacking in the artistic but powerful to effect great ends; that restless, nervous energy; that dominant individualism, working for good and for evil; and withal, that buoyancy and exuberance which comes with freedom—these are traits of the frontier, or traits called out elsewhere because of the existence of the frontier.

A significant but somewhat unnoticed aspect of Turner's treatment is the fact that, in his quest to discover the traits of the American character, he relied for proof not upon descriptive evidence that given traits actually prevailed, but upon the argument that given conditions in the environment would necessarily cause the development of certain traits. Thus the cheapness of land on the frontier would make for universal landholding which in turn would make for equalitarianism in the society. The absence of division of labor on the frontier would force each man to do most things for himself, and this would breed self-reliance. The pitting of the individual man against the elemental forces of the wilderness and of nature would further reinforce this self-reliance. Similarly, the fact that a man had moved out in advance of society's institutions and its stratified structure would mean that he could find independence, without being overshadowed by the institutions, and could enjoy an equality unknown to stratified society. All of this argument was made without any sustained effort to measure exactly how much recognizable equalitarianism and individualism and self-reliance actually were in evidence either on the American frontier or in American society. There is little reason to doubt that most of his arguments were valid or that most of the traits which he emphasized did actually prevail, but it is nevertheless ironical that Turner's interpretation, which exercised such vast influence upon historians, was not based upon the historian's kind of proof, which is from evidence, but upon an argument from logic which so often fails to work out in historical experience.

But no matter how he arrived at it, Turner's picture reaffirmed some by-now-familiar beliefs about the American character. The American was equalitarian, stoutly maintaining the practices of both social and political democracy; he had a spirit of freedom reflected in his buoyance and exuberance; he was individualistic—hence "practical and inventive," "quick to find expedients," "restless, nervous, acquisitive." Turner was too much a scholar to let his evident fondness for the frontiersman run away with him entirely, and he took pains to point out that this development was not without its sordid aspects. There was a marked primitivism about the frontier, and with it, to some extent, a regression from civilized standards. The buoyant and exuberant frontiersman sometimes emulated his Indian neighbors in taking the scalps of his adversaries. Coarse qualities sometimes proved to have more survival values than gentle ones. But on the whole this regression was brief, and certainly a rough-and-ready society had its compensating advantages. Turner admired his frontiersman, and thus Turner's American, like Jefferson's American, was partly a realistic portrait from life and partly an idealized model from social philosophy. Also, though one of these figures was an agrarian and the other was a frontiersman, both were very much the same man—democratic, freedom-loving, self-reliant, and individualistic.

An essay like this is hardly the place to prove either the validity or the invalidity of the Jeffersonian and Turnerian conception of the American character. The attempt to do so would involve a review of the entire range of American historical experience, and in the course of such a review the proponents of this conception could point to a vast body of evidence in support of their interpretation. They could argue, with much force, that Americans have consistently been zealous to defend individualism by defending the rights and the welfare of the individual, and that our whole history is a protracted record of our government's recognizing its responsibility to an ever broader range of people—to men without property, to men held in slavery, to women, to small enterprises threatened by monopoly, to children laboring in factories, to industrial workers, to the ill, to the elderly, and to the unemployed. This record, it can further be argued, is also a record of the practical idealism of the American people, unceasingly at work.

But without attempting a verdict on the historical validity of this image of the American as individualist and idealist, it is important to bear in mind that this image has been partly a portrait, but also partly a model. In so far as it is a portrait—a likeness by an observer reporting on Americans whom he knew—it can be regarded as authentic testimony on the American character. But in so far as it is a model—an idealization of what is best in Americanism, and of what Americans should strive to be, it will only be misleading if used as evidence of what ordinary Americans are like in their everyday lives. It is also important to recognize that the Jefferson–Turner image posited several traits as distinctively American, and that they are not all necessarily of equal validity. Particularly, Jefferson and Turner both believed that love of equality and love of liberty go together. For Jefferson the very fact, stated in the Declaration of Independence, that "all men are created equal," carried with it the corollary that they are all therefore "entitled to (and would be eager for) life, liberty, and the pursuit of happiness." From this premise it is easy to slide imperceptibly into the position of holding that equalitarianism and individualism are inseparably linked, or even that they are somehow the same thing. This is, indeed, almost an officially sanctioned ambiguity in the American creed. But it requires only a little thoughtful reflection to recognize that equalitarianism and individualism do not necessarily go together. Alexis de Tocqueville understood this fact more than a century ago, and out of his recognition he framed an analysis which is not only the most brilliant single account of the American character, but is also the only major alternative to the Jefferson–Turner image.

After traveling the length and breadth of the United States for ten months at the height of Andrew Jackson's ascendancy, Tocqueville felt no doubt of the depth of the commitment of Americans to democracy. Throughout two volumes which ranged over every aspect of American life, he consistently emphasized democracy as a pervasive factor. But the democracy which he wrote about was far removed from Thomas Jefferson's dream.

"Liberty," he observed of the Americans, "is not the chief object of their desires; equality is their idol. They make rapid and sudden efforts to obtain liberty, and if they miss their aim resign themselves to their disappointment; but nothing can satisfy them without equality, and they would rather perish than lose it."

This emphasis upon equality was not, in itself, inconsistent with the most orthodox Jeffersonian ideas, and indeed Tocqueville took care to recognize that under certain circumstances equality and freedom might "meet and blend." But such circumstances would be rare, and the usual effects of equality would be to encourage conformity and discourage individualism, to regiment opinion and to inhibit dissent. Tocqueville justified this seemingly paradoxical conclusion by arguing that:

> When the inhabitant of a democratic country compares himself individually with all those about him, he feels with pride that he is the equal of any one of them; but when he comes to survey the totality of his fellows, and to place himself in contrast with so huge a body, he is instantly overwhelmed by the sense of his own insignificance and weakness. The same equality that renders him independent of each of his fellow citizens, taken severally, exposes him alone and unprotected to the influence of the greater number. The

public, therefore, among a democratic people, has a singular power, which
aristocratic nations cannot conceive; for it does not persuade others to its
beliefs, but it imposes them and makes them permeate the thinking of
everyone by a sort of enormous pressure of the mind of all upon the individual intelligence.

At the time when Tocqueville wrote, he expressed admiration for the
American people in many ways, and when he criticized adversely his tone
was abstract, bland, and free of the petulance and the personalities that
characterized some critics, like Mrs. Trollope and Charles Dickens. Consequently, Tocqueville was relatively well received in the United States,
and we have largely forgotten what a severe verdict his observations implied. But, in fact, he pictured the American character as the very embodiment of conformity, of conformity so extreme that not only individualism but even freedom was endangered. Because of the enormous weight
with which the opinion of the majority pressed upon the individual, Tocqueville said, the person in the minority "not only mistrusts his strength,
but even doubts of his right; and he is very near acknowledging that he is
in the wrong when the greater number of his countrymen assert that he is
so. The majority do not need to force him; they convince him." "The principle of equality," as a consequence, had the effect of "prohibiting him
from thinking at all," and "freedom of opinion does not exist in America."
Instead of reinforcing liberty, therefore, equality constituted a danger to
liberty. It caused the majority "to despise and undervalue the rights of private persons," and led on to the pessimistic conclusion that "Despotism
appears . . . peculiarly to be dreaded in democratic times."

Tocqueville was perhaps the originator of the criticism of the American as conformist, but he also voiced another criticism which has had
many echoes, but which did not originate with him. This was the con-
demnation of the American as a materialist. As early as 1805 Richard
Parkinson had observed that "all men there (in America) make it (money)
their pursuit," and in 1823 William Faux had asserted that "two selfish
gods, pleasure and gain, enslave the Americans." In the interval between
the publication of the first and second parts of Tocqueville's study, Washington Irving coined his classic phrase concerning "the almighty dollar,
that great object of universal devotion throughout the land." But it remained for Tocqueville, himself, to link materialism with equality, as he
had already linked conformity.

"Of all passions," he said, "which originate in or are fostered by equality,
there is one which it renders peculiarly intense, and which it also infuses
into the heart of every man: I mean the love of well-being. The taste for well-

being is the prominent and indelible feature of democratic times. . . . The effort to satisfy even the least wants of the body and to provide the little conveniences of life is uppermost in every mind."

He described this craving for physical comforts as a "passion," and affirmed that "I know of no country, indeed, where the love of money has taken stronger hold on the affections of men."

For more than a century we have lived with the contrasting images of the American character which Thomas Jefferson and Alexis de Tocqueville visualized. Both of these images presented the American as an equalitarian and therefore as a democrat, but one was an agrarian democrat while the other was a majoritarian democrat; one an independent individualist, the other a mass-dominated conformist; one an idealist, the other a materialist. Through many decades of self-scrutiny Americans have been seeing one or the other of these images whenever they looked into the mirror of self-analysis.

The discrepancy between the two images is so great that it must bring the searcher for the American character up with a jerk, and must force him to grapple with the question whether these seemingly antithetical versions of the American can be reconciled in any way. Can the old familiar formula for embracing opposite reports—that the situation presents a paradox—be stretched to encompass both Tocqueville and Jefferson? Or is there so grave a flaw somewhere that one must question the whole idea of national character and call to mind all the warnings that thoughtful men have uttered against the very concept that national groups can be distinguished from one another in terms of collective group traits.

Certainly there is a sound enough basis for doubting the validity of generalizations about national character. To begin with, many of these generalizations have been derived not from any dispassionate observation or any quest for truth, but from superheated patriotism which sought only to glorify one national group by invidious comparison with other national groups, or from a pseudoscientific racism which claimed innately superior qualities for favored ethnic groups. Further, the explanations which were offered to account for the ascribed traits were as suspect as the ascriptions themselves. No one today will accept the notions which once prevailed that such qualities as the capacity for self-government are inherited in the genes, nor will anyone credit the notion that national character is a unique quality which manifests itself mystically in all the inhabitants of a given country. Between the chauvinistic purposes for which the concept of national character was used, and the irrationality with which it was supported, it fell during the 1930s into a disrepute from which it has by no means fully recovered.

Some thinkers of a skeptical turn of mind had rejected the idea of national character even at a time when most historians accepted it without question. Thus, for instance, John Stuart Mill as early as 1849 observed that "of all vulgar modes of escaping from the consideration of the effect of social and moral influences on the human mind, the most vulgar is that of attributing diversities of character to inherent natural differences." Sir John Seely said, "no explanation is so vague, so cheap, and so difficult to verify."

But it was particularly at the time of the rise of Fascism and Naziism, when the vicious aspects of extreme nationalism and of racism became glaringly conspicuous, that historians in general began to repudiate the idea of national character and to disavow it as an intellectual concept, even though they sometimes continued to employ it as a working device in their treatment of the peoples with whose history they were concerned. To historians whose skepticism had been aroused, the conflicting nature of the images of the American as an individualistic democrat or as a conformist democrat would have seemed simply to illustrate further the already demonstrated flimsiness and fallacious quality of all generalizations about national character.

But to deny that the inhabitants of one country may, as a group, evince a given trait in higher degree than the inhabitants of some other country amounts almost to a denial that the culture of one people can be different from the culture of another people. To escape the pitfalls of racism in this way is to fly from one error into the embrace of another, and students of culture—primarily anthropologists, rather than historians—perceived that rejection of the idea that a group could be distinctive, along with the idea that the distinction was eternal and immutable in the genes, involved the ancient logical fallacy of throwing out the baby along with the bath. Accordingly, the study of national character came under the special sponsorship of cultural anthropology, and in the forties a number of outstanding workers in their field tackled the problem of national character, including the American character, with a methodological precision and objectivity that had never been applied to the subject before. After their investigations, they felt no doubt that national character was a reality—an observable and demonstrable reality. One of them, Margaret Mead, declared that "In every culture, in Samoa, in Germany, in Iceland, in Bali, and in the United States of America, we will find consistencies and regularities in the way in which newborn babies grow up and assume the attitudes and behavior patterns of their elders—and this we may call 'character formation.' We will find that Samoans may be said to have a Samoan character structure and Americans an American character structure." Another, the late Clyde Kluckhohn, wrote: "The statistical prediction can safely be made that a hundred Americans, for example, will display certain defined characteristics more frequently than will a hundred Englishmen comparably distributed as to age, sex, social class, and vocation."

If these new students were correct, it meant that there was some kind of identifiable American character. It might conform to the Jeffersonian image; it might conform to the Tocqueville image; it might conform in part to both; or it might conform to neither. But in any event discouraged investigators were enjoined against giving up the quest with the conclusion that there is no American character. It has been said that a philosopher is a blind man in a dark room looking for a black cat that isn't there; the student of national character might also, at times, resemble a blind man in a dark room, looking for a black cat, but the cultural anthropologists exhorted him to persevere in spite of the problems of visibility, for the cat was indubitably there.

Still confronted with the conflicting images of the agrarian democrat and the majoritarian democrat, the investigator might avoid an outright rejection of either by taking the position that the American character has changed, and that each of these images was at one time valid and realistic, but that in the twentieth century the qualities of conformity and materialism have grown increasingly prominent, while the qualities of individualism and idealism have diminished. This interpretation of a changing American character has had a number of adherents in the last two decades, for it accords well with the observation that the conditions of the American culture have changed. As they do so, of course the qualities of a character that is derived from the culture might be expected to change correspondingly. Thus, Henry S. Commager, in his *The American Mind* (1950), portrayed in two contrasting chapters "the nineteenth-century American" and "the twentieth-century American." Similarly, David Riesman, in *The Lonely Crowd* (1950), significantly subtitled *A Study of the Changing American Character*, pictured two types of Americans, first an "inner-directed man," whose values were deeply internalized and who adhered to these values tenaciously, regardless of the opinions of his peers (clearly an individualist), and second an "other-directed man," who subordinated his own internal values to the changing expectations directed toward him by changing peer groups (in short, a conformist).

Although he viewed his inner-directed man as having been superseded historically by his other-directed man, Riesman did not attempt to explain in historical terms the reason for the change. He made a rather limited effort to relate his stages of character formation to stages of population growth, but he has since then not used population phase as a key. Meanwhile, it is fairly clear, from Riesman's own context, as well as from history in general, that there were changes in the culture which would have accounted for the transition in character. Most nineteenth-century Americans were self-employed; most were engaged in agriculture; most produced a part of their own food and clothing. These facts meant that their well-being did not depend on the goodwill or the services of their associates, but upon their resourcefulness in wrestling with the elemental forces of Nature. Even their physical isolation from their fellows added something to the independence of their natures. But most twentieth-century Americans work for wages or salaries, many of them in very large employee groups; most are engaged in office or factory work; most are highly specialized; and are reliant upon many others to supply their needs in an economy with an advanced division of labor. Men now do depend upon the goodwill and the services of their fellows. This means that what they achieve depends less upon stamina and hardihood than upon their capacity to get along with other people and to fit smoothly into a cooperative relationship. In short the culture now places a premium upon the qualities which will enable the individual to function effectively as a member of a large organizational group. The strategic importance of this institutional factor has been well recognized by William H. Whyte, Jr., in his significantly titled book *The Organization Man* (1956)—for the conformity of Whyte's bureaucratized individual results from the fact that he lives under an imperative to succeed in a situation where promotion and even survival depend upon effective interaction with others in an hierarchical structure.

Thus, by an argument from logic (always a treacherous substitute for direct observation in historical study), one can make a strong case that the nineteenth-century American should have been (and therefore must have been) an individualist, while the twentieth-century American should be (and therefore is) a conformist. But this formula crashes headlong into the obdurate fact that no Americans have ever been more classically conformist than Tocqueville's Jacksonian democrats—hardy specimens of the frontier breed, far back in the nineteenth century, long before the age of corporate images, peer groups, marginal differentiation, and status frustration. In short, Tocqueville's nineteenth-century American, whether frontiersman or no, was to some extent an other-directed man. Carl N. Degler has pointed out this identity in a very cogent paper . . . in which he demonstrates very forcibly that most of our easy assumptions about the immense contrast between the nineteenth-century American and the twentieth-century American are vulnerable indeed.

This conclusion should, perhaps, have been evident from the outset, in view of the fact that it was Tocqueville who, in the nineteenth century, gave us the image which we now frequently identify as the twentieth-century American. But in any case, the fact that he did so means that we can hardly resolve the dilemma of our individualist democrat and our majoritarian democrat by assuming that both are historically valid but that one replaced the other. The problem of determining what use we can make of either of these images, in view of the fact that each casts doubt upon the other, still remains. Is it possible to uncover common factors in these apparently contradictory images, and thus to make use of them both in our quest for a definition of the national character? For no matter whether either of these versions of the American is realistic as a type or image, there is no doubt that both of them reflect fundamental aspects of the American experience.

There is no purpose, at this point in this essay, to execute a neat, pre-arranged sleight-of-hand by which the individualist democrat and the conformist democrat will cast off their disguises and will reveal themselves as identical twin Yankee Doodle Dandies, both born on the fourth of July. On the contrary, intractable, irresolvable discrepancies exist between the two figures, and it will probably never be possible to go very far in the direction of accepting the one without treating the other as a fictitious image, to be rejected as reflecting an antidemocratic bias and as at odds with the evidence from actual observation of the behavior of *Homo Americanus* in his native haunts. At the same time, however, it is both necessary to probe for the common factors, and legitimate to observe that there is one common factor conspicuous in the extreme—namely the emphasis on equality, so dear both to Jefferson's American and to Tocqueville's. One of these figures, it will be recalled, has held no truth to be more self-evident than that all men are created equal, while the other has made equality his "idol," far more jealously guarded than his liberty.

If the commitment to equality is so dominant a feature in both of these representations of the American, it will perhaps serve as a key to various facets of the national character, even to contradictory aspects of this character. In a society as complex as that of the United States, in fact, it may be that the common factors underlying the various manifestations are all that our quest should seek. For it is evident that American life and American energy have expressed themselves in a great diversity of ways, and any effort to define the American as if nearly two hundred million persons all corresponded to a single type would certainly reduce complex data to a blunt, crude, and oversimplified form. To detect what qualities Americans share in their diversity may be far more revealing than to superimpose the stereotype of a fictitious uniformity. If this is true, it means that our quest must be to discover the varied and dissimilar ways in which the commitment to equality expresses itself—the different forms which it takes in different individuals—rather than to regard it as an undifferentiated component which shows in all individuals in the same way. Figuratively, one might say that in seeking for what is common, one should think of the metal from which Americans are forged, no matter into how many shapes this metal may be cast, rather than thinking of a die with which they all are stamped into an identical shape. If the problem is viewed in this way, it will be readily apparent that Tocqueville made a pregnant statement when he observed that the idea of equality was "the fundamental fact from which all others seem to be derived."

The term "equality" is a loose-fitting garment and it has meant very different things at very different times. It is very frequently used to imply parity or uniformity. The grenadiers in the King of Prussia's guard were equal in that they were all, uniformly, over six feet six inches tall. Particularly, it can mean, and often does mean in some social philosophies, uniformity of material welfare—of income, of medical care, etc. But people are clearly not uniform in strength or intelligence or beauty, and one must ask, therefore, what kind of uniformity Americans believed in. Did they believe in an equal sharing of goods? Tocqueville himself answered this question when he said, "I know of no country . . . where a profounder contempt is expressed for the theory of the permanent equality of property."

At this point in the discussion of equality, someone, and very likely a business man, is always likely to break in with the proposition that Americans believe in equality of opportunity—in giving everyone what is called an equal start, and in removing all handicaps such as illiteracy and all privileges such as monopoly or special priority, which will tend to give one person an advantage over another. But if a person gains the advantage without having society give it to him, by being more clever or more enterprising or even just by being stronger than someone else, he is entitled to enjoy the benefits that accrue from these qualities, particularly in terms of possessing more property or wealth than others.

Historically, equality of opportunity was a particularly apt form of equalitarianism for a new, undeveloped frontier country. In the early stages of American history, the developed resources of the country were so few that an equality in the division of these assets would only have meant an insufficiency for everyone. The best economic benefit which the government could give was to offer a person free access in developing undeveloped resources for his own profit, and this is what America did offer. It was an ideal formula for everyone: for the individual it meant a very real chance to gain more wealth than he would have secured by receiving an equal share of the existing wealth. For the community, it meant that no one could prosper appreciably without activities which would develop undeveloped resources, at a time when society desperately needed rapid economic development. For these reasons, equality of opportunity did become the most highly sanctioned form of equalitarianism in the United States.

Because of this sanction, Americans have indeed been tolerant of great discrepancies in wealth. They have approved of wealth much more readily when they believed that it had been earned—as in the case, for instance, of Henry Ford—than when they thought it had been acquired by some special privilege or monopoly. In general, however, they have not merely condoned great wealth; they have admired it. But to say that the ideal of equality means only equality of opportunity is hardly to tell the whole story. The American faith has also held, with intense conviction, the belief that all men are equal in the sense that they share a common humanity—that all are alike in the eyes of God—and that every person has a certain dignity, no matter how low his circumstances, which no one else, no matter how high *his* circumstances, is entitled to disregard. When this concept of the nature of man was translated into a system of social arrangements, the crucial point on which it came to focus was the question of rank. For the concept of rank essentially denies that all men are equally worthy and argues that some are better than others—that some are born to serve and others born to command. The American creed not only denied this view, but even condemned it and placed a taboo upon it. Some people, according to the American creed, might be more fortunate than others, but they must never regard themselves as better than others. Pulling one's rank has therefore been the unforgivable sin against American democracy, and the American people have, accordingly, reserved their heartiest dislike for the officer class in the military, for people with upstage or condescending manners, and for anyone who tries to convert power or wealth (which are not resented) into overt rank or privilege (which are). Thus it is permissible for an American to have servants (which is a matter of function), but he must not put them in livery (which is a matter of rank); permissible to attend expensive schools, but not to speak with a cultivated accent; permissible to rise in the world, but never to repudiate the origins from which he rose. The most palpable and overt possible claim to rank is, of course, the effort of one individual to assert authority, in a personal sense, over others, and accordingly the rejection of authority is the most pronounced of all the concrete expressions of American beliefs in equality.

In almost any enterprise which involves numbers of people working in conjunction, it is necessary for some people to tell other people what to do. This function cannot be wholly abdicated without violating the taboos against authority. The result is that the American people have developed an arrangement which skillfully combines truth and fiction, and maintains that the top man does not rule, but leads; and does not give orders, but calls signals; while the men in the lower echelons are not underlings, but members of the team. This view of the relationship is truthful in the sense that the man in charge does depend upon his capacity to elicit the voluntary or spontaneous co-operation of the members of his organization, and he regards the naked use of authority to secure compliance as an evidence of failure; also, in many organizations, the members lend their support willingly, and contribute much more on a voluntary basis than authority could ever extact from them. But the element of fiction sometimes enters, in terms of the fact that both sides understand that in many situations authority would have to be invoked if voluntary compliance were not forthcoming. This would be humiliating to all parties—to the top man because it would expose his failure as a leader and to the others because it would force them to recognize the carefully concealed fact that in an ultimate sense they are subject to coercion. To avoid this mutually undesirable exploration of the ultimate implications, both sides recognize that even when an order has to be given, it is better for it to be expressed in the form of a request or a proposal, and when compliance is mandatory, it should be rendered with an appearance of consent.

It is in this way that the antiauthoritarian aspect of the creed of equality leads to the extraordinarily strong emphasis upon permissiveness, either as a reality or as a mere convention in American life. So strong is the taboo against authority that the father, once a paternal authority, is now expected to be a pal to his children, and to persuade rather than to command. The husband, once a lord and master, to be obeyed under the vows of matrimony, is now a partner. And if, perchance, an adult male in command of the family income uses his control to bully his wife and children, he does not avow his desire to make them obey, but insists that he only wants them to be co-operative. The unlimited American faith in the efficacy of discussion as a means of finding solutions for controversies reflects less a faith in the powers of rational persuasion than a supreme reluctance to let anything reach a point where authority will have to be invoked. If hypocrisy is the tribute that vice pays to virtue, permissiveness is, to some extent, the tribute that authority pays to the principle of equality.

When one recognizes some of these varied strands in the fabric of equalitarianism it becomes easier to see how the concept has contributed to the making both of the Jeffersonian American and the Tocquevillian American. For as one picks at the strands they ravel out in quite dissimilar directions. The strand of equality of opportunity, for instance, if followed out, leads to the theme of individualism. It challenged each individual to pit his skill and talents in a competition against the skill and talents of others and to earn the individual rewards which talent and effort might bring. Even more, the imperatives of the competitive race were so compelling that the belief grew up that everyone had a kind of obligation to enter his talents in this competition and to "succeed." It was but a step from the belief that ability and virtue would produce success to the belief that success was produced by—and was therefore an evidence of—ability and virtue. In short, money not only represented power, it also was a sign of the presence of admirable qualities in the man who attained it. Here, certainly, an equalitarian doctrine fostered materialism, and if aggressiveness and competitiveness are individualistic qualities, then it fostered individualism also.

Of course, neither American individualism nor American materialism can be explained entirely in these terms. Individualism must have derived great strength, for instance, from the reflection that if all men are equal, a man might as well form his own convictions as accept the convictions of someone else no better than himself. It must also have been reinforced by the frontier experience, which certainly compelled every man to rely upon himself. But this kind of individualism is not the quality of independent-mindedness, and it is not the quality which Tocqueville was denying when he said that Americans were conformists. A great deal of confusion has resulted, in the discussion of the American character, from the fact that the term individualism is sometimes used (as by Tocqueville) to mean willingness to think and act separately from the majority, and sometimes (as by Turner) to mean capacity to get along without help. It might be supposed that the two would converge, on the theory that a man who can get along by himself without help will soon recognize that he may as well also think for himself without help. But in actuality, this did not necessarily happen. Self-reliance on the frontier was more a matter of courage and of staying power than of intellectual resourcefulness, for the struggle with the wilderness challenged the body rather than the mind, and a man might be supremely effective in fending for himself, and at the same time supremely conventional in his ideas. In this sense, Turner's individualist is not really an antithesis of Tocqueville's conformist at all.

Still, it remains true that Jefferson's idealist and Tocqueville's conformist both require explanation, and that neither can be accounted for in the terms which make Jefferson's individualist and Tocqueville's materialist understandable. As an explanation of these facets of the American character, it would seem that the strand of equalitarianism which stresses the universal dignity of all men, and which hates rank as a violation of dignity, might be found quite pertinent. For it is the concept of the worth of every man which has stimulated a century and a half of reform, designed at every step to realize in practice the ideal that every human possesses potentialities which he should have a chance to fulfill. Whatever has impeded this fulfillment, whether it be lack of education, chattel slavery, the exploitation of the labor of unorganized workers, the hazards of unemployment, or the handicaps of age and infirmity, has been the object, at one time or another, of a major reforming crusade. The whole American commitment to progress would be impossible without a prior belief in the perfectibility of man and in the practicability of steps to bring perfection nearer. In this sense, the American character has been idealistic. And yet its idealism is not entirely irreconcilable with its materialism, for American idealism has often framed its most altruistic goals in materialistic terms—for instance, of raising the standard of living as a means to better life. Moreover, Americans are committed to the view that materialistic means are necessary to idealistic ends. Franklin defined what is necessary to a virtuous life by saying "an empty sack cannot stand upright," and Americans have believed that spiritual and humanitarian goals are best achieved by instrumentalities such as universities and hospitals which carry expensive price tags.

If the belief that all men are equal of worth has contributed to a feature of American life so much cherished as our tradition of humanitarian reform, how could it at the same time have contributed to a feature so much deplored as American conformity? Yet it has done both, for the same respect of the American for his fellow men, which has made many a reformer think that his fellow citizens are worth helping, has also made many another American think that he has no business to question the opinions that his neighbors have sanctioned. True, he says, if all men are equal, each ought to think for himself, but on the other hand, no man should consider himself better than his neighbors, and if the majority have adopted an opinion on a matter, how can one man question their opinion, without setting himself up as being better than they. Moreover, it is understood that the majority are pledged not to force him to adopt their opinion. But it is also understood that in return for this immunity he will voluntarily accept the will of the majority in most things. The absence of a formal compulsion to conform seemingly increases the obligation to conform voluntarily. Thus, the other-directed man is seen to be derived as much from the American tradition of equalitarianism as the rugged individualist, and the compulsive seeker of an unequally large share of wealth as much as the humanitarian reformer striving for the fulfillment of democratic ideals.

To say that they are all derived from the same tradition is by no means to say that they are, in some larger, mystic sense, all the same. They are not, even though the idealism of the reformer may seek materialistic goals, and though men who are individualists in their physical lives may be conformists in their ideas. But all of them, it may be argued, do reflect circumstances which are distinctively American, and all present manifestations of a character which is more convincingly American because of its diversity than any wholly uniform character could possibly be. If Americans have never reached the end of their quest for an image that would represent the American character, it may be not because they failed to find one image but because they failed to recognize the futility of attempting to settle upon one, and the necessity of accepting several.

QUESTIONS TO CONSIDER

1. What are the two basic categories of theories on the American character?
2. What is so disconcerting about the existence of two schools of thought about the American character?
3. What grounds are there for doubting the validity of generalizations about national character?
4. How did sociologist David Riesman reconcile the differences in the two generalizations in *The Lonely Crowd* (1950)? What is the crucial flaw in his explanation?
5. How does Potter reconcile Turner's individualist with de Tocqueville's conformist?
6. Summarize the thesis of the article in your own words in such a way that you could teach your roommate the basic thrust of Potter's thinking.

5

Religion and Politics
in America from the First
Settlements to the Civil War*

John M. Murrin

Carl Degler tackled some venerable myths in his article on the Puritans. In this selection, John Murrin also takes on some highly contentious beliefs about the nature of the American past. Partially in response to the rise of the religious right in the 1980s and 1990s, he explores the motivations of the original English settlers in America and the evolution of American practices of religious orthodoxy and freedom. He finds that orthodoxy was the norm in the seventeenth century, but that by the early nineteenth century religious freedom and toleration had triumphed. In the process, the Founding Fathers had consciously created a Constitution that did not include God, reflecting a prevailing attitude among them of what is today termed secular humanism by many on the religious right. Although many Americans want to believe that somehow early America was both solidly Christian and religiously free, this article suggests that the two conditions are not compatible. The United States, as a nation, has been from its beginning committed to religious freedom and pluralism.

John Murrin, professor of history at Princeton University, writes widely on all aspects of American life in the colonial and revolutionary periods. He edited *Saints and Revolutionaries: Essays on Early American History* in 1984.

*From *Religion and American Politics from the Colonial Period to the 1980s,* edited by Mark A. Noll. Footnotes omitted. Copyright © 1990 by Oxford University Press. Reprinted by permission.

Religion in America, we like to believe, is not only freer than in Europe and the rest of the world, but has always been so—or nearly always. One of the most enduring American myths—I intend nothing pejorative by this term, which I use in the anthropological sense of a body of folklore or a series of stories that organizes the way a particular culture tries to understand the world—remains the belief that this country was peopled largely by settlers fleeing religious persecution and yearning for the opportunity to worship openly and without fear. It was never that simple. At one level even popular culture provides a corrective in the equally persistent stereotype of the Puritan as cold, hard, bigoted, unimaginative, humorless—terrified by human sexuality and the enemy of all fun. "The Puritans hated bearbaiting," Thomas Babington Macaulay once remarked, "not because it gave pain to the bear, but because it gave pleasure to the spectators." American undergraduates still respond warmly to this quotation. Like their elders, they prefer to believe both clichés about religion in early America.

Of course, neither stereotype does justice to the religious complexity of early New England, much less colonial America as a whole. Most New England Puritans came to these shores not to establish religious liberty, but to practice their own form of orthodoxy. They experienced moments of tension and open conflict when they discovered that John Winthrop's orthodoxy was not Roger Williams's or Anne Hutchinson's. Perhaps Thomas Hooker's was not even John Cotton's. They spent much of the 1630s and 1640s trying to agree on what their orthodoxy was, a process that achieved institutional expression in the Cambridge Platform of 1648, bolstered on the civil side by the Body of Liberties of 1641 as it transformed itself into the law code of 1648. By 1648 most had made compromises that few had anticipated in 1630, but beyond any doubt they meant to narrow, not expand, the religious options available to people in seventeenth-century England.

They succeeded. Outside of Rhode Island, religious belief and practice became far more uniform in early New England than in the mother country at the same time. Bishops, altars, vestments, choirs, the liturgical calendar, and *The Book of Common Prayer* all failed to survive this particular Atlantic crossing, but persecution did in a limited form. Puritans used the law courts to harass and punish the small number of Quakers and Baptists that remained among them. But even though they hanged four Quakers around 1660, few Puritans were comfortable with this behavior. They preferred to cope with dissent by shunning the dissenters. Advocates of severe repression always spoke in the name of a larger religious unity, but serious efforts to implement their program ended by dividing the community, not uniting it.

Something analogous happened in seventeenth-century Virginia. The options available in England diminished sharply in the colony, but in this case dissent, not the establishment, failed to win a secure place in the new settlement. Governor Sir William Berkeley was delighted. "I thank God *there are no free schools* nor *printing,* and I hope we shall not have [either] these hundred years," he exulted; "for *learning* has brought disobedience, and heresy, and sects into the world; and *printing* has divulged them, and libels against the best government. God keep us from both." Although Virginia never obtained its own bishop in the colonial era and clergymen were usually in short supply, the colony managed fairly well as a low-key, very Low Church Anglican establishment. It kept most dissenters far away even during the turbulent 1640s and 1650s, when the Church of England collapsed at home. During the last quarter of the seventeenth century and the first quarter of the eighteenth, the church made striking institutional gains in Virginia just when dissenting energies seemed to be flagging elsewhere. Few planters lamented these restrictions on their choices.

Maryland, of course, began very differently. Although planned by the Calverts as a refuge for persecuted Roman Catholics, the proprietary family always encouraged a high degree of toleration and welcomed Presbyterian and Quaker dissenters to the province. But the hostility between Catholic and Protestant would not disappear. In the wake of the Glorious Revolution of 1688–89, Catholics were disfranchised and the Church of England became established by law. When a large majority of planters rapidly accepted the new order, dissent in all forms, Protestant or Catholic, became increasingly marginalized. The religious complexion of Maryland began to resemble that of Virginia ever more closely. Partly because they had experienced directly the bitter conflict that religious choice could foster, most Marylanders seemed relieved to be delivered from the anguish of this particular liberty. They, too, were content to enjoy fewer options than those who had remained in England.

In 1740 about 63 percent of the people of British North America lived in the New England or Chesapeake colonies under a Congregational or Anglican establishment with few real religious choices. Some dissent did exist, of course, but for the most part it was stagnant or declining. Baptists and Quakers had ceased to grow in New England before the end of the seventeenth century; in that region only Anglicans were still expanding at Congregational expense, and their numbers were still very small. Dissent had been shrinking rapidly in Maryland since the 1690s and had never achieved significance in Virginia. In both regions the clergy worried more about popular indifference and laxity than about overt denominational challenges to the established order. More than a century after the first settlements, most of the people in British America lived within a narrower band of religious choices than fellow subjects enjoyed in England. A mere half-century before the drafting of the Bill of Rights, a well-informed observer could not easily have detected in most of the American colonies much of a popular base for the active separation of church and state as proclaimed in the First Amendment.

But the Chesapeake and New England were not the whole story. What was happening among the other third of the colonial population would help to shatter this older pattern and characterize all of nineteenth-century America.

Religion in the Middle Atlantic colonies marked the most striking departure from the European norm of an established church. In New Netherland, the Dutch Reformed Church was actively supported by government, and Peter Stuyvesant grimly persecuted Quakers and other dissenters. But the church lost its privileges after the English conquest of 1664, and the Church of England never came close to providing a substitute. No regular Anglican parish was established anywhere in the colony before the 1690s. The vast bulk of the English-speaking population consisted of dissenters, mostly New Englanders with little affection for formal Anglican ways. Few settlers from a non-English background would support an Anglican establishment. Even though the legislature did establish the church in the four southern counties of the province in the 1690s, the institution remained weak, incapable of attracting the loyalties of most colonists. Toleration vanquished establishment if only because even those who favored establishment were divided over which church to support. The established churches of England, Scotland, and the Netherlands all had committed adherents by the eighteenth century. None could win preeminence in either New York or neighboring New Jersey.

In Pennsylvania and Delaware toleration became much more the preferred choice of the community as a whole. Lutheran, German Reformed, and Presbyterian clergymen lamented the "disorder" they detected all around them and sometimes all but despaired of bringing the proper worship of God to the American wilderness. But, beginning in the 1680s, the Quakers had set the tone for the Delaware Valley. At no point thereafter did an established church seem even a remotely viable option. Churches became voluntary societies that people joined only if they so desired and then supported through private contributions. They had to compete with one another for members and they received no special privileges from government. Within its small corner of New England, Rhode Island had already moved in this direction beginning in the 1630s. Somewhat less directly, North Carolina stumbled in the same direction within the colonial South. The Church of England was established there by law shortly after 1700, but most settlers seldom saw an Anglican clergyman. Dissent became the norm despite the law.

Before 1740 the Chesapeake and New England colonies narrowed the religious choices that had been generally available in England. The Middle Atlantic colonies along with Rhode Island and North Carolina expanded them. Were these trends utterly contradictory, or can we find any underlying uniformities between them?

Two points seem relevant here: the institutional possibilities that America created and the potential for sustained and effective governmental coercion. Colonial North America was not a place where everyone was "doomed" to be free. It was an institutional void. Because it lacked the fixed structures of European societies, people could try out in the wilderness a whole range of ideas and experiments impossible to attempt in Europe. Some had a liberating vision that we still find bracing. The Quakers of West New Jersey drafted and implemented a constitutional system that was as radical as anything yet tried by Europeans. Other novelties could be extremely repressive. The Americas, not Europe, witnessed the resurrection of chattel slavery on a gigantic scale.

Puritans erected their godly commonwealth in New England because the English crown would not let them do so in England. To be sure, those who had remained behind overturned the monarchy and established their own Puritan regime, but it collapsed much more quickly than the one in America. Unlike Oliver Cromwell's Protectorate, the New England Way survived long enough to expose the tensions and contradictions inherent within the Puritan vision itself. So did William Penn's Holy Experiment. Only in America did pacifists have three-fourths of a century to demonstrate whether they could or could not govern a complex society in a world often at war. Even Lord Baltimore's Maryland, too often dismissed as a stodgy anachronism, embodied an equally bold vision. Where else did a Catholic elite try to rule a Protestant majority through toleration, disestablishment, and broad political participation? To the Calverts, the emphasis on feudal hierarchy probably seemed a necessary cement for an otherwise fragile structure. The manorial system had little impact after the first decade or two, but the rest of the experiment lasted more than half a century. After 1660 it was getting stronger, not weaker, until it was undermined by the Glorious Revolution in England.

America may be, as Daniel Boorstin once argued, the burial ground for Europe's utopias. More important, it was the only place where these experiments could receive a serious trial. All were doomed to failure in

Europe. In America they got the chance to prove what they could accomplish. Only in America did several of them survive long enough to expose their inherent contradictions and to fail, not primarily because of conflict with outsiders, but through their own momentum or social dynamic. This pattern has long been clear for the New England Way and the Holy Experiment, but the logic even applies to the Church of England in colonial Virginia.

Well into the first quarter of the eighteenth century, the planters seemed quite content to remain a colonial outpost of the mother church. Then this aspiration began to collide with the underlying demographic realities of North America, which affected even public worship in profound ways. Few planters hoped to become clergymen or to have their sons ordained. William and Mary College, organized around the turn of the century, did little to change this situation. The Anglican church had to import clergy to survive. Just after 1700, the Society for the Propagation of the Gospel in Foreign Parts (SPG) made concerted efforts to send Oxford and Cambridge graduates into the colonies. In the Chesapeake the ratio of clergy to settlers reached its highest point in the 1710s. But the population of the colonies doubled every twenty-five years. Oxford and Cambridge were stagnant. Even by sustaining its efforts the SPG could not hope to keep pace with demand in North America. It too would have had to double its efforts every generation. Although it did draw increasingly upon more dynamic universities in Scotland and Ireland, it was already losing the struggle by the 1720s. Especially in the Piedmont, the Southside, and the Valley, many of the laity were slipping out of touch with the established church. The Great Awakening would soon give them a chance to improvise their own solutions to this religious dilemma.

In other societies governmental coercion might succeed in imposing orthodoxy despite these difficulties, but in all of the colonies these instruments were weak. No governor commanded a permanent military force of any significant size. No reliable hierarchy of social and economic clientage or patronage helped to ensure that lesser people would accept the religious judgments of their social superiors. To an extraordinary degree, government relied instead on voluntary cooperation to be effective. The results could be quite authoritarian when the broader population accepted such goals, as New Haven's rigid Puritan regime well illustrates. But when any sizable portion of the population rejected the values of those in office, government had little chance of securing broad compliance. The Quaker magistrates of West Jersey could not surmount the open defiance of non-Quaker settlers by the 1690s. When the justices of Albany County, New York, summoned individuals to court in the eighteenth century, a large majority never bothered to appear. If any one feature of early

America tells us how settlers who did not deliberately choose religious freedom got it anyway, the weakness of government is that factor.

For most people during the first century of settlement and beyond, religious choice remained narrower, not greater, than what England allowed. After 1740 that pattern changed irreversibly. The reasons are not hard to find—the First and Second Great Awakenings with the Revolution sandwiched between them.

Together these events generated the most important denominational reshuffling in American history. Into the 1730s the prevailing denominations were Congregationalist in New England, Anglican in the South, and—somewhat less firmly—the Quakers and their sectarian German allies in the Delaware Valley. New York and New Jersey were already a mosaic of competing denominations that no one group could dominate, a pattern that also characterized Rhode Island and North Carolina. But Congregationalists, Anglicans, and Quakers remained far more influential than all other rivals. The First Great Awakening, a series of intense revivals concentrated in the 1730s and 1740s, made New England and Virginia far more pluralistic than they had ever been before. The Revolution disestablished the Church of England from Maryland through Georgia. The Second Great Awakening, which spread throughout the continent after 1800, captured the religious loyalties of most settlers in the South and West and also disestablished the Congregational Church in the New England states. By the 1820s religious pluralism, the lack of an establishment, and full toleration had become the traditional pattern. It prevailed everywhere but in Massachusetts, which finally came into line by 1833. By then even most clergymen considered the transformation a good thing. They believed that voluntaristic religion produced healthier varieties of Christian commitment than any form of state support could generate.

In denominational terms, this shift meant that the three prevailing faiths prior to 1740 would lose influence and adherents to three newcomers by 1820. Baptists and Methodists vied for the largest membership in the United States, a contest that Methodists would win by a narrow margin before the Civil War. A distant third, but well ahead of all other rivals, were the Presbyterians. These three denominations shared one major feature—all had embraced evangelical piety in the eighteenth century. Anglicans and Quakers had rejected the Awakenings. Congregationalists in New England were divided fiercely over the revivals. Old Lights generally prevailed in eastern Massachusetts and western Connecticut, the traditional heart of each colony; New Light strength was greatest on the periphery of each. In the Middle Atlantic, the revivals also split the young Presbyterian church by 1741. Because Old Side antirevivalists outnumbered New Side awakeners at that point, the revivalists seceded from the Philadelphia Synod and organized their own synod in New York City by 1745, with the most dynamic leadership coming from the Tennent family in New Jersey and Jonathan Dickinson on Long Island. By the time this rift was healed in 1758, the New Side clergy had become far more numerous than their opponents simply because—first at the Log College in Neshaminy, Pennsylvania, and later at the College of New Jersey, finally located at Nassau Hall in Princeton in the 1750s—the New Side had acquired the means to train its own clergy. Old Side Presbyterians still relied on Ulster and Scotland as their source of ministers.

Methodists and Baptists had even greater advantages in this respect. By not insisting on a college education and by emphasizing charismatic qualities over formal learning, they could train men quickly and were ideally situated to conquer the West. The three denominations that had dominated the colonies before 1740 never made much headway in the West. Anglican settlers who crossed the mountains almost never brought the Church of England with them, although many may have preferred Methodism to other evangelical faiths because it was an offshoot of Anglicanism. Similarly, New Englanders loyal to their ancestral faith rarely remained Congregationalists when they moved west. They were much more likely to become Presbyterians. Except for a few pockets in Indiana and elsewhere, Quakers made almost no headway in the West. From the 1750s through the War of 1812, the American frontier was an exceptionally violent place, as the Iroquois, Delaware, Shawnee, Creeks, Cherokee, and Seminoles organized the last heroic phase of their resistance to settler encroachment. Quaker pacifism did not thrive in this environment.

The Revolution brought another momentous change to North America. By the late eighteenth century, the churches were no longer the only official spokesmen for public values. They had rivals. Today many Americans like to think of the Revolutionary generation as quiet and confident custodians of our fundamental values. They were less confused by their world than we are by ours. When we get into trouble, we can always turn to them to regain our moral bearings.

This vision has a fatal weakness. The Revolutionary generation never shared a single set of fundamental values. Then, as now, people had to decide which of a half-dozen sets of competing fundamental values they wished to uphold. These choices became urgent, even agonizing, as the century roared to its passionate conclusion in the violence of the French Revolution, an upheaval that shook America almost as profoundly as Europe.

At least six discernible value systems competed for the allegiance of

Americans: Calvinist orthodoxy, Anglican moralism, civic humanism, classical liberalism, Tom Paine radicalism, and Scottish moral sense and common sense philosophy. They did not exhaust the possibilities. For example, Roman Catholics and Jews affirmed very different constellations of values, but far into the nineteenth century both still remained well on the margins of American life.

The prevailing six differed dramatically. While some of their emphases could be reconciled with one another, many could not. Calvinist orthodoxy achieved its most systematic and eloquent statement in America in the writings of Jonathan Edwards and his students. It was no anachronism in the age of the Revolution. Edwardsians insisted on predestination, the inerrancy of Scripture, and the centrality of the conversion experience in the life of a Christian. To be converted, a person must first recognize his or her utter lack of merit in the eyes of God. Only then would God bestow saving grace on someone to whom He owed nothing whatever. Anglican moralists, by contrast, rejected the necessity of a conversion experience and emphasized the need to lead an ethical life in this world. This tradition left few systematic expressions in eighteenth-century America, but it undoubtedly made a deep impact on gentleman planters and other elite groups. Civic humanism went even farther in its concentration upon this worldly activities. The fullest life, its apologists insisted, is that of the citizen who must always be willing to sacrifice self-interest for the common good. Civic humanists gloried in their own rectitude and incorruptibility. Although many evangelical Calvinists could embrace the ethic of sacrifice that civic humanists demanded, few men who began as civic humanists could ever become evangelical Calvinists. They could not persuade themselves that their best deeds stank in the nostrils of the Lord. They could not achieve the humility essential to an orthodox conversion experience.

Classical liberalism—the philosophy that society will be much better off if individuals are left free to pursue their self-interest with minimal governmental restraint—clashed with all three of the older value systems. In many ways it grew out of the natural rights philosophy of John Locke, a Socinian (or proto-Unitarian) in theology. Its principal European spokesmen after 1740—David Hume, Adam Smith, Jeremy Bentham, and, later, John Stuart Mill—were all atheists, although Smith never advertised his loss of faith. Liberalism seemed to transform the Christian sin of greed into a civic virtue. It seemed to mock the civic humanist commitment to disinterested patriotism. Tom Paine's admirers posed equally dramatic challenges. Many were deists rather than unbelievers, but their challenge to Protestant orthodoxy drove many clergymen close to panic in the 1790s. Radicals also challenged an assumption common among moderate and conservative civic humanists, that gentlemen of leisure made the best citizens and officeholders. To radicals, this claim was but a disguised assertion of aristocratic privilege. Only men who worked for a living deserved the confidence of other citizens.

Scottish moral sense philosophy derived mostly from Francis Hutcheson of Glasgow and from the Edinburgh literati, a remarkably talented group that made important contributions to most fields of knowledge in the last half of the eighteenth century. The Scots tried to synthesize the best of existing knowledge. Moral sense philosophy tried to find a more compelling basis for human ethics than John Locke's highly cerebral reliance upon explicit understanding of natural law among people living in the state of nature. The Scots, whose curiosity drove them to read much of the descriptive literature about American Indians, had difficulty imagining the Iroquois, for example, rationally deducing the laws of nature in their long houses before embarking on moral behavior. Instead the Scots endowed every human with a moral sense, an ingrained and instantaneous response to external stimuli. Until corrupted by their cultures or by habit, people react positively to benevolent actions (for example, a mother nursing her infant) and negatively to malevolence (for instance, teenagers clubbing a grandmother). Common sense philosophy provided an antedote to the skepticism of David Hume by trying to establish, first, what people can take for granted and then by building larger philosophical systems upon this foundation. At first, many Calvinists regarded moral sense philosophy as a challenge to the doctrine of original sin, but by the end of the century Scottish learning had triumphed almost completely in American academic life. Scottish common sense philosophy is still taught today in fundamentalist schools. Its original enemies have become its warmest advocates.

Partly because disestablishment took government out of the business of proclaiming and defending fundamental values, the struggle among these systems was passionate but seldom violent. The state did not execute nonjuring clergymen—unlike the government of revolutionary France, which brought many priests to the guillotine. Although the officeholding class in the United States was probably no more orthodox than its counterparts in Britain and France, nearly all public officials deliberately minimized rather than emphasized how far they had strayed from ancestral beliefs. Thomas Jefferson and James Madison cooperated actively with Baptists and Presbyterians in Virginia politics to disestablish the Protestant Episcopal Church, but to the dismay of many Presbyterians they also refused to sanction tax support for any other denomination or combination of denominations. Jefferson and Madison along with

George Washington, John Adams, Benjamin Franklin, and nearly all of the Founding Fathers claimed to be Christians; but, by virtually any standard of doctrinal orthodoxy, hardly any of them was. They demanded the right to think for themselves on the most sensitive questions of faith, doctrine, and morals, but they did not try to impose their conclusions on others by force.

Yet these were precisely the men who led the way in drafting the nation's fundamental laws—its most admired constitutions, state and national, and its bills of rights at both levels. The first state constitutions usually invoked God somewhere in the text. "The People of this State, being by the Providence of God, free and independent," declared Connecticut in converting its royal charter into a constitution in 1776, "have the sole and exclusive Right of governing themselves as a free, sovereign, and independent State. . . ." The preamble of the Massachusetts Constitution of 1780 explicitly recognized the providence of God while "imploring His direction" in framing a government derived from the people. New Hampshire in 1784 based all "due subjection" to government upon "morality and piety, rightly grounded on evangelical principles."

The explicit theism of these pronouncements made them exceptional at the time. Other constitutions were more perfunctory, or they used the language of the Enlightenment rather than Scripture or the ritual phrases of any of the Protestant churches. The preamble to the Pennsylvania Constitution, for instance, proclaimed that government exists to protect natural rights "and the other blessings which the Author of existence has bestowed upon man" and acknowledges "the goodness of the great Governour of the universe" for the people's opportunity "to form for themselves such just rules as they shall think best for governing their future society." Even Massachusetts, while explicitly invoking providence, avoided the word "God." Instead the drafters acknowledged "with grateful hearts, the goodness of the Great Legislator of the Universe" in permitting the people of the commonwealth to assemble peaceably and create their own "original, explicit and solemn compact with each other." The preamble to the Vermont Constitution of 1777 saluted natural rights "and the other blessings which the Author of existence has bestowed upon man." Neither Pennsylvania nor Vermont joined Massachusetts in recognizing divine providence. Both assumed that the people had to make their political decisions for themselves. Even the Articles of Confederation, something less than a full organic document, explicitly invoked God, "the Great Governor of the world," who, however, assumed something more than a deistical role when He "incline[d] the hearts of the legislatures we represent in Congress, to approve of . . . the said articles of confederation and perpetual union."

In some states the reference to God was casual and incidental, but it did reveal something about popular expectations. Virginia mentioned God only in the last clause of the Declaration of Rights, which guaranteed full religious freedom because "Religion, or the duty which we owe to our Creator, and the manner of discharging it, can be directed only by reason and conviction, not by force or violence." The New Jersey Constitution closely followed this model. Georgia acknowledged a deity only in prescribing specific texts for several oaths. Maryland made no explicit mention of God's blessings, but in requiring all officeholders to be Christians, its constitution was in fact far more traditional than most others of the period. In a slightly weaker clause, North Carolina, after barring all clergymen from public office (as did several other states), required all officeholders to believe in God, an afterlife, the truth of the Protestant religion, and the divine authority of both the Old and New Testaments.

In the light of this pattern, the failure of the Federal Constitution to mention God becomes all the more significant. The delegates to the Philadelphia Convention must have realized that they were doing something singular in this respect. They used the text of the Articles of Confederation quite often for specific clauses of the Constitution, but they omitted the passage that invoked God. They were used to seeing chaplains in their state legislatures and in the Continental Congress, but they invited none to participate in their deliberations. This choice was no mere oversight. When disagreements became particularly ferocious in late June 1787, Franklin moved to invite one or more clergymen to lead them in prayer at the beginning of each day. Hamilton objected on grounds of realpolitik. The delegates had sent for no chaplain until then; to do so at that moment could only inform the world how badly at odds they were. Edmund Randolph countered with the shrewd suggestion that they first invite a minister for the Fourth of July celebration and then continue the practice thereafter. The public would not realize that a transition had occurred. But the resolution won little support in either form—four votes, in all probability, with only Roger Sherman and Jonathan Dayton joining Franklin and Randolph. Yet even in a convention closed to the public, the majority was much too prudent to vote directly against God. Instead, Hamilton and Madison carried a motion to adjourn.

The Federal Constitution was, in short, the eighteenth-century equivalent of a secular humanist text. The delegates were not a very orthodox group of men in any doctrinal sense. The only born-again Christian among them was probably Richard Bassett of Delaware, a Methodist who generously supported the labors of Francis Asbury and other missionaries but who said nothing at the Convention. Roger Sherman may have been another, but his advocacy of New Light causes in Connecticut seems more political than religious. One cliché often applied to the Constitution is not correct in any literal sense—that at least the Founders, unlike the wildly optimistic French, believed in original sin and its implications for government and politics.

Quite possibly not a single delegate accepted Calvinist orthodoxy on original sin—that man is irretrievably corrupted and damned unless redeemed from the outside. Washington, Franklin, Madison, Hamilton, James Wilson, and Gouverneur Morris gave no sign of such a belief at this phase of their lives. As a Methodist, even Bassett was probably an Arminian in theology, willing—like John Wesley—to give individuals some effective agency in their own salvation.

But if the delegates did not think that man is irrevocably corrupted, they did believe that he is highly corruptible and that a surrender to corruption had destroyed nearly every republic before their day. When combined with the vestige of aristocratic honor that most Founders shared, this fear came to mean something rather different, a conviction that *other people* are corrupt. The typical Founding Father repeatedly insisted that *his* motives were pure, disinterested, patriotic—a judgment often extended to one's close friends in public life as well. Jefferson had no higher praise for Madison, but he always suspected Hamilton of sinister designs.

Although the dread of corruption had a genuine affinity for orthodox Christian values, it drew far more directly from civic humanist sources, the effort by the seventeenth and eighteenth centuries to understand why republics had failed in the past and how they could be constructed to endure. The Convention's answer to this problem, although not always civic humanist in content and emphasis, came very close in most particulars to what today's evangelicals mean by secular humanist.

In their television sermons, Jerry Falwell and Jimmy Swaggart usually define three components as the essential ingredients of secular humanism. First is the willingness to elevate human reason above divine revelation whenever a conflict appears between them. Beyond any doubt nearly all of the Founders qualify on this score. Jefferson and Adams certainly fit that description. Madison, although he probably contemplated entering the ministry as a young college graduate and affirmed some basic Calvinist tenets as late as 1778, seemed much more comfortable with nature's supreme being than with the God of revelation by the 1780s. He looked increasingly to history, not to the Bible, for political guidance. James Wilson also believed that the Bible usefully reinforced moral precepts that we learn through our moral sense and reason, not the other way around.

As a group, the Founders took Protestant private judgment a step beyond earlier eras and used it to evaluate the plausibility of Scripture itself.

Most of them were extremely reluctant to use the word "God" or "Christ." They flatly rejected miracles, whether attested by Scripture or not. As Jefferson advised his nephew, one should read the Bible as one would any other book, accepting what is edifying and rejecting what is fantastic. He chose a sensitive issue on which to make his point. The Virgin Birth being impossible, Jesus of Nazareth must have been a bastard. "And the day will come," he assured John Adams several decades later, "when the mystical generation of Jesus by the supreme being as his father in the womb of a virgin will be classed with the fable of the generation of Minerva in the brain of Jupiter."

A second criterion of secular humanism is the conviction that human solutions are adequate for human problems. Politicians need not invoke God or providence. At the Philadelphia Convention, a large majority explicitly refused to do so, as we have seen, and they proceeded to devise a constitution that, in the words of one nineteenth-century admirer, became "a machine that would go of itself." Built-in checks and balances pitted one human passion against another. The separation of powers kept Congress, the president, and the courts warily watching one another. The House and Senate likewise checked each other and within the broader federal system, so did the state and national governments as a whole. Madison hoped that he had created a political system that would routinely produce leaders who could identify and pursue the common good above narrow and selfish interests. In this respect he left little to chance—or providence. Instead, he put his confidence in the structure of the constitutional system as a whole.

Ethical relativism has become the third component of secular humanism, at least as defined by televangelists. In the modern sense of a truly relative or situational ethics, the term does not apply to the Founders. But while they admired the moral precepts of Jesus of Nazareth, virtually all of them also believed that man can do better than what the Bible prescribes. Anticlerical in a rather gentle way, they were extremely reluctant to let any minister or church define their moral priorities for them. They believed that man was still making tremendous improvements in the moral character of public life, which, on the whole, they valued above traditional private morality. The churches, they noted quietly from time to time, had contributed much misery to the world through internal conflict and persecution. Rational man, they assumed, ought to do better. They aspired, in short, to something more perfect than the organized Christianity of their own day. They differed from ethical relativists of today in their expectation that reasonable men would someday find a loftier moral code that all could affirm and implement. When Jefferson predicted shortly before he died that most American youths would enter adulthood as Unitarians, he proved to be a terrible prophet. But what he really meant is that he expected them to embody a stronger morality than traditional churches had espoused.

On all of these grounds the Founders meet the definition of secular humanism. If it is now ruining the republic, they started the process. At a minimum they expanded the content of American pluralism. Secular values became so prominent in the overall revolutionary achievement that, fully as much as the Puritan vision of an earlier age, they emerged as an essential part of the American experience. Of course, the two systems of thought overlapped at many points. Defenders of the Puritan tradition were already recasting its original emphasis on religious and civil liberty (which in 1630 had meant the political freedom to practice religious orthodoxy unrestrained from abroad) into a new hierarchy that valued civil over religious liberty. Secular apologists for the republic, if they had a taste for historical precedents, usually learned to admire Roger Williams and Anne Hutchinson, George Fox and William Penn. Yet, despite genuine similarities, the underlying motivations between seventeenth-century religious radicals and eighteenth-century revolutionaries were quite different. Williams and the Quakers favored a sharp separation of church and state because they were convinced that in any formal union, the state will always corrupt the church. Jefferson and Madison also favored rigid separation, but for the opposite reason. They believed that when any church is established by law, it will corrupt the polity.

The potential for conflict between secular leaders and the defenders of orthodoxy remained quite strong throughout the era of the Revolution and the early republic. At times clerical denunciations of the new godlessness became shrill and even hysterical, particularly in the assault upon the Bavarian Illuminati in 1798, a secret and conspiratorial group credited with the destruction of religion in France and who were now, supposedly, trying to repeat that triumph in America. When Jefferson ran for president in 1800, his religious convictions—or lack thereof—became a major campaign issue in New England.

And yet the truly remarkable feature about the age as a whole is how contained this struggle was. About half of the clergy of France could not accept the Civil Constitution of the Clergy and became enemies of the revolutionary regime. In the United States nearly all of the clergy (including even a majority of Anglicans) supported the Revolution, the Constitution, and later the War of 1812. Some of them perfectly understood the secular vision of the Founding Fathers. "We formed our Constitution without any acknowledgment of God . . . ," reflected Timothy Dwight as the War of 1812 threatened to engulf the land in a new calamity. "The Convention, by which it was formed, never asked, even once, his direction, or his blessing upon their labours. Thus we commenced our national existence under the present system, without God." But this tone was never the predominant one even among the clergy, most of whom greatly preferred the Constitution to the Articles of Confederation in 1788 and never saw reason to change their mind.

How can we explain this conflict that never quite happened? Several reasons come to mind. One is the most obvious contrast between religion and revolution in France and America. France's radical republicans gloried in their assault upon orthodoxy, while the Founding Fathers all claimed to be "Christians." They used the word in a way that aroused the suspicions of numerous ministers, but in doing so they also signaled their unwillingness to fight, at least in public, about such issues. New England Federalists denounced Jefferson's godlessness in 1800. He never replied. Madison kept his religious opinions very much to himself as he drifted away from orthodoxy. Second, although the Constitution was in no explicit way a religious text, it was also not antireligious. It provided no overt threat to anybody's doctrinal convictions. Firm believers in original sin could find much to admire in it even if its drafters did not share their conviction. Finally, the secular humanists of 1787 eventually had to confront Madison's own logic about how things really worked in America. By 1798, as part of his own defense of the states' rights position of the Jeffersonian opposition, Madison insisted that the Philadelphia Convention never had power to implement and therefore define the meaning of the Constitution. That act took place through the process of ratification. Only the people in their separate state conventions had the power to put the Constitution into practice. Through the same process, only they could decide what it means.

In the nineteenth century, the American public sacralized the Constitution. The extreme case is the Mormon church, which still teaches that the Convention was inspired by God, that the Constitution is thus the product of explicit divine intervention in history. Others did not go that far, but by the 1820s, mostly because of Jonathan Dayton's garbled recollections, they were quite happy to believe that Franklin's prayer motion at the Convention not only carried but was passed with at most a single dissent, and that it also marked the turning point in the debates. Soon after sending for a minister, according to Dayton's version, the large and small states agreed upon the Great Compromise, and the republic was saved. No effective answer to this claim was available until 1840, when Madison's notes were finally published. By then the public's eagerness to sanctify the secular had probably gone too far to reverse.

Americans are indeed a peculiar people. The enormous range of religious choice available to the public since the late eighteenth century has generally favored evangelical Protestants over more traditional ones, but it has also energized Roman Catholics to a startling degree. While Catholicism faced a serious threat of decline nearly everywhere in nineteenth-century Europe, it built a larger and more faithful base of communicants in the United States than anywhere else in the world. American Catholics were also less inclined to heresy and more loyal to the pope than just about any other large body of Catholics in the world. Somehow the most traditional as well as the most evangelical of Christian churches were able to thrive in America. The land foreordained nobody's success, but it did provide amazing opportunities that groups and institutions could learn to use if they had sufficient energy and imagination.

The Revolution also liberated an important group of gentlemen from the constraints of orthodoxy long enough for them to draft the constitutions and bills of rights at both the state and federal levels. Major elements of the broader public have been trying to Christianize these texts ever since.

The real meaning of America and the American Revolution is not in one alternative rather than the other, but in their continuing and dramatic interaction. Neither the orthodox nor the skeptics have ever been able to destroy one another. Neither can ever do so without drastically redefining the whole of the American experience. At some periods, such as the New Deal era, this tension has been very much muted. At other times it has come close to defining the central issues of the age. Without the Northern evangelical assault upon slavery, there would have been no Civil War. Without the evangelical resurgence in the United States from the 1960s to the present, there probably would have been no Reagan Revolution—a lesser matter, to be sure, but hardly a trivial one.

The tension between secular humanist and orthodox or evangelical values has been an active part of American public life for two centuries. It shows no sign of abating.

QUESTIONS TO CONSIDER

1. What does Murrin cite as an enduring American myth? What equally mythologocial antidote does he offer?
2. By 1740, what had become of religious freedom in New England, Virginia, and Maryland?
3. What feature of colonial America best explains how settlers got considerable religious freedom whether or not they sought it? Explain.
4. What three events in the century after 1740 transformed America from having narrower religious choices than England to having broader options? Which three denominations replaced which other three as dominant during that century, and why?

5. What six value systems does Murrin suggest competed for American allegiance in the late eighteenth century? Which most appeals to you?

6. How did the values of the Founding Fathers affect the writing of the United States Constitution? How did their view of human sinfulness differ from Calvinist orthodoxy?

7. How did the Founding Fathers embody the three essential elements of secular humanism?

8. How did the American revolutionary experience differ from the French in the area of religion?

6

England's Vietnam: The American Revolution*

Richard M. Ketchum

Richard Ketchum (1922–   ), a former editor of *American Heritage* magazine, has written and edited numerous books, including *The American Heritage Book of the Revolution* (1958) and *The Battle for Bunker Hill* (1962).

While history never exactly repeats itself, events frequently follow patterns surprisingly close to those of the past. One of the primary values of the study of history is to make us aware of the parallels between present problems and those of the past. Failure to perceive such similarities can doom us to repeat past mistakes. In this article Ketchum notes a number of remarkable parallels between Great Britain's attitude toward the American Revolution and American attitudes toward the Vietnam War two hundred years later. He wrote this article in 1971 in hopes of convincing Americans of the error of their involvement in Vietnam. The facts speak eloquently for themselves. If only, he laments, Presidents Kennedy, Johnson, and Nixon had paid more attention in class when they were studying the American Revolution.

This article, along with observation of the behavior of England and the United States as great powers, suggests that the national character of a country, like the character of a person, is a blend of heredity and environment. Understanding this hereditary simi-

*Reprinted by permission of *American Heritage* magazine, a division of Forbes, Inc. © Forbes, Inc., 1971.

larity should help clarify the way in which the American character was forged.

If it is true that those who cannot remember the past are condemned to repeat it, America's last three Presidents might have profited by examining the ghostly footsteps of America's last king before pursuing their adventure in Vietnam. As the United States concludes a decade of war in Southeast Asia, it is worth recalling the time, two centuries ago, when Britain faced the same agonizing problems in America that we have met in Vietnam. History seldom repeats itself exactly, and it would be a mistake to try to equate the ideologies or the motivating factors involved; but enough disturbing parallels may be drawn between those two distant events to make one wonder if the Messrs. Kennedy, Johnson, and Nixon had their ears closed while the class was studying the American Revolution.

Britain, on the eve of that war, was the greatest empire since Rome. Never before had she known such wealth and power; never had the future seemed so bright, the prospects so glowing. All, that is, except the spreading sore of discontent in the American colonies that, after festering for a decade and more, finally erupted in violence at Lexington and Concord on April 19, 1775. When news of the subsequent battle for Bunker Hill reached England that summer, George III and his ministers concluded that there was no alternative to using force to put down the insurrection. In the King's mind, at least, there was no longer any hope of reconciliation—nor did the idea appeal to him. He was determined to teach the rebellious colonials a lesson, and no doubts troubled him as to the righteousness of the course he had chosen. "I am not sorry that the line of conduct seems now chalked out," he had said even before fighting began; later he told his prime minister, Lord North, "I know I am doing my Duty and I can never wish to retract." And then, making acceptance of the war a matter of personal loyalty, "I wish nothing but good," he said, "therefore anyone who does not agree with me is a traitor and a scoundrel." Filled with high moral purpose and confidence, he was certain that "when once these rebels have felt a smart blow, they will submit . . . ."

In British political and military circles there was general agreement that the war would be quickly and easily won. "Shall we be told," asked one of the King's men in Commons, "that (the Americans) can resist the powerful efforts of this nation?" Major John Pitcairn, writing home from Boston in March, 1775, said "I am satisfied that one active campaign, a smart action, and burning two or three of the towns, will set everything to rights." The man who would direct the British navy during seven years of war, the unprincipled, inefficient Earl of Sandwich, rose in the House of Lords to express his opinion of the provincial fighting man. "Suppose the Colonies do abound in men," the First Lord of the Admiralty asked, "what does that signify? They are raw, undisciplined, cowardly men. I wish instead of forty or fifty thousand of these *brave* fellows they would produce in the field at least two hundred thousand; the more the better, the easier would be the conquest; if they did not run away, they would starve themselves into compliance with our measures. . . ." And General James Murray, who had succeeded the great Wolfe in 1759 as commander in North America, called the native American "a very effeminate thing, very unfit for and very impatient of war." Between these estimates of the colonial militiaman and a belief that the might of Great Britain was invincible, there was a kind of arrogant optimism in official quarters when the conflict began. "As there is not common sense in protracting a war of this sort," wrote Lord George Germain, the secretary for the American colonies, in September, 1775, "I should be for exerting the utmost force of this Kingdom to finish the rebellion in one campaign."

Optimism bred more optimism, arrogance more arrogance. One armchair strategist in the House of Commons, William Innes, outlined for the other members an elaborate scheme he had devised for the conduct of the war. First, he would remove the British troops from Boston, since that place was poorly situated for defense. Then, while the people of the Massachusetts Bay Colony were treated like the madmen they were and shut up by the navy, the army would move to one of the southern colonies, fortify itself in an impregnable position, and let the provincials attack if they pleased. The British could sally forth from this and other defensive enclaves at will, and eventually "success against one-half of America will pave the way to the conquest of the whole. . . ." What was more, Innes went on, it was "more than probable you may find men to recruit your army in America." There was a good possibility, in other words, that the British regulars would be replaced after a while by Americans who were loyal to their king, so that the army fighting the rebels would be Americanized, so to speak, and the Irish and English lads sent home. General James Robertson also believed that success lay in this scheme of Americanizing the combat force: "I never had an idea of subduing the Americans," he said, "I meant to assist the good Americans to subdue the bad."

This notion was important not only from the standpoint of the fighting, but in terms of administering the colonies once they were beaten; loyalists would take over the reins of government when the British pulled out, and loyalist militiamen would preserve order in the pacified colonies. No one knew, of course, how many "good" Americans there were; some thought they might make up half or more of the population. Shortly after arriving in the colonies in 1775, General William Howe, for one, was convinced that "the insurgents are very few, in comparison with the whole of the people."

Before taking the final steps into full-scale war, however, the King and his ministers had to be certain about one vitally important matter: They had to be able to count on the support of the English people. On several occasions in 1775 they were able to read the public pulse (that part of it, at least, that mattered) by observing certain important votes in Parliament. The King's address to both Houses on October 26, in which he announced plans to suppress the uprising in America, was followed by weeks of angry debate; but when the votes were counted, the North ministry's majority was overwhelming. Each vote indicated the full tide of anger that influenced the independent members, the country gentlemen who agreed that the colonials must be put in their place and taught a lesson. A bit out of touch with the news, highly principled, and content in the belief that the King and the ministry must be right, none of them seem to have asked what would be the best for the empire; they simply went along with the vindictive measures that were being set in motion. Eloquent voices—those of Edmund Burke, Charles James Fox, the Earl of Chatham, John Wilkes, among others—were raised in opposition to the policies of the Crown, but as Burke said, ". . . it was almost in vain to contend, for the country gentlemen had abandoned their duty, and placed an implicit confidence in the Minister."

The words of sanity and moderation went unheeded because the men who spoke them were out of power and out of public favor; and each time the votes were tallied, the strong, silent, unquestioning majority prevailed. No one in any position of power in the government proposed, after the Battle of Bunker Hill, to halt the fighting in order to settle the differences; no one seriously contemplated conversations that might have led to peace. Instead the government—like so many governments before and since—took what appeared to be the easy way out and settled for war.

George III was determined to maintain his empire, intact and undiminished, and his greatest fear was that the loss of the American colonies would set off a reaction like a line of dominoes falling. Writing to Lord North in 1779, he called the contest with America "the most serious in which any country was ever engaged. It contains such a train of consequences that they must be examined to feel its real weight. . . . Independence is (the Americans') object, which every man not willing to sacrifice every object to a momentary and inglorious peace must concur with me in thinking this country can never submit to. Should America succeed in that, the West Indies must follow, not in independence, but for their own interest they must become dependent on America. Ireland would soon follow, and this island reduced to itself, would be a poor island indeed."

Despite George's unalterable determination, strengthened by his domino theory; despite the wealth and might of the British empire; despite all the odds favoring a quick triumph, the problems facing the King and his ministers and the armed forces were formidable ones indeed. Surpassing all others in sheer magnitude was the immense distance between the mother country and the rebellious colonies. As Edmund Burke described the situation in his last, most eloquent appeal for the conciliation, "Three thousand miles of ocean lie between you and them. No contrivance can prevent the effect of this distance in weakening government. Seas roll, and months pass, between the order and the execution; and the want of a speedy explanation of a single point is enough to defeat a whole system." Often the westerly passage took three months, and every soldier, every weapon, every button and gaiter and musket ball, every article of clothing and great quantities of food and even fuel, had to be shipped across those three thousand miles of the Atlantic. It was not only immensely costly and time consuming, but there was a terrifying wastefulness to it. Ships sank or were blown hundreds of miles off course, supplies spoiled, animals died en route. Worse yet, men died, and in substantial numbers: Returns from regiments sent from the British Isles to the West Indies between 1776 and 1780 reveal that an average of 11 percent of the troops was lost on these crossings.

Beyond the water lay the North American land mass, and it was an article of faith on the part of many a British military man that certain ruin lay in fighting an enemy on any large scale in that savage wilderness. In the House of Lords in November, 1775, the Duke of Richmond warned the peers to consult their geographies before turning their backs on a peaceful settlement. There was, he said, "one insuperable difficulty with which an army would have to struggle"—America abounded in vast rivers that provided natural barriers to the progress of troops; it was a country in which every bush might conceal an enemy, a land whose cultivated parts would be laid waste, so that "the army (if any army could march or subsist) would be obliged to draw all its provisions from Europe, and all its fresh meat from Smithfield market." The French, the mortal enemies of the Great Britain, who had seen a good deal more of the North American wilds than the English had, were already laying plan to capitalize on the situation when the British army was bogged down there. In Paris, watchfully eyeing his adversary's every move, France's foreign minister, the Comte de Vergennes, predicted in July, 1775, that "it will be vain for the English to multiply their forces" in the colonies; "no longer can they bring that vast continent back to dependence by force of arms." Seven years later, as the war drew to a close, one of Rochambeau's aides told a friend of Charles James Fox: "No opinion was clearer than that though the people of America might be conquered by well-disciplined European troops, the country of America was unconquerable."

Yet even in 1775 some thoughtful Englishmen doubted if the American people or their army could be defeated. Before the news of Bunker

Hill arrived in London, the adjutant general declared that a plan to defeat the colonials militarily was "as wild an idea as ever controverted common sense," and the secretary-at-war, Lord Barrington, had similar reservations. As early as 1774 Barrington ventured the opinion that a war in the wilderness of North America would cost Britain far more than she could ever gain from it; that the size of the country and the colonials' familiarity with firearms would make victory questionable—or at best achievable only at the cost of enormous suffering; and finally if Britain would win such a contest, Barrington believed that the cost of maintaining the colonies in any state of subjection would be staggering. John Wilkes, taunting Lord North on this matter of military conquest, suggested that North—even if he rode out at the head of the entire English cavalry—would not venture ten miles into the countryside for fear of guerrilla fighters. "The Americans," Wilkes promised, "will dispute every inch of territory with you, every narrow pass, every strong defile, every Thermopylae, every Bunker's Hill."

It was left to the great William Pitt to provide the most stirring warning against fighting the Americans. Now Earl of Chatham, he was so crippled in mind and body that he rarely appeared in the House of Lords, but in May, 1777, he made the supreme effort, determined to raise his voice once again in behalf of conciliation. Supported on canes, his eyes flashing with the old fire and his beak-like face thrust forward belligerently, he warned the peers: "You cannot conquer the Americans. You talk of your numerous friends to annihilate the Congress, and of your powerful forces to disperse their army, but I might as well talk of driving them before me with this crutch. . . . You have been three years teaching them the art of war, and they are apt scholars. I will venture to tell your lordships that the American gentry will make officers enough fit to command the troops of all the European powers. What you have sent there are too many to make peace, to few to make war. You cannot make them respect you. You cannot make them wear your cloth. You will plant an invincible hatred in their breast against you . . ."

"My lords," he went on, "you have been the aggressors from the beginning. I say again, this country has been the aggressor. You have made descents upon their coasts. You have burnt their towns, plundered their country, made war upon the inhabitants, confiscated their property, proscribed and imprisoned their persons. . . . The people of America look upon Parliament as the authors of their miseries. Their affections are estranged from their sovereign. Let then, reparation come from the hands that inflicted the injuries. Let conciliation succeed chastisement. . . ." But there was no persuading the majority; Chatham's appeal was rejected and the war went on unabated.

It began to appear, however, that destruction of the Continental

Army—even if that goal could be achieved—might not be conclusive. After the disastrous campaign around Manhattan in 1776, George Washington had determined not to risk his army in a major engagement, and he began moving away from the European battle style in which two armies confronted each other head to head. His tactical method became that of the small, outweighed prizefighter who depends on his legs to keep him out of range of his opponent and who, when the bigger man begins to tire, darts in quickly to throw a quick punch, then retreats again. It was an approach to fighting described by Nathanael Greene, writing of the campaign in the South in 1780: "We fight, get beat, rise, and fight again." In fact, between January and September of the following year, Greene, short of money, troops, and supplies, won a major campaign without ever really winning a battle. The battle at Guilford Courthouse, which was won by the British, was typical of the results. As Horace Walpole observed, "Lord Cornwallis has conquered his troops out of shoes and provisions and himself out of troops."

There was, in the colonies, no great political center like Paris or London, whose loss might have been demoralizing to the Americans; indeed, Boston, New York, and Philadelphia, the seat of government, were all held at one time or another by the British without irreparable damage to the rebel cause. The fragmented political and military structure of the colonies was often a help to the rebels, rather than a hindrance, for it meant that there was almost no chance of the enemy striking a single crushing blow. The difficulty, as General Frederick Haldimand, who succeeded Carleton in Canada, saw it, was the seemingly unending availability of colonial militiamen who rose up out of nowhere to fight in support of the nucleus of regular troops called the Continental Army. "It is not the number of troops Mr. Washington can spare from his army that is to be apprehended," Haldimand wrote, "it is the multitude of militia and men in arms ready to turn out at an hour's notice at the shew of a single regiment of Continental Troops. . . ." So long as the British were able to split up their forces and fan out over the countryside in relatively small units, they were fairly successful in putting down the irregulars' activities and cutting off their supplies; but the moment they had to concentrate again to fight the Continentals, guerrilla warfare burst out like so many brush fires on their flank and rear. No British regular could tell if an American was friend or foe, for loyalty to King George was easy to attest; and the man who was a farmer or merchant when a British battalion marched by his home was a militiaman as soon as it had passed by, ready to shoulder his musket when an emergency or an opportunity to confound the enemy arose.

Against an unnumberable supply of irregular forces the British could bring to bear only a fixed quantity of troops—however many, that is, they happened to have on the western side of the Atlantic Ocean at any given moment. Early in the war General James Murray had foreseen the difficulties that would undoubtedly arise. Writing to Lord Barrington, he warned that military conquest was no real answer. If the war proved to be a long one, their advantage in numbers would heavily favor the rebels, who could replace their losses while the British could not. Not only did every musket and grain of powder have to be shipped across the ocean; but if a man was killed or wounded, the only way to replace him was to send another man in full kit across the Atlantic. And troop transports were slow and small: Three or four were required to move a single battalion.

During the summer of 1775 recruiting went badly in England and Ireland, for the war was not popular with a lot of the people who would have to fight it, and there were jobs to be had. It was evident that the only means of assembling a force large enough to suppress the rebellion in the one massive stroke that had been determined upon was to hire foreign troops. And immediately this word was out, the rapacious petty princes of Brunswick, Hesse-Cassel, and Waldeck, and the Margrave of Anspach-Bayreuth, generously offered up a number of their subjects—at a price—fully equipped and ready for duty, to serve His Majesty George III. Frederick the Great of Prussia, seeing the plan for what it was, announced that he would "make all the Hessian troops, marching through his dominions to America, pay the usual cattle tax, because, although human beings, they had been sold as beasts." But George III and the princes regarded it as a business deal, in the manner of such dubious alliances ever since: Each foot soldier and trooper supplied by the Duke of Brunswick, for instance, was to be worth seven pounds, four shillings, fourpence halfpenny in levy money to his Most Serene Highness. Three wounded men were to count as one killed in action, and it was stipulated that a soldier killed in combat would be paid for at the same rate as levy money. In other words the life of a subject was worth precisely seven pounds, four shillings, fourpence halfpenny to the Duke.

As it turned out, the large army that was assembled in 1776 to strike a quick, overpowering blow that would put a sudden end to the rebellion proved—when that decisive victory never came to pass—to be a distinct liability, a hideously expensive and at times vulnerable weapon. In the indecisive hands of men like William Howe and Henry Clinton, who never seemed absolutely certain about what they should do or how they should do it, the great army rarely had an opportunity to realize its potential; yet, it remained a ponderous and insatiable consumer of supplies, food, and money.

The loyalists, on whom many Englishmen had placed such high

hopes, proved a will-o'-the-wisp. Largely ignored by the policy makers early in the war despite their pleas for assistance, the loyalists were numerous enough but were neither well organized nor evenly distributed throughout the colonies. Where the optimists in Britain went wrong in thinking that loyalist strength would be an important factor was to imagine that anything like a majority of Americans *could* remain loyal to the Crown if they were not continuously supported and sustained by the mother country. Especially as the war went on, as opinions hardened, and as the possibility increased that the new government in America might actually survive, it was a very difficult matter to retain one's loyalty to the King unless friends and neighbors were of like mind and unless there was a British force nearby for the British command to satisfy the loyalists, who were bitterly angry over the persecution and physical violence and robbery they had to endure and who charged constantly that the British generals were too lax in their treatment of rebels.

While the problems of fighting the war in distant America mounted, Britain found herself unhappily confronted with the combination of circumstances the Foreign Office dreaded most: with her armies tied down, the great European maritime powers—France and Spain—vengeful and adventurous and undistracted by war in the Old World, formed a coalition against her. When the American war began, the risk of foreign intervention was regarded as minimal, and the decision to fight was made on the premise that victory would be early and complete and that the armed forces would be released before any threatening European power could take advantage of the situation. But as the war continued without any definite signs of American collapse, France and Spain seized the chance to embarrass and perhaps humiliate their old antagonist. At first they supported the rebels surreptitiously with shipments of weapons and other supplies; then, when the situation appeared more auspicious, France in particular furnished active support in the form of an army and a navy, with catastrophic results for Great Britain.

One fascinating might-have-been is what would have happened had the Opposition in Parliament been more powerful politically. It consisted, after all, of some of the most forceful and eloquent orators imaginable, men whose words still have the power to send shivers up the spine. Not simply vocal, they were highly intelligent men whose concern went beyond the injustice and inhumanity of war. They were quick to see that the personal liberty of the King's subjects was as much an issue in London as it was in the colonies, and they foresaw irreparable damage to the empire if the government followed its unthinking policy of coercion. Given a stronger power base, they might have headed off war or the ultimate disaster; had the government been in the hands of men like Chatham or

Burke or their followers, some accommodation with America might conceivably have evolved from the various proposals for reconciliation. But the King and North had the votes in their pockets, and the antiwar Opposition failed because a majority that was largely indifferent to reason supported the North ministry until the bitter end came with Cornwallis's surrender. Time and again a member of the Opposition would rise to speak out against the war for one reason or another: "This country," the Earl of Shelburne protested, "already burdened much beyond its abilities, is now on the eve of groaning under new taxes, for the purpose of carrying on this cruel and destructive war." Or, from Dr. Franklin's friend David Hartley: "Every proposition for reconciliation has so constantly and uniformly been crushed by Administration, that I think they seem not even to wish for the appearance of justice. The law of force is that which they appeal to. . . ." Or, from Sir James Lowther, when he learned that the King had rejected an "Olive Branch Petition" from the provincials: "Why have we not peace with a people who, it is evident, desire peace with us?" Or this, from General Henry Seymour Conway, inviting Lord North to inform members of the House of Commons about his overall program: "I do not desire the detail; let us have general outline, to be able to judge of the probability of its success. It is indecent not to lay before the House some plan, or the outlines of a plan. . . . If (the) plan is conciliation, let us see it, that we may form some opinion of it; if it be hostility and coercion, I do repeat, that we have no cause for a minute's consideration; for I can with confidence pronounce, that the present military armament will never succeed." But all unavailing, deafened by self-righteousness and minds hardened against change.

Although it might be said that the arguments raised by the Opposition did not change the course of the war, they nevertheless affected the manner in which it was conducted, which in turn led to the ultimate British defeat. Whether Lord North was uncertain of that silent majority's loyalty is difficult to determine, but it seems clear that he was sufficiently nervous about public support to decide that a bold policy which risked defeats was not for him. As a result, the war of the American Revolution was a limited war—limited from the standpoint of its objectives and the force with which Britain waged it.

In some respects the aspect of the struggle that may have had the greatest influence on the outcome was an intangible one. Until the outbreak of hostilities in 1775 no more than a small minority of the colonials had seriously contemplated independence, but after a year of war the situation was radically different. Now the mood was reflected in words such as these—instructions prepared by the county of Buckingham, in Virginia, for its delegates to a General Convention in Williamsburg: " . . . as far as your voices are admitted, you (will) cause a free and happy Constitution to be established, with a renunciation of the old, and so much thereof as has been found inconvenient and oppressive." That simple and powerful idea—renunciation of the old and its replacement with something new, independently conceived—was destined to sweep all obstacles before it. In Boston James Warren was writing the news of home to John Adams in Philadelphia and told him: "Your Declaration of Independence came on Saturday and diffused a general joy. Every one of us feels more important than ever; we now congratulate each other as Freemen." Such winds of change were strong, and by contrast all Britain had to offer was a return to the status quo. Indeed, it was difficult for the average Englishman to comprehend the appeal that personal freedom and independence held for a growing number of Americans. As William Innes put it in a debate in Commons, all the government had to do to put an end to the nonsense in the colonies was to "convince the lower class of those infatuated people that the imaginary liberty they are so eagerly pursuing is not by any means to be compared to that which the Constitution of this happy country already permits them to enjoy."

With everything to gain from victory and everything to lose by defeat, the Americans could follow Livy's advice, that "in desperate matters the boldest counsels are the safest." Frequently beaten and disheartened, inadequately trained and fed and clothed, they fought on against unreasonably long odds because of that slim hope of attaining a distant goal. And as they fought on, increasing with each passing year the possibility that independence might be achieved, the people of Britain finally lost the will to keep going.

In England the goal had not been high enough, while the cost was too high. There was nothing compelling about the limited objective of bringing the colonies back into the empire, nothing inspiring about punishing the rebels, nothing noble in proving that retribution awaited those who would change the nature of things.

After the war had been lost and the treaty of peace signed, Lord North looked back on the whole affair and sadly informed the members of the House of Commons where, in his opinion, the fault lay. With a few minor changes, it was a message as appropriate to America in 1971 as to Britain in 1783: "The American war," he said, "has been suggested to have been the war of the Crown, contrary to the wishes of the people. I deny it. It was the war of Parliament. There was not a step in it that had not the sanction of Parliament. It was the war of the people, for it was undertaken for the express purpose of maintaining the just rights of Parliament, or, of the empire. For this reason, it was popular at its commencement, and eagerly embraced by the people and Parliament. . . . Nor did it ever cease to be popular until a series of unparalleled disasters and calamities caused the people, wearied out with almost uninterrupted ill-success and misfortune, to call out as loudly for peace as they had formerly done for war."

QUESTIONS TO CONSIDER

1. How tough an opponent did Britain expect the Americans to be?
2. What was the biggest problem facing the British and how serious was it?
3. Why did some critics feel the American colonies would be impossible to conquer?
4. What military strategy did Washington and Greene pursue? What advantages did this strategy give the colonists?
5. Why were the loyalists so little help to the British?
6. Whom does Lord North blame for the Revolutionary War (and, by implication, whom does Ketchum blame for the Vietnam War)?

7

The Revolutionary Context of the Constitutional Convention*

Lance Banning

Lance Banning (1942–   ), awarded his Ph.D. by Washington University in St. Louis in 1971, is a professor of history at the University of Kentucky. A specialist in the revolutionary and early national periods, he wrote this article in 1985 as part of the celebration of the bicentennial of the Constitution. As the title implies, he sees the times as having been revolutionary.

The years 1774–1789 encompassed a whirlwind of events, but it is important to keep the Declaration of Independence, the Revolutionary War, the Articles of Confederation, and the Constitution separate in our minds. The revolution is often viewed as conservative because it did not cause immediate social or economic upheaval like the French and Russian models. Banning argues that it was not only radical but that it was generally viewed that way at the time on both sides of the Atlantic. Yet the Articles of Confederation emerged not from careful reflection, but more as a codification of the ad hoc arrangements that had emerged in the years 1774 to 1777. The shortcomings of the new government seemed likely to result in chaos and a loss of both union and liberty. Out of this morass, once chronicled by John Fiske as "the critical period," came the impetus for the Constitution, the culmination of the revolutionary age.

*Reprinted by permission of The American Political Science Association from the spring 1985 issue of *This Constitution*.

The political debates of the era reflected the tensions inherent in conflicting perceptions of the American character. On the one hand, a healthy skepticism about human nature (sinfulness, in Calvinist terms) led to effective controls on governors to prevent their abuse of power, and then to a Constitution with checks and balances to avert the same. On the other hand, the optimistic view embodied in Jefferson's independent idealists encouraged reductions in property requirements for the vote and started the nation toward a distant day when virtually everyone over the age of eighteen could vote. The egalitarian genie was out of the bottle, and despite persistent resistance, this key aspect of the American character would not be headed.

Most Americans recall our Revolution in decidedly selective ways. As a people, we are not as eager as we used to be to recollect how truly revolutionary are our roots. Our Bicentennial celebration, for example, focused overwhelmingly on independence and the war with Britain, not on the genuinely revolutionary facets of the struggle. Too often, we commemorated even independence with hoary myths about tyrannical King George and clever minutemen who used the woods and fences to defeat the British regulars. Perhaps, then, it is not so inexcusable as it would first appear for some Americans to think that Thomas Jefferson wrote the Constitution as well as the Declaration of Independence in 1776. If we think of the American Revolution as no more than a sudden, brave attempt to shake off English rule, perverse consistency leads easily to a mistake that lumps together all the documents and incidents connected with the Founding. For a better understanding, . . . we would do well to fit the Constitution back into the revolutionary process from which it emerged.

As John Adams said, the American Revolution was not the war against Great Britain; it should not be confused with independence. The Revolution started in the people's minds at least ten years before the famous shots at Lexington and Concord. It was well advanced before the colonies declared their independence. It continued for perhaps a quarter of a century after the fighting came to an end. It dominated the entire life experience of America's greatest generation of public men. And it was fully revolutionary in many of the strictest definitions of that term. The men who made it wanted not just independence, but a change that would transform their own societies and set a new example for mankind. They wanted to create, as they put it on the Great Seal of the United States, "a new order of the ages" which would become a foundation for the happiness of all of their descendants and a model for the other peoples of the world. To their minds, the federal Constitution was a Revolutionary act, an episode in their experimental quest for such an order.

A REPUBLICAN EXPERIMENT

From a twentieth-century perspective, the American Revolution may appear conservative and relatively tame. There were no mass executions. Social relationships and political arrangements were not turned upside down in an upheaval of shattering violence, as they would be later on in France or Russia or any of a dozen other countries we might name. To people living through it, nonetheless—or watching it from overseas—the American Revolution seemed very radical indeed. It was not self-evident in 1776 that all men are created equal, that governments derive their just authority from popular consent, or that good governments exist in order to protect God-given rights. These concepts are not undeniable in any age. From the point of view of eighteenth-century Europeans, they contradicted common sense. The notions that a sound society could operate without the natural subordination customary where men were either commoners or nobles or that a stable government could be based entirely on elections seemed both frightening and ridiculously at odds with the obvious lessons of the past. A republican experiment had been attempted once before on something like this scale—in England during the 1640s and 1650s—and the ultimate result had been a Cromwellian dictatorship and a quick return to the ancient constitution of King, Lords, and Commons.

Nevertheless, the Americans dreamed revolutionary visions of perfection, comparable in many ways to revolutionary visions of later times. They sought a new beginning, a rebirth, in which hereditary privilege would disappear and all political authority would derive exclusively from talent, public service, and the people's choice. And their commitment to the principles of liberty and equal rights did touch and change most aspects of their common life.

No essay of this length can possibly describe all of the ways in which the Revolution altered American society. To understand the Constitution, though, we have to realize, at minimum, that as they fought the War for Independence, Americans were equally involved in a fundamental transformation of political beliefs and thus of political institutions. The decision to separate from England was also a decision that Americans were a people different from the English, a separate nation with a special mission in the world. This people had no way to understand their new identity except in terms of their historical mission, no way to define or perfect their national character except by building their new order. To be an American, by 1776, was to be a republican, and to become consistently republican required a thorough reconstruction of existing institutions.

A republican experiment, in fact, required rebuilding governments afresh. For in the months between the clash at Lexington and the Declaration of Independence, formal governments dissolved in one American colony after another. The people, who had ordinarily elected only one branch of their local governments, simply transferred their allegiance from their legal governmental institutions to extra-legal revolutionary committees, state conventions, and the Continental Congress. Through the first months of the fighting, the conventions and committees managed very well. Power rested with the people in a wholly literal sense, the people followed the directives of these revolutionary bodies, and those bodies turned the popular determination into armies and materials of war.

Some revolutionaries might have been content to see their states continue indefinitely under governmental bodies of this sort. Many patriots were intensely localistic, and they had learned a fierce distrust of any power much beyond the people's easy reach. Other patriots, however, many more of those who exercised great influence, never saw the revolutionary agencies as anything but temporary. A structure that depended so immediately on the people was good enough for an emergency, but hardly suitable for the longer term. For permanence, most patriots admired a governmental structure that balanced and divided power between different and independent parts, not one that concentrated it in single bodies which performed both legislative and executive functions.

The revolutionaries had been reared as Englishmen, in a tradition that instructed them that liberty was incompatible with the unchecked rule of the majority or with a government composed of only a single branch. Proper constitutions, they believed, depended on consent, but governments existed in order to protect the liberties of all. The revolutionaries had decided that good governments should have no place for aristocrats or kings, but they continued to believe that immediate and undiluted rule by the majority could not provide the wisdom and stability that governments require, nor could it offer proper safeguards for the rights of all. Thus, as they moved toward independence, the revolutionaries started a long search for a governmental structure in which liberty and representative democracy could be combined. This was what they meant by a "republic."

Most of the revolutionary states established written constitutions before the end of 1776. Although they differed greatly in details, these constitutions tended to be similar in broader lines. The colonial experience, together with the quarrel with Great Britain, had taught a powerful fear of the executive and of the executive's ability to undermine the independence of the other parts of government by use of patronage or "influence." Accordingly, most states created governors too weak to do such harm. Most stripped the governors of the majority of their traditional powers of appointment and deprived them of the traditional right to veto legislation. Most provided for election of the governors by the legislative branch. Most confined the chief executives, in short, to the job of enforcing the legislatures' wills.

According to these constitutions, the legislative power would remain within the people's hardy grip. The concept of a balance required two legislative houses, but hostility to privilege was far too sharp to let the second house become a bastion for any special group, in imitation of the English House of Lords. Moreover, in societies without hereditary ranks, it was difficult to reach agreement on a genuinely republican method for selecting the few men of talent and leisure whose superior wisdom, lodged in an upper house, was traditionally supposed to check the passions of the multitude. The revolutionary senates differed relatively little in their makeup from the lower houses of assembly. Democratic Pennsylvania did without an upper house at all and placed executive authority in the hands of a council, rather than a single man, though this was such a radical departure from general ideas that it quickly created an anticonstitutional party in that state.

Nearly all the revolutionaries would have failed a modern test of loyalty to democratic standards. Even the most dedicated patriots were eighteenth-century men, and eighteenth-century thinking normally excluded many portions of the people from participation in the politics of a republic: adherents to unpopular religions, women, blacks, and even very poor white males.

Accordingly, not even Pennsylvania departed so far from tradition as to give the vote to every male adult. And yet most states moved noticeably in that direction. Most lowered the amount of property one had to own in order to possess the franchise. Several gave the vote to every man who paid a tax. All the states provided for annual elections of the lower house of legislature and, often, for annual elections of the senate and governor as well. Every part of these new governments would be chosen by the people or by those the people had elected. And the legislatures in particular were filled with men whose modest means and ordinary social rank would have excluded them from higher office in colonial times. In a variety of ways, these governments were far more responsive to the people than the old colonial governments had been. They were also far more closely watched. The revolutionary air was full of popular awareness of the people's rights.

The revolutionary movement disestablished churches, altered attitudes toward slavery, and partly redefined the role of women in American society. Eventually, of course, revolutionary concepts paved the way for an extension of the rights of citizens to all the groups that eighteenth-century patriots excluded. But whatever else the Revolution was or would become, its essence lay originally in these thirteen problematic experiments in constructing republican regimes. It would succeed or fail, in revolutionary minds, according to the success of these regimes in raising the new order and fulfilling expectations that republicanism would defend and perfect this special people and the democratic social structure that they hoped would become the envy of the world.

A PERMANENT CONFEDERATION

Americans did not intend, at the beginning, to extend the revolutionary experiment in republican government from the states to the nation as a whole. Republics were expected to be small. The Revolution had begun as an attempt to protect the old colonial governments from external interference by a distant Parliament and king. Traditional loyalties and revolutionary ideas were both keyed to the states.

Still, the argument with Britain taught Americans to think that they were a single people, and the War for Independence built a growing sense of nationhood. There was a Continental Congress before there were any independent states. *Congress* declared American independence and recommended that new state governments be formed. *Congress* assumed the direction of the war.

The Continental Congress was an extralegal body. It had simply emerged in the course of the imperial quarrel and continued to exert authority with the approval of the people and the states, all of which sent an unspecified number of delegates to help take care of common concerns. As early as June 12, 1776, these delegates initiated consideration of a plan to place their authority on formal grounds. But the experiences that had led to independence made Americans powerfully suspicious of any central government, and there were many disagreements in the Congress. Meanwhile, there was also the necessity of managing a war.

Not until November 17, 1777, did Congress finally present a formal proposal to the states. This plan, the Articles of Confederation, called upon the sovereign states to join in a permanent confederation presided over by a Congress whose authority would be confined to matters of interest to all: war and peace; foreign relations; trade with the Indians; disputes between states; and other common concerns. Each state would continue to have a single vote in Congress. In matters of extreme importance, such as war and peace, Congress would act only when nine of the thirteen states agreed. Since Congress would not directly represent the people, troops or money could be raised only by requisitioning the states.

The Articles of Confederation did not issue from a systematic, theoretical consideration of the problems of confederation government. For the most part, they only codified the structure and procedures that had emerged in practice in the years since 1774. Most of the country scarcely noticed when they finally went into effect, which was not until February 1781—three years after they were first proposed. Maryland, which had a definite western border, refused its consent until Virginia and the other giant states, whose colonial charters gave them boundaries which might stretch from coast to coast, agreed to cede their lands beyond the mountains to the Confederation as a whole. Then, for the most of the rest of the 1780s, Americans lived in a confederation of this sort.

Historians have long since given up the old idea that the Confederation years were a period of governmental folly and unmixed disaster. The Articles established a genuine federal government, not merely a league of states. The union was to be permanent, and Congress was granted many of the usual attributes of sovereign authority. Great things were accomplished. The states secured their independence and won a generous treaty of peace, which placed their western border at the Mississippi River. The country weathered a severe postwar depression. Congress organized the area northwest of the Ohio for settlement and eventual statehood. In fact, the Northwest Ordinance of 1787 established the pattern for all the rest of the continental expansion of the United States, providing that new territories would eventually enter the union on terms of full equality with its original members and thus assuring that America would manage to escape most of the problems usually confronted by an expanding empire. It was not an unimpressive record.

THIRTEEN SQUABBLING STATES

Nevertheless, the Articles of Confederation came under increasing criticism from an influential minority even before they formally went into practice. This minority was centered in the Congress itself and around the powerful executive officials created by the Congress, especially Robert Morris, a Philadelphia merchant who was appointed Superintendent of Finance in 1781. Morris and his allies were necessarily concerned with the Confederation as a whole, and they found it almost impossible to meet their responsibilities under this kind of government. By the time the war was over, the Confederation's paper money was entirely worthless—"not worth a Continental," as the phrase still goes. The Confederation owed huge debts to army veterans, to citizens who had lent supplies or money during the war, and to foreign governments and foreign subjects who had purchased American bonds. Dependent on the states for revenues, Congress could not even pay the interest on these obligations. All the states had war debts of their own, and in the midst of a depression, their citizens were seldom willing or even able to pay taxes high enough to make it possible for the republics to handle their own needs and meet their congressional requisitions as well. By 1783, Morris, Alexander Hamilton, James Madison, and many other continental-minded men were insisting on reform. They demanded, at the very least, that Congress be granted the authority to levy a tax on foreign imports, which might provide it with a steady, independent source of revenue.

The need for revenue, however, was only the most urgent of several concerns. Lacking a direct connection with the people, Congress had to work through and depend on the states for nearly everything. Unable to compel cooperation, its members watched in futile anger as the sovereign republics went their separate ways. Some states quarreled over boundaries. Troubled by the depression, others passed competitive duties on foreign imports. The states ignored Confederation treaties, fought separate wars with Indians, and generally neglected congressional pleas for money.

As this happened, American ambassadors in foreign lands—John Adams in England and Thomas Jefferson in France—discovered that the European nations treated the American confederation with contempt. The European powers refused to make commercial treaties that would lower their barriers to freer trade and ease America's commercial problems. England refused to remove her soldiers from forts in the American northwest, insisting that she would abide by the treaty of peace only when the states began to meet their own obligations to cease prosecuting returning loyalists and to open their courts to British creditors who wanted to collect their debts.

Nevertheless, the nationalists in Congress were frustrated in their desire for reform. The Articles of Confederation could be amended only by unanimous consent, but when Congress recommended an amendment that would give it the authority to levy a 5 percent duty on imports, little Rhode Island refused to agree. When Congress asked for power to retaliate against Great Britain's navigation laws, the states again could not concur.

Repeatedly defeated in their efforts at reform, increasingly alarmed by mutual antagonisms between the states, which had grown serious enough by 1786 to threaten an immediate fragmentation of the union into several smaller confederacies, the men of continental vision turned their thoughts to fundamentals. A much more sweeping change, they now suspected, might be necessary to resolve the pressing problems of the current central government. And if the change went far enough, a few of them began to think, it might accomplish something more. It might restore the Revolution to its proper course.

The Revolution, after all, involved a dream of national greatness; and the dream was going wrong. A people who had hoped to be a model for the world was fragmented into thirteen petty, squabbling states. The states would not—or could not—subordinate their separate interests to the good of the Confederation as a whole. Even worse, too many of the states fell short of fulfilling revolutionary expectations within their individual bounds. The early revolutionary constitutions had delivered overwhelming power to the people's immediate representatives in the lower houses of assembly. As these lower houses struggled to protect the people from hard times, they frequently neglected private rights and seldom seemed to give a due consideration to the long-term good. As clashing groups in different states competed to control their house of representatives, nobody could feel certain what the law might be next year, when one majority replaced another. The lower houses of assembly were essentially unchecked by the other parts of government, and to many revolutionaries it appeared that the assemblies proceeded on their ways with slight regard for justice and little thought about tomorrow. The rule of law appeared to be collapsing into a kind of anarchy in which the liberty and property of everyone might depend on the good will of whichever temporary majority happened to control his state. No one could feel secure in the enjoyment of his rights.

LIBERTY IN PERIL

During the 1780s, in other words, the feeling grew that liberty was once again in peril. Alarm was most intense among the men whose duties, education, or experience encouraged them to pin their patriotic feelings on the continent as a whole: certain members of Congress; most of the best-known revolutionary thinkers; most of the former officers of the continental army; many merchants, public creditors, and other men of wealth. Men of social standing were distressed with the way in which the revolutionary principles of liberty and equality seemed to shade into a popular contempt for talent or distinction. Too often, to their minds, the best men lost elections in the states to self-serving, scrambling demagogues, and the revolutionary constitutions made it far too easy for these demagogues to set an ill-considered course or even to oppress the propertied minority in order to secure the people's favor. Continued confiscations of the property of people who had sympathized with Britain and continued use of paper money, which threatened men's investments and their right to hold their property secure, were grievances of particular importance to those who had investments and positions to defend.

And yet the sense of fading hopes and failing visions was not exclusively confined to men of wealth. Anyone whose life had been immersed in revolutionary expectations might share in the concern. Every state seemed full of quarrels. Every individual seemed to be on the scrape for himself. No one seemed to have a real regard for common interests, a willingness to recognize that selfish interests must be limited by some consideration for the good of all. Public virtue, to use the phrase the revolutionaries used, seemed to be in danger of completely disappearing as every man and every social group sought private goods at the expense of harmony and other people's rights. But virtue, revolutionaries thought, was the indispensable foundation for republics, without which they could not survive. If public virtue was collapsing, then the Revolution was about to fail. It would degenerate into a kind of chaos, from which a tyrant might emerge, or else the people, in disgust, might eventually prefer to return to hereditary rule.

So, at least, did many fear. Guided by the same ideas that had impelled them into independence, they saw a second crisis, as dangerous to liberty as the crisis that had led them into Revolution. As they had done in 1776, they blamed their discontents on governments that lacked the character to mold a virtuous people and fit them for their special role. Once more, they turned to constitutional reform. They saw in the problems of the Confederation government not merely difficulties that would have to be corrected, but an opportunity that might be seized for even greater ends, an opportunity to rescue revolutionary hopes from their decay.

The constitutional reformers of the 1780s had several different motives and several different goals. Some had an economic interest in a constitutional reform that would enable the central government to pay its debts and act to spur the economic revival. All wanted to make the government adequate to its tasks and able to command more respect from the rest of the world. Some wanted more: to reconstruct the central government in such a way that its virtues might override the mistakes that had been made in some of the states. They wanted to redeem the reputation of democracy and save the republican experiment from a process of degeneration which threatened to destroy all that they had struggled for.

Shays's Rebellion handed them their chance. Out in western Massachusetts, hard times, large debts, and the high taxes prompted by the state's attempt to handle its revolutionary debt drove many farmers to distress. They first petitioned for relief, but when the legislature refused to issue paper money or to pass the laws required to protect their property from seizure, petitions gave way to rebellion. Farmers forced the courts to close in several counties, and Daniel Shays, a revolutionary captain, organized an armed resistance. The rebels were defeated with surprising ease. The state called out the militia during the winter of 1786, and Shays' forces disintegrated after a minor fight. The incident was nonetheless, for many, the final straw atop a growing load of fears. Armed resistance to a republican government seemed the ultimate warning of a coming collapse.

Earlier in 1786, delegates from five states had met at Annapolis, Maryland, to consider better means of regulating interstate and international trade. Nationalist sentiment was strong among the delegates. Hamilton and Madison were there. The participants quickly agreed that little could be done about commercial problems without a revision of the Articles of Confederation. They said as much in a report to Congress and their states, and Congress endorsed their recommendation for the meeting of a national convention to consider ways to make the central government "adequate to the exigencies of the union." Badly frightened by events in Massachusetts, whose constitution was widely thought to be among the best, every state except Rhode Island answered the call. From this context and in hope that it might save both liberty and union, the Constitutional Convention emerged.

QUESTIONS TO CONSIDER

1. Why do many twentieth-century historians view the American Revolution as conservative?
2. Why does Banning contend that the revolution was seen as radical at the time?
3. Characterize the state constitutions that emerged in 1776.
4. How did the Continental Congress develop? What was its relation to the states and independence? How do you think this might become an important factor in the debate over states rights at the time of the Civil War?
5. What were the significant governmental accomplishments under the Articles of Confederation?
6. What were the motivations for the calling of the Constitutional Convention.

8

Hamilton's Legacy*
Michael Lind

Michael Lind is a senior editor at *The New Republic*. In this article he traces the importance of the ideas of one of the founding fathers who has suffered serious neglect over the past half century. Alexander Hamilton has at various points in American history been regarded as second only to George Washington among the founders, but his star has waned. Today, Lind contends, all politicians see themselves as Jeffersonians. Nevertheless, as the author traces the course of Hamilton's reputation, he finds that a lot of his ideas continue to exist, even though his authorship is not acknowledged. His policy of economic nationalism may be resurgent if GATT and NAFTA, the free trade agreements of the nineties, fail to bring the anticipated prosperity. A strong national security state, standard in post-World War II national thought, derives from Hamilton's thinking. Lind concludes that the United States would be wise to rethink its antipathy to Hamilton and recognize the wisdom of his ideas.

After the revolutions of 1989 brought down communism in Eastern Europe, many of the political and intellectual leaders of the emerging democracies turned for guidance to the United States. Americans of all political persuasions recommended the writings of such sages as Thomas Jefferson, James Madison, and Abraham Lincoln. Alexander Hamilton was seldom mentioned, even though his contributions to that compendium of political wisdom, *The Federalist*, far outweigh those of his co-authors Madison and John Jay. No one suggested that the theories and example of Hamilton might be far more relevant to the new democratic regimes struggling to consolidate their rule and build new governmental, financial, and military institutions on the remnants of Soviet colonialism.

This oversight is puzzling, if not tragic, because Hamilton was perhaps the most practical nation builder among the Founding Fathers. Thanks largely to his vision and energy, the United States became what it is today: a relatively centralized nation-state with a military second to none in the world, a powerful presidency, a strong judiciary, and an industrial capitalist economy. John Marshall, the first chief justice of the Supreme Court, who did so much to fix Hamilton's expansive view of federal authority in law, thought that Hamilton and his mentor George Washington were the greatest of the Founders. One contemporary acquaintance, Judge Ambrose Spencer, who had clashed with Hamilton, nevertheless declared that he was "the greatest man this country ever produced. . . . He, more than any man, did the thinking of the time." The great French diplomat and statesman Talleyrand, who worked with Hamilton during the Revolution and the early years of the republic, put his "mind and character . . . on a par with [those of] the most distinguished statesmen of Europe, not even excepting Mr. Pitt and Mr. Fox."

Such praise was anything but fulsome. As well as serving as George Washington's valued aide-de-camp during most of the Revolutionary War (and successfully reorganizing the Continental Army as one of his tasks), Hamilton helped to initiate the move toward a more centralized union that resulted in the Philadelphia convention of 1787 and the federal constitution. His view of the Constitution as the source of implied as well as enumerated powers became the dominant interpretation, thanks to his admirers and students John Marshall, Joseph Storey, and Daniel Webster, and his conception of expansive presidential war and foreign policy powers would prevail in the twentieth century. As secretary of the treasury (1789–95), Hamilton established the fiscal infrastructure of the new republic, including the Bank of the United States, precursor of the Federal Reserve. He not only articulated the theory of tariff-based industrial policy (an inspiration to later American, German, and Japanese modernizers) but organized the Society for Useful Manufactures (SUM), the first American research institute and industrial conglomerate, sited on 38 acres by the Passaic River falls in Paterson, New Jersey.

Today, however, those who remember the mastermind of the Washington administration (1789–97) tend to know only a caricature of Hamilton as a champion of the rich—the prototype of such Wall Street wizards as Andrew Mellon and Michael Milken. Now and then Hamilton's ideas are invoked by those seeking to justify policies of economic nationalism, but more often "Hamiltonianism" is used as shorthand for a blend of plutocracy and authoritarianism, the antithesis of democratic idealism associated with his lifelong political rival Thomas Jefferson. (Jefferson placed a bust of Hamilton on the right side of the entrance hall at Monticello, across from his own portrait on the left. He explained to visitors: "Opposed in death as in life.") Regardless of political orientations, American politicians all claim to be Jeffersonians. Few, if any, will admit to being Hamiltonians. In the late twentieth century, it appears, the consensus holds that Noah Webster was right to name Hamilton "the evil genius of this country."

It is far easier to understand why Hamilton has been maligned than why he has been forgotten. His life was as dramatic as any in the annals of the early American republic. The only nonnative among the Founding Fathers, he was born in the British West Indies, probably in 1755, the illegitimate son of an aristocratic Scot and a French Huguenot. Orphaned at 13, he supported himself as a clerk in the St. Croix office of a New York import-export firm, acquiring a head for commerce that would further distinguish him from all the other Founders but Franklin. Hamilton so impressed his employers with his intelligence and industry that they and other sponsors, sent him to the North American colonies to further his education. He enrolled in King's College (later Columbia) in 1773, but academic pursuits were cut short by his involvement in the writing of anti-British pamphlets and the subsequent outbreak of war. Nevertheless, wide and thorough reading kept Hamilton abreast of intellectual developments in Britain and continental Europe. Perhaps one of the strongest influences on his thought was the work of the Scottish philosopher David Hume, whose skepticism about classical republicanism and yeoman virtues made him anathema to Jefferson and other American republican idealists.

Psychobiographers eager to explain away Hamilton's devotion to the principle of a strong military need look no farther than his years in the inner circle of Washington's headquarters. As a member of what Washington called his "family," Hamilton made himself so indispensable that he almost missed his chance for martial glory. (That finally came at the Battle of Yorktown, where the slight, still boyish-looking officer personally led his battalion in an assault on a British position.) The bond forged with Washington, though subject to strains, would eventually bring Hamilton into the first president's administration. But between the war's end and Washington's inauguration, Hamilton was never idle. He read and practiced the law, started a family with Elizabeth Schuyler (a New York patrician's daughter whom he had married in 1780), and became increasingly involved in New York and national politics. To the latter he brought his strong conviction that the weakly knit confederation could not work, a conviction that spurred his cogent defense of the proposed constitution in the essays that he and his collaborators Madison and Jay wrote between October 1787 and May 1788. (At least two thirds of the 85 essays eventually published as *The Federalist* came from Hamilton's pen.)

As an immigrant, Hamilton lacked any ties to a particular region that might have qualified his intense devotion to the American nation in its entirety. Installed as Washington's secretary of the treasury, he took decisive steps to strengthen the standing and power of the federal government. To that end, and to make the nation creditworthy, he arranged for the federal government to assume the debts accumulated by the states during and after the Revolution and devised a system of taxation to pay off the debt. (A political pragmatist, he won support for his plan, a bitterly contested assertion of sovereignty by the federal government, by agreeing to back Thomas Jefferson and other southerners in their ambition to move the nation's capital to a site on the Potomac River.) Though at first opposed to political parties because of their disruptive character, Hamilton helped to create and then took the helm of the Federalist Party to push his policies through the legislature. His rivals in the newly formed Republican Party, including Secretary of State Thomas Jefferson, fought just as hard to thwart Hamilton's agenda, which they labeled crudely as probusiness, antidemocratic, and monarchical. Hamilton's disposition to favor England over France—and to hold up England's powerful civil administration as a model—only stoked his enemies' animosity. The Republicans' efforts to drive their foe from office, including unfounded accusations of wrongdoing, finally succeeded in 1795, two years before the end of Washington's second term.

Still wielding power in private life—among other ways, through the *New York Post*, which he founded (and which survives to this day)—Hamilton began to make enemies even among his fellow Federalists, opposing John Adams's reelection to the presidency in 1800 and supporting the Louisiana Purchase in 1803. Hamilton, who, like Napoleon, preferred to make war on allies, enraged another Federalist by speaking ill of his candidacy for the governorship of New York. The offended party, Aaron Burr, demanded satisfaction. Hamilton accepted, though in the resulting duel he took care to aim away from his challenger. Burr was not so gracious. Hamilton, who as a boy had hoped to become a physician, offered an immediate evaluation of his condition: "This is a mortal wound, Doctor." He died the next day—July 14, 1804.

His ideas could not be so easily extinguished. Like his rival Jefferson, Hamilton was a theorist as well as a statesman. His premature death prevented him from writing the "full investigation of the history and science of civil government and the various modifications of it upon the freedom and happiness of mankind," to which he had planned to devote his later years, according to his admirer Chancellor Joseph Kent, an early chief justice of the Supreme Court of New York. Though he never wrote his treatise on government, Hamilton lived to see the republication of *The Federalist* and his polemical *Pacificus* letters defending presidential authority in foreign affairs. These and other occasional writings, together with the three great reports he made to Congress as secretary of the treasury—*The Report on the Public Credit* (1790), *The Report on the Bank of the United States* (1790), and *The Report on Manufactures* (1791)—constitute a substantial body of work explicating the principles of Hamiltonianism.

As Hamilton saw it, the United States was (and should always remain) a nation-state in which the states are clearly subordinated to a strong but not oppressive federal government. The federal government must possess the military force not only to secure America's interests abroad but to suppress domestic insurrection quickly and effectively—a lesson he learned in the Whiskey Rebellion, which President Washington, with Hamilton's aid, put down in 1794. The success of the federal government, for Hamilton and his followers, depends upon an efficient and competent executive branch and a powerful federal judiciary, both insulated to a degree from the popularly elected legislature. "The test of good government," Hamilton wrote, "is its aptitude and tendency to produce a good administration." Holding that good administration requires first-rate officers with long tenure, Hamilton firmly rejected the Jeffersonian notion that a great and powerful state can be administered by amateur politicians and short-term, inexperienced appointees.

One of the duties of the federal government, in Hamilton's view, is the active promotion of a dynamic, industrial capitalist economy—not by government ownership of industry (which Hamilton favored only for military contractors) but by establishment of sound public finance, public investment in infrastructure, and promotion of new industrial sectors unlikely to be profitable in their early stages. "Capital is wayward and timid in lending itself to new undertakings, and the State ought to excite the confidence of capitalists, who are ever cautious and sagacious, by aiding them to overcome the obstacles that lie in the way of all experiments," Hamilton wrote in *The Report on Manufactures*.

Hamilton, who had studied Adam Smith's *Wealth of Nations,* agreed with the Scottish philosopher on most points but criticized two of his ideas. He rejected Smith's notion that agriculture was preferable to manufacturing industry. And though Hamilton saw many benefits in trade and foreign investment, he believed that free trade was a mistaken policy in some circumstances. Hamilton had learned during the Revolutionary War how important it was for a country not to depend on others for "the manufactories of all the necessary weapons of war." He also advocated protection of infant American industries such as textiles, at least until they were capable of competing on an equal basis with foreign products. Finally, Hamilton thought it foolish for a country to open its markets to countries that protected theirs. In short, Hamilton held that economic policymakers should be guided by results rather than by dogmas in promoting state interests such as national security and the diversification of the national economy.

With the collapse of the Federalist Party a few years after Hamilton's death in 1804, his philosophy of a strong, centralized national government promoting industrial capitalism and defending America's concrete interests abroad with an effective professional military passed into partial eclipse for a couple of generations. Quite different conceptions—states' rights, minimal government, agrarianism, isolationism, a militia-based defense—inspired the Jeffersonian and Jacksonian Democrats who dominated antebellum American politics. "National Republicans" such as John Quincy Adams, and later Whigs such as Daniel Webster and Henry Clay, kept the Hamiltonian legacy alive. The Whigs, fusing with antislavery Jacksonian Democrats in the 1850s, formed the new Republican Party, which under Lincoln and his successors crushed the Confederacy, abolished slavery, and made America into a strong union linked by a federally sponsored railroad infrastructure and industrializing behind high tariff walls.

The triumph of the Union was in many ways a vindication of Hamilton's vision, as was the rise of the United States as one of the world's great powers by the time of the Spanish-American War. "For many decades after the Civil War," Hamilton biographer Forrest McDonald writes, "his niche in the pantheon of American demigods was beneath only Washington's, if indeed it was not at Washington's right hand." Even so, the industrial magnates of the Gilded Age—the Jay Goulds and Edward H. Harrimans and J. P. Morgans—were not as a rule Hamiltonian in their philosophy. They tended to follow Herbert Spencer, the English philosopher of laissez-faire Social Darwinism. Moreover, many American business leaders were pacifists, believing that international capitalism, by increasing interdependence, would render war and economic rivalry between states obsolete.

The intellectual and political heirs of Hamilton operated largely outside the realm of business. Harvard political scientist Samuel P. Huntington, in *The Soldier and the State* (1957), describes the rise and fall of a neo-Hamiltonian school between 1890 and 1920. It included politicians such as Theodore Roosevelt and Massachusetts Senator Henry Cabot Lodge as well as intellectuals such as Herbert Croly, Brooks Adams, and Alfred Thayer Mahan, the prophet of American navalism and great-power politics. This congeries of like-minded men often combined *realpolitik* in foreign policy with support for progressive reforms at home—more in the interest of national efficiency than of abstract social justice. They rejected the Gilded Age's celebration of the entrepreneur in favor of the patrician-military ideal of an elite that serves the public by serving the state. According to Huntington, "Brooks Adams even went so far as to suggest openly that America would do well to substitute the values of West Point for the values of Wall Street." (It should come as no surprise to learn that West Point was a scaled-down version of Hamilton's grandiose vision of a comprehensive military academy.)

At the beginning of this century, Hamilton's reputation reached its peak. The most influential of his proponents was Herbert Croly, the founding editor of the *New Republic*. In *The Promise of American Life* (1909), Croly contrasted Hamilton's view that "the central government is to be used, not merely to maintain the Constitution, but to promote the national interest and to consolidate the national organization" with the Jeffersonian theory that "there should be as little government as possible." The latter view rested on what Croly considered a naive belief in "the native goodness of human nature." To Croly and his allies, Jeffersonian doctrines, if they had ever been relevant, were obsolete in the new era of national and multinational corporations, mass organizations, technological warfare, and imperialism. Croly conceded that Hamilton's version of American nationalism had been inadequate because of its excessive distrust of popular democracy, but he held that the basic conception of an activist national government promoting the common good was as compatible with egalitarian as with aristocratic notions of a good social order.

Croly's beau ideal of an American statesman was Theodore Roosevelt, whom he praised for emancipating "American democracy from its Jeffersonian bondage." TR united progressive nationalism in domestic policy with an assertive realism, based on military power, in foreign affairs—a realism seen in his seizure of Panama and his mediation of the Russo-Japanese War in the interest of the Pacific balance of power, for which he won the Nobel Peace Prize in 1906. Roosevelt, like his friend Henry Cabot Lodge, chairman of the Senate Foreign Relations Committee, favored U.S. intervention in World War I but opposed Wilson's League of Nations Treaty because it committed the United States to a vague collective security arrangement rather than a traditional limited alliance. In his own biography of Hamilton, published in 1883, Lodge predicted that "so long as the people of the United States form one nation, the name of Alexander Hamilton will be held in high and lasting honor, and even in the wreck of governments that noble intellect would still command the homage of men."

Lodge spoke too soon. After World War I, Hamilton's reputation, along with Hamiltonianism, went into sudden decline. The defeat of the progressive TR-Robert La Follette wing of the Republican Party by the representatives of the conventional business elite made the Republicans hostile to overseas military intervention, high levels of military spending, and ideas of government activism in the economy, even on behalf of business. The liberal wing of the Democratic Party inherited the legacy of Hamiltonian progressivism. But New Deal liberalism, as it evolved in the 1930s, was quite different from the nationalism of earlier Progressives such as TR and Croly.

The claim is often made that the New Deal resulted in a fusion of the two great American traditions of government—the pursuit of Jeffersonian ends by Hamiltonian means. The historian Merrill D. Peterson writes that during the New Deal, "national power and purpose grew without disturbing the axis of the democratic faith. For all practical purposes, the New Deal ended the historic Jefferson-Hamilton dialogue in American history." One might more plausibly argue that New Deal liberals abandoned the democratic and technocratic Hamiltonianism of Herbert Croly in favor of the ideal of the lobby-based broker state.

Partly to shield themselves from accusations that the New Deal was the American version of fascism or communism, New Dealers stressed the *absence* of centralized state direction of the economy. The journalist John Chamberlain described Roosevelt's broker state as a liberal-democratic alternative to the directive state of the Progressives (and totalitarians). Interest-group liberalism was seen as a pragmatic, democratic, American version of corporatism or syndicalism. "We have equilibrated power," theologian Reinhold Niebuhr wrote. "We have attained a certain equilibrium in economic society itself by setting organized power against organized power" in the form of unions, corporations, and professional associations.

New Deal liberals found a patron saint for interest-group liberalism not in Hamilton but in Madison, particularly in his *Federalist* no. 10, with its theory of factions in a democracy. They reinterpreted Madison to stress the idea not of conflict but of harmony and equilibrium through pluralism. In the 1940s and '50s, Madison was elevated to the status of a patron saint of interest-group liberalism, while Hamilton, the moving force behind *The Federalist,* was denounced by, among others, historian Douglass Adair for favoring "an overruling, irresponsible, and unlimited government."

Franklin D. Roosevelt himself played an important role in expelling Hamilton from the American pantheon. FDR, a tory Democrat from the landed gentry of the Hudson River, saw himself in the tory democrat from the Virginia Tidewater. In his mind, Jefferson stood for popular government, not necessarily for weak or decentralized government, while Hamilton was a forerunner of Andrew Mellon and identified with the worst excesses of callous plutocracy. Reviewing a book by Claude G. Bowers, *Jefferson and Hamilton: The Struggle for Democracy in America,* Roosevelt suggested in 1925 that the common people needed a champion against the forces of plutocracy: "I have a breathless feeling, too, as I wonder if, a century and a quarter later, the same contending forces are not mobilizing." At the 1928 Democratic national convention, FDR, the keynote speaker, declared, "Hamiltons we have today. Is a Jefferson on the horizon?" Soon enough, Jefferson—or at least a sanitized Jefferson, whose racial views and small-government, states' rights preferences were conveniently underplayed—came to stand at the head of a line leading, by way of Andrew Jackson, to President Franklin D. Roosevelt himself. The work of rewriting American history as a prelude to the New Deal was completed by the moderate-liberal consensus historians of the 1950s and '60s, including Arthur Schlesinger, Jr., and Richard Hofstadter. At least one dissenting historian, Samuel Eliot Morison, considered this dismissal of the Federalist-Whig-Republican tradition "unbalanced and unhealthy, tending to create a neoliberal stereotype." But Hamilton's stock remained low.

To the extent that the Hamiltonian tradition lived on, it was in foreign policy. The logic of the broker state did not apply to the centralized national-security state that was assembled during World War II and consolidated into a permanent structure during the Korean War. Samuel Huntington notes "the curious way in which Theodore Roosevelt was the intellectual godfather of Democratic administrations after 1933" in foreign policy, and he sees a "clear line" from such neo-Hamiltonians as TR and Elihu Root to "Stimson to Marshall, Lovett, and McCloy."

One might have expected the leaders of the civil rights movement of the 1950s and '60s to have looked to Hamilton for inspiration. The civil rights struggle, after all, was largely carried out in the name of federal authority by federal judges, whose power and independence Hamilton strenuously defended (notably in *Federalist* no. 76). What is more, Hamilton was one of the more ardent opponents of slavery and racism among the Founding Fathers. When he was aide-de-camp to Washington, Hamilton favored giving blacks their freedom and citizenship and arming them as soldiers: "The contempt we have been taught to entertain for the blacks, makes us fancy many things that are founded neither in reason nor experience. . . . [T]he dictates of humanity and true policy equally interest me in favour of this unfortunate class of men." After the war, Hamilton—who had grown up in the slave society of the West Indies—helped organize the Society for Promoting the Manumission of Slaves. Jefferson, by contrast, opposed emancipation if it could not be accompanied by the immediate colonization of black Americans abroad, and his speculations about alleged black racial inferiority in his *Notes on the State of Virginia* (1784–85) made him a hero to generations of pseudoscientific racists. Nevertheless, the modern habit of attributing everything good in American life to the inspiration of Jefferson alone has resulted in his being given the credit for convictions about black equality and freedom that are, in fact, closer to those of Hamilton.

The New Left and the modern conservative movement both draw on Jeffersonian distrust of concentrated authority, whether commercial or governmental, and on Jeffersonian individualism. The Jeffersonian Left stresses sexual rights, while the Jeffersonian Right stresses property rights; Left-Jeffersonians attack big business, while Right-Jeffersonians attack big government. For all that, there is a striking similarity in the paeans to the virtue of the people and the suspicion of authority and organization shared by the leaders of both the sexual revolution and the tax revolt—and a common dislike of Alexander Hamilton, the socially conservative proponent of big business *and* big government.

While liberals were redefining their tradition as one that stretched from Jefferson to Lincoln to FDR, leaving out Hamilton and TR, the conservatives of the 1950s were reading Hamilton out of the lineage of the contemporary Right. Conservative writer Russell Kirk, who repeated the hoary Jeffersonian libel that Hamilton sought to ensure that the rich and well born "could keep their saddles and ride . . . like English squires," criticized him as an unwitting precursor of the New Deal welfare state. "A man on the Right," according to historian Clinton Rossiter in 1955, "is not necessarily a conservative, and if Hamilton was a conservative, he was the only one of his kind." The McCarthy-Buckley-Goldwater conservative movement owed more to the old southern Democrats than to the Federalist-Whig-Republican tradition. Its philosophical roots sank deep in Jeffersonian antistatism, states' rights, and free-market libertarianism, and its antielitism and anti-intellectualism originated in southern and western populism. The defense of the Hamiltonian tradition fell to northeastern moderate Republicans such as Senator Jacob Javits of New York. In *Order of Battle* (1964), Javits sought to defend his conception of the Republican Party against the ex-Democratic Goldwaterite conservatives of the South and West: "This is the spirit which has represented the most dominant strain in Republican history. Hamilton-Clay-Lincoln-Theodore Roosevelt: they represent the line of evolution embodying this tradition." Arguably the last great Hamiltonians in American politics were Richard Nixon—a foreign-policy realist who admired TR—and John Connally, who, as one of Hamilton's distant successors as secretary of the treasury, shocked foreign governments and American critics with his unapologetic economic nationalism.

By the time Ronald Reagan was elected in 1980, the Republican Party had become a completely libertarian, antistatist party in economics, with serious disagreements in its ranks only over social issues such as abortion and school prayer. Though Kevin Phillips, a graduate of the Nixon-Connally wing of the GOP, published a book, *Staying on Top: The Business Case for National Industry Strategy* (1984), advocating a conservative industrial policy that would target federal aid to "basic industries like steel or automobiles, or high-technology industry," his was an isolated voice. (Phillips was decisively read out of the Right for attacking its plutocratic tendencies in his 1990 best seller, *The Politics Rich and Poor.*) Former Reagan trade negotiator Clyde Prestowitz founded the Economic Strategy Institute (ESI) to contest orthodox laissez-faire notions and advocate government-business partnership and a results-oriented trade policy.

Nevertheless, the dominant group in the Republican Party today consists of southern and western Jeffersonians in the Dixiecrat tradition, along with ex-Democratic intellectuals who, while retaining a strong cultural nationalism, have repudiated the New Deal and the Great Society for laissez-faire economics and the libertarian ideal of minimal government. In 1990, George Will named Jefferson the "Person of the Millennium," writing that Jefferson "is what a free person looks like—confident, serene, rational, disciplined, temperate, tolerant, curious." Ronald Reagan, himself an apostate Democrat, recommended that we "pluck a flower from Thomas Jefferson's life and wear it in our soul forever."

Hamilton probably would have thought as little of the contemporary Republican Right as it thinks of him. Reagan's brand of populist conservatism, contrasting the virtue of the people with the evils of the elite, would have found no favor with the elitist Hamilton. He despised politicians concerned with "what will *please* (and) not what will *benefit* the people." Though often maligned as a champion of plutocracy, Hamilton favored imposts on the luxuries of the rich as a means of "taxing their superior wealth," praised inheritance laws that would "soon melt down those great estates which, if they continued, might favor the power of the few," and denounced the poll tax in order "to guard the least wealthy part of the community from oppression." Though Hamilton was not alarmed by a moderate deficit, he would have been shocked by deficits produced, like Reagan's, by an unwillingness to levy taxes to match spending. In his *Second Report on the Public Credit* (1795), he noted that runaway debt is "the natural disease of all governments" and that it is difficult "to conceive anything more likely than this to lead to great and convulsive revolutions of empire." The first and greatest secretary of the treasury, who during the Whiskey Rebellion helped President Washington to mobilize the militia to collect excise taxes, would not have smiled upon the tax-revolt rhetoric of Howard Jarvis and Ronald Reagan.

Having seen the consequences of feeble government during the Revolutionary War and the years of the Articles of Confederation, Hamilton would have been appalled by Reagan's assertion that "government is not part of the solution; it is the problem." Indeed, during the French Revolution, Hamilton contemptuously dismissed the "pernicious system" that maintained "that but a small portion of power is requisite to Government . . . and that as human nature shall refine and ameliorate by the operation of a more enlightened plan, government itself will become useless, and Society will subsist and flourish free from its shackles."

"The American nation reached the peak of its greatness in the middle of the twentieth century," historian Forrest McDonald has lamented. "After that time it became increasingly Jeffersonian, governed by coercion and the party spirit, its people progressively more dependent and less self-reliant, its decline candy-coated with the rhetoric of liberty and equality and justice for all: and with that decline Hamilton's fame declined apace." Repudiated by *ersatz* Jeffersonians and Jacksonians of the Left and Right alike, Hamilton, by the mid-twentieth century, was even being cast as a villain in American fiction and poetry. In his book-length poem *Paterson* (1946–58) William Carlos Williams, one of America's leading mid-century modernist poets, chose the site of Hamilton's early industrial experiments as a symbol of the blighting of the American spirit in the era of centralized government and concentrated industry. (The poem is interlarded with quotations from a pamphlet Williams had read attacking Hamilton and the Federal Reserve, entitled "Tom Edison on the Money Subject.") In the ultimate insult—from an eccentric populist perspective—Gore Vidal's best selling historical novel *Burr* (1986) cast Hamilton as a sinister foil to the man who murdered him in a duel. Never had Hamilton's reputation been lower.

In recent years, Hamiltonianism has been reintroduced into American political debate by way of Japan. Whereas the neo-Hamiltonians of the late nineteenth century looked to Hamilton as a guide to power politics, the Hamiltonians of today are more likely to view him as the patron saint of industrial policy and economic nationalism.

The architects of the postwar Japanese economic miracle in the Ministry of International Trade and Industry (MITI) and the Ministry of Finance (MOF) were inspired not only by the examples of nineteenth-century Germany and America, but by the theories of the nineteenth-century German economic nationalist Friedrich List, who, when he lived for a time in Pennsylvania, absorbed Hamilton's ideas about the protection of infant industries. By the late 1970s, the remarkable success of modern Japan in promoting its high-tech industry and banking sectors by combining protectionism and industrial policy with the targeting of open foreign markets—including that of the United States—was presenting a challenge to orthodox American economists and politicians, who had been committed to free trade since the aftermath of World War II. Working within the neoclassical paradigm, architects of "the new trade theory" (which is little more than a recycling of the old Hamilton-List theory of tariff-driven industrial policy) began to question the orthodox view that free trade is always beneficial to a country.

By the early 1980s, a growing number of American thinkers and politicians was advocating the emulation, in the United States, of aspects of Japanese industrial policy. It would be a mistake to describe all American proponents of industrial policy as "Hamiltonian." Most of the industrial-policy advocates were Left-liberals such as Robert Reich, Robert Kuttner, and Lester Thurow, whose interest in different (and sometimes conflicting) versions of industrial policy grew out of a desire to help American workers threatened by foreign competition. Also in this school is Laura Tyson, who left the Berkeley Roundtable on the International Economy, an influential forum for the new trade theory, to chair President Clinton's Council of Economic Advisers. Many of these liberals are reluctant nationalists. Given a choice, they would prefer a "global New Deal" regulating the excesses of transnational capitalism to American economic nationalism in the service of American self-sufficiency and geopolitical pre-eminence. They are better described as neo-Keynesians than as Hamiltonians. As for Ross Perot's brand of economic nationalism, it owes more to southwestern populism than to Hamilton's principles.

The genuine Hamiltonians, one can argue, are the politicians and national-security experts more concerned about the U.S. defense industrial base than about union jobs in Detroit. The United States has long had its own military-led industrial policy, in the form of Pentagon-funded research and development. Military procurement has been largely responsible for the postwar U.S. lead in industries characterized by high risk and high research costs requiring government support: computers, aircraft, and communications equipment. The chief Pentagon agency—the American MITI—was the Defense Advanced Research Projects Agency (DARPA).* During the 1980s, DARPA funded R&D in sectors including very high speed integrated circuits (VHSIC), fiber optics, advanced lasers, computer software, and composite materials, which promised to have commercial applications as well as military uses.

The leading Hamiltonians to emerge from the military-industrial complex have not fared well in politics or in the private sector. DARPA director Craig Fields, an advocate of industrial policy, was forced out of his job by the Bush administration in 1990. The view that prevailed in that administration was one attributed to Michael J. Boskin, chairman of the Council of Economic Advisers: "It doesn't matter whether the United States makes computer chips or potato chips." Admiral Bobby Ray Inman, the former National Security Agency (NSA) director who grew concerned about American technological dependence in the mid-80s, left government for an unsuccessful stint as the head of a government-backed computer consortium, Microelectronics and Computer Technology Corporation (MCC), in Austin, Texas. (It might be useful to recall, however, that Hamilton failed both in his political efforts to promote an industrial policy and in his private attempt to jump-start American industrialization with his Society for Useful Manufactures in Paterson—only to be posthumously vindicated by later generations that adopted certain aspects of his program for national development.)

Among recent American politicians, only the "Atari Democrats," led by Gary Hart and Al Gore, combined interests with military innovation and domestic technology policy in true Hamiltonian fashion. Gore's advocacy of military intervention in the Persian Gulf, technology policy, and the building of an "information highway"—the modern version of canals and railroads—makes this southern Democrat the philosophical descendant of northern Federalists, Whigs, and Republicans. One influential thinker among the neoliberal Democrats, journalist James Fallows, is the author of a book on high-tech military reform, *National Defense* (1981) as well as a study of the application of the Hamilton-List economic theory in modern Japan, *Looking at the Sun* (1994). Hamiltonian economic ideas, currently out of favor, can be expected to make a comeback if the contemporary panacea of free-trade agreements such as the North American Free Trade Agreement (NAFTA) and the General Agreement on Tariffs and

*President Clinton has since dropped the word "Defense" from the agency's name.

Trade (GATT) fails to produce the promised results in terms of employment and the revitalization of the American industrial base.

If the neo-Hamiltonians of the 1890s gave a one-sided emphasis to Hamilton's foreign policy realism, the Hamiltonians of today may be overstressing his approach to trade and industry. To Hamilton, foreign policy and economic policy alike were mere means to achieving the goal to which he devoted his life—the unity of the American nation and the competence of its agent, the national state. The circumstances of the 1990s are far different from those of the 1890s, and the United States is a far different country—thanks, in no small part, to Hamilton and his successors. And yet the questions of national unity and competent government are as important in our day as in his.

Today the greatest threat to national unity comes not from sectionalism but from multiculturalism—from the idea that there is no single nation comprising Americans of all races, ancestries, and religions but only an aggregate of biologically defined "cultures" coexisting under a minimal framework of law. Neither Hamilton nor any of his contemporaries gave any thought to the necessity of a multiracial but unicultural society. Still, Hamilton's impassioned vision of a "continentalist" American society can inspire us indirectly as we seek to integrate the American nation in the aftermath of both segregation and multiculturalism.

When it comes to the problem of effective democratic government, Hamilton's legacy is more relevant today than ever. For a generation, the United States has suffered from political gridlock, symbolized by, but not limited to, an inability to make tax revenues match spending. What Jonathan Rauch has called "demosclerosis" is a lethal by-product of the interest-group liberalism of the New Deal, a system now in advanced decay. Rauch, along with other conservatives and libertarians, argues for a "Jeffersonian" solution involving the radical reduction of government at all levels and the dispersal of authority from the central government to the states. However, in the conditions of the twenty-first century, when the United States will likely face geopolitical competition with rising technological powers, mercantilist economic rivalries, and the threat of mass immigration from the Third World, minimal government will almost certainly not be a realistic alternative. Because the quantity of national government will not be significantly reduced, the quality of national governance will have to be improved. That will mean repudiating the ideal of the directionless broker state—now three-quarters of a century old—and attempting to realize the Hamiltonian and Progressive ideal of a strong but not authoritarian executive branch that is led by a meritocratic elite and capable of resisting interest-group pressures without ceasing to be ultimately accountable to elected representatives.

The 1992 campaigns of Clinton and Perot—both of whom, in essence, promised more "businesslike" government rather than less government—are signs that the American public is disenchanted with New Deal interest-group liberalism and with the nostalgic antigovernment libertarianism of the Reagan Right. Journalist David Frum sees American politicians on both Left and Right slowly returning to "the political formula that has won more presidential elections than any other: active government intervention in the economy to promote welfare and assist private business, conservative moral reform at home, and the assertion of American nationality." If Frum is right, then in the decades ahead Hamiltonian nationalism may once again define the political mainstream.

Elsewhere in the world, the Hamiltonian approach to building democratic capitalism in ex-communist and Third World societies could not be more timely. In the immediate aftermath of the Cold War, Americans urged a "Jeffersonian" model of reconstruction on societies everywhere, thinking that immediate elections and rapid marketization of statist economies would solve all problems. The result, in Russia and much of Eastern Europe and the Third World, has been economic collapse, popular disillusionment with democracy and capitalism, and the acquisition of local industries by foreigners at fire-sale prices. The leaders of new democracies can learn from Hamilton and his mentor Washington that it is not enough to hold elections and establish free markets. A struggling new democratic government must be able to defend its borders against foreign enemies, suppress insurrection and criminality, gradually construct a system of sound finance, and guide industrial reform and development in the nation's interest—if necessary, at the expense of free trade.

Not only contemporary Americans, then, but people everywhere have much to learn from Hamilton and Hamiltonianism in the century ahead. In the words of Clinton Rossiter, Hamilton "was conservative and radical, traditionalist and revolutionary, reactionary and visionary, Tory and Whig all thrown into one. He is a glorious source of inspiration and instruction to modern conservatives, but so is he to modern liberals." Earlier in this century, when the threats were totalitarian imperialism and domestic conformity and repression, Americans and freedom-loving peoples around the world may have been right to look for inspiration to apostles of revolution and individualism such as Thomas Jefferson. In the aftermath of successful revolutions, however, a quite different kind of leadership is called for. The task of the coming generation is not to tear down, but to rebuild and build anew. In that task, Alexander Hamilton, the master architect among America's Founders, must be our pre-eminent guide.

QUESTIONS TO CONSIDER

1. What were Alexander Hamilton's most significant achievements?
2. What were Hamilton's ideas on economics and the role the government should play in the economy?
3. How was Hamilton adapted to the modern world at the peak of his popularity in the early twentieth century? What political leader most embodied his thinking?
4. How did FDR transform the nature of Jefferson's legacy and cast himself as Jefferson's heir? What did he and modern Jeffersonians ignore about the Virginian's thinking?
5. What political figures does Lind cite as recent and current Hamiltonians? Why? What nation seems to embody much of his thinking?
6. Why does Lind feel that Hamilton is needed today? How does the national political debate in the wake of the 1994 elections involve him?

9

The Secret Life of a
Developing Country (Ours)*

Jack Larkin

While the ideas and actions of Founding Fathers like Alexander
Hamilton have greatly influenced the lives of Americans down to
the present, most of the populace lived more mundane lives. Like
us, they carried on the routine practices of life, often without thinking about them. Yet the way they lived—their greetings, their diet,
their social activities, their attitudes—in many ways seems strikingly
different from the way we live today. This portrait of the lives of
common folk in the early nineteenth century demonstrates that in
many ways morality was far more questionable in the idyllic past
than today, and also suggests that it is possible to change behavior in substantial ways through both religious and secular campaigns. The American character is not fixed, but evolving.

Author Jack Larkin is Chief Historian at Old Sturbridge Village in
Massachusetts. This article is adapted from his book *The Reshaping
of Everyday Life in the United States, 1790–1840,* published in 1988.

Contemporary observers of early-nineteenth-century America left a fragmentary but nonetheless fascinating and revealing picture of the manner
in which rich and poor, Southerner and Northerner, farmer and city
dweller, freeman and slave presented themselves to the world. To begin

---

*Reprinted from *American Heritage,* September/October 1988, by permission of the author.

with, a wide variety of characteristic facial expressions, gestures, and ways of carrying the body reflected the extraordinary regional and social diversity of the young republic.

When two farmers met in early-nineteenth-century New England, wrote Francis Underwood, of Enfield, Massachusetts, the author of a pioneering 1893 study of small-town life, "their greeting might seem to a stranger gruff or surly, since the facial muscles were so inexpressive, while, in fact, they were on excellent terms." In courtship and marriage, countrymen and women were equally constrained, with couples "wearing all unconsciously the masks which custom had prescribed; and the onlookers who did not know the secret would think them cold and indifferent."

Underwood noted a pervasive physical as well as emotional constraint among the people of Enfield; it was rooted, he thought, not only in the self-denying ethic of their Calvinist tradition but in the nature of their work. The great physical demands of unmechanized agriculture gave New England men, like other rural Americans, a distinctively ponderous gait and posture. Despite their strength and endurance, farmers were "heavy, awkward and slouching in movement" and walked with a "slow inclination from side to side."

Yankee visages were captured by itinerant New England portraitists during the early nineteenth century, as rural storekeepers, physicians, and master craftsmen became the first more or less ordinary Americans to have their portraits done. The portraits caught their caution and immobility of expression as well as recording their angular, long-jawed features, thus creating good collective likenesses of whole communities.

The Yankees, however, were not the stiffest Americans. Even by their own impassive standards, New Englanders found New York Dutchmen and Pennsylvania German farmers "clumsy and chill" or "dull and stolid." But the "wild Irish" stood out in America for precisely the opposite reason. They were not "chill" or "stolid" enough, but loud and expansive. Their expressiveness made Anglo-Americans uncomfortable.

The seemingly uncontrolled physical energy of American blacks left many whites ill at ease. Of the slaves celebrating at a plantation ball, it was "impossible to describe the things these people did with their bodies," Frances Kemble Butler, an English-born actress who married a Georgia slave owner, observed, "and above all with their faces. . . ." Blacks' expressions and gestures, their preference for rhythmic rather than rigid bodily motion, their alternations of energy and rest made no cultural sense to observers who saw only "antics and frolics," "laziness," or "savagery." Sometimes perceived as obsequious, childlike, and dependent, or sullen and inexpressive, slaves also wore masks—not "all unconsciously" as Northern farm folk did, but as part of their self-protective strategies for controlling what masters, mistresses, and other whites could know about their feelings and motivations.

American city dwellers, whose daily routines were driven by the quicker pace of commerce, were easy to distinguish from "heavy and slouching" farmers attuned to slow seasonal rhythms. New Yorkers, in particular, had already acquired their own characteristic body language. The clerks and commercial men who crowded Broadway, intent on their business, had a universal "contraction of the brow, knitting of the eyebrows, and compression of the lips . . . and a hurried walk." It was a popular American saying in the 1830s, reported Frederick Marryat, an Englishman who traveled extensively in the period, that "a New York merchant always walks as if he had a good dinner before him, and a bailiff behind him."

Northern and Southern farmers and city merchants alike, to say nothing of Irishmen and blacks, fell well short of the standard of genteel "bodily carriage" enshrined in both English and American etiquette books and the instructions of dancing masters: "flexibility in the arms . . . erectness in the spinal column . . . easy carriage of the head." It was the ideal of the British aristocracy, and Southern planters came closest to it, expressing the power of their class in the way they stood and moved. Slave owners accustomed to command, imbued with an ethic of honor and pride, at ease in the saddle, carried themselves more gracefully than men hardened by toil or preoccupied with commerce. Visiting Washington in 1835, the Englishwoman Harriet Martineau contrasted not the politics but the postures of Northern and Southern congressmen. She marked the confident bearing, the "ease and frank courtesy . . . with an occasional touch of arrogance" of the slaveholders alongside the "cautious . . . and too deferential air of the members of the North." She could recognize a New Englander "in the open air," she claimed, "by his deprecatory walk."

Local inhabitants' faces became more open, travelers observed, as one went west. Nathaniel Hawthorne found a dramatic contrast in public appearances only a few days' travel west of Boston. "The people out here," in New York State just west of the Berkshires, he confided to his notebook in 1839, "show out their character much more strongly than they do with us," in his native eastern Massachusetts. He compared the "quiet, silent, dull decency . . . in our public assemblages" with Westerners' wider gamut of expressiveness, "mirth, anger, eccentricity, all showing themselves freely." Westerners in general, the clergyman and publicist Henry Ward Beecher observed, had "far more freedom of manners, and more frankness and spontaneous geniality" than did the city or country people of the New England and Middle Atlantic states, as did the "odd mortals that wander in from the western border," that Martineau observed in Washington's political population.

Early-nineteenth-century Americans lived in a world of dirt, insects, and pungent smells. Farmyards were strewn with animal wastes, and farmers wore manure-spattered boots and trousers everywhere. Men's and women's working clothes alike were often stiff with dirt and dried sweat, and men's shirts were often stained with "yellow rivulets" of tobacco juice. The locations of privies were all too obvious on warm or windy days. Unemptied chamber pots advertised their presence. Wet baby "napkins," today's diapers, were not immediately washed but simply put by the fire to dry. Vats of "chamber lye"—highly concentrated urine used for cleaning type or degreasing wool—perfumed all printing offices and many households. "The breath of that fiery bar-room," as Underwood described a country tavern, "was overpowering. The odors of the hostlers' boots, redolent of fish-oil and tallow, and of buffalo-robes and horse-blankets, the latter reminiscent of equine ammonia, almost got the better of the all-pervading fumes of spirits and tobacco."

Densely populated, but poorly cleaned and drained, America's cities were often far more noisome than its farmyards. Horse manure thickly covered city streets, and few neighborhoods were free from the spreading stench of tanneries and slaughterhouses. New York City accumulated so much refuse that it was generally believed the actual surfaces of the streets had not been seen for decades. During her stay in Cincinnati, the English writer Frances Trollope followed the practice of the vast majority of American city housewives when she threw her household "slops"—refuse food and dirty dishwater—out into the street. An irate neighbor soon informed her that municipal ordinances forbade "throwing such things at the sides of the streets" as she had done; "they must just all be cast right into the middle and the pigs soon takes them off." In most cities hundreds, sometimes thousands, of free-roaming pigs scavenged the garbage; one exception was Charleston, South Carolina, where buzzards patrolled the streets. By converting garbage into pork, pigs kept city streets cleaner than they would otherwise have been, but the pigs themselves befouled the streets and those who ate their meat—primarily poor families—ran greater than usual risks of infection.

The most visible symbols of early American sanitation were privies or "necessary houses." But Americans did not always use them; many rural householders simply took to the closest available patch of woods or brush. However, in more densely settled communities and in regions with cold winters, privies were in widespread use. They were not usually put in out-of-the-way locations. The fashion of some Northern farm families, according to Robert B. Thomas's *Farmer's Almanack* in 1826, had long been to have their "necessary planted in a garden or other conspicuous place." Other countryfolk went even further in turning human wastes to agricultural account and built their outhouses "within the territory of a hog yard, that the swine may root and ruminate and devour the nastiness thereof." Thomas was a long-standing critic of primitive manners in the countryside and roundly condemned these traditional sanitary arrangements as demonstrating a "want of taste, decency, and propriety." The better-arranged necessaries of the prosperous emptied into vaults that could be opened and cleaned out. The dripping horse-drawn carts of the "nocturnal goldfinders," who emptied the vaults and took their loads out for burial or water disposal—"night soil" was almost never used as manure—were a familiar part of nighttime traffic on city streets.

The humblest pieces of American household furniture were the chamber pots that allowed people to avoid dark and often cold nighttime journeys outdoors. Kept under beds or in corners of rooms, "chambers" were used primarily upon retiring and arising. Collecting, emptying, and cleaning them remained an unspoken, daily part of every housewife's routine.

Nineteenth-century inventory takers became considerably more reticent about naming chamber pots than their predecessors, usually lumping them with miscellaneous "crockery," but most households probably had a couple of chamber pots; genteel families reached the optimum of one for each bedchamber. English-made ceramic pots had become cheap enough by 1820 that few American families within the reach of commerce needed to go without one. "Without a pot to piss in" was a vulgar tag of long standing for extreme poverty; those poorest households without one, perhaps more common in the warm South, used the outdoors at all times and seasons.

The most decorous way for householders to deal with chamber-pot wastes accumulated during the night was to throw them down the privy hole. But more casual and unsavory methods of disposal were still in wide use. Farm families often dumped their chamber pots out the most convenient door or window. In densely settled communities like York, Pennsylvania, the results could be more serious. In 1801, the York diarist Lewis Miller drew and then described an event in North George Street when "Mr. Day an English man [as the German-American Miller was quick to point out] had a bad practice by pouring out of the upper window his filthiness . . . one day came the discharge . . . on a man and wife going to a wedding, her silk dress was fouled."

Sleeping accommodations in American country taverns were often dirty and insect-ridden. The eighteenth-century observer of American life

Isaac Weld saw "filthy beds swarming with bugs" in 1794; in 1840 Charles Dickens noted "a sort of game not on the bill of fare." Complaints increased in intensity as travelers went south or west. Tavern beds were uniquely vulnerable to infestation by whatever insect guests travelers brought with them. The bedding of most American households was surely less foul. Yet it was dirty enough. New England farmers were still too often "tormented all night by bed bugs," complained *The Farmer's Almanack* in 1837, and books of domestic advice contained extensive instructions on removing them from feather beds and straw ticks.

Journeying between Washington and New Orleans in 1828, Margaret Hall, a well-to-do and cultivated Scottish woman, became far more familiar with intimate insect life than she had ever been in the genteel houses of London or Edinburgh. Her letters home, never intended for publication, gave a graphic and unsparing account of American sanitary conditions. After sleeping in a succession of beds with the "usual complement of fleas and bugs," she and her party had themselves become infested: "We bring them along with us in our clothes and when I undress I find them crawling on my skin, nasty wretches." New and distasteful to her, such discoveries were commonplace among the ordinary folk with whom she lodged. The American children she saw on her Southern journey were "kept in such a state of filth," with clothes "dirty and slovenly to a degree," but this was "nothing in comparison with their heads . . . [which] are absolutely crawling!" In New Orleans she observed women picking through children's heads for lice, "catching them according to the method depicted in an engraving of a similar proceeding in the streets of Naples."

Americans were not "clean and decent" by today's standards, and it was virtually impossible that they should be. The furnishings and use of rooms in most American houses made more than the most elementary washing difficult. In a New England farmer's household, wrote Underwood, each household member would "go down to the 'sink' in the lean-to, next to the kitchen, fortunate if he had not to break ice in order to wash his face and hands, or more fortunate if a little warm water was poured into his basin from the kettle swung over the kitchen fire." Even in the comfortable household of the prominent minister Lyman Beecher in Litchfield, Connecticut, around 1815, all family members washed in the kitchen, using a stone sink and "a couple of basins."

Southerners washed in their detached kitchens or, like Westerners in warm weather, washed outside, "at the doors . . . or at the wells" of their houses. Using basins and sinks outdoors or in full view of others, most Americans found anything more than "washing the face and hands once a-day," usually in cold water, difficult, even unthinkable. Most men and women also washed without soap, reserving it for laundering clothes; instead they used a brisk rubbing with a course towel to scrub the dirt off their skins.

Gradually the practice of complete bathing spread beyond the topmost levels of American society and into smaller towns and villages. This became possible as families moved washing equipment out of kitchens and into bedchambers, from shared space to space that could be made private. As more prosperous households furnished one or two of their chambers with washing equipment—a washstand, a basin, and a ewer, or large-mouthed pitcher—family members could shut the chamber door, undress, and wash themselves completely. The daughters of the Larcom family, living in Lowell, Massachusetts, in the late 1830s, began to bathe in a bedchamber in this way; Lucy Larcom described how her oldest sister started to take "a full cold bath every morning before she went to her work . . . in a room without a fire," and the other young Larcoms "did the same whenever we could be resolute enough." By the 1830s better city hotels and even some country taverns were providing individual basins and pitchers in their rooms.

At a far remove from "primitive manners" and "bad practices" was the genteel ideal of domestic sanitation embodied in the "chamber sets"—matching basin and ewer for private bathing, a cup for brushing the teeth, and a chamber pot with cover to minimize odor and spillage—that American stores were beginning to stock. By 1840 a significant minority of American households owned chamber sets and washstands to hold them in their bedchambers. For a handful there was the very faint dawning of an entirely new age of sanitary arrangements. In 1829 the new Tremont House hotel in Boston offered its patrons indoor plumbing: eight chambers with bathtubs and eight "water closets." In New York City and Philadelphia, which had developed rudimentary public water systems, a few wealthy households had water taps and, more rarely, water closets by the 1830s. For all other flush toilets and bathtubs remained far in the future.

The American people moved very slowly toward cleanliness. In "the backcountry at the present day," commented the fastidious author of the *Lady's Book* in 1836, custom still "requires that everyone should wash at the pump in the yard, or at the sink in the kitchen." Writing in 1846, the physician and health reformer William Alcott rejoiced that to "wash the surface of the whole body in water daily" had now been accepted as a genteel standard of personal cleanliness. But, he added, there were "multitudes who pass for models of neatness and cleanliness, who do not perform this work for themselves half a dozen times—nay once—a year." As the better-off became cleaner than ever before, the poor stayed dirty.

In the early part of the century America was a bawdy, hard edged, and violent land. We drank more than we ever had before or ever would again. We smoked and chewed tobacco like addicts and fought and quarreled on the flimsiest pretexts. The tavern was the most important gateway to the primarily male world of drink and disorder: in sight of the village church in most American communities, observed Daniel Drake, a Cincinnati physician who wrote a reminiscence of his Kentucky boyhood, stood the village tavern, and the two structures "did in fact represent two great opposing principles."

The great majority of American men in every region were taverngoers. The printed street directories of American cities listed tavernkeepers in staggering numbers, and even the best-churched parts of New England could show more "licensed houses" than meetinghouses. In 1827 the fast-growing city of Rochester, New York, with a population of approximately eight thousand, had nearly one hundred establishments licensed to sell liquor, or one for every eighty inhabitants.

America's most important centers of male sociability, taverns were often the scene of excited gaming and vicious fights and always of hard drinking, heavy smoking, and an enormous amount of alcohol-stimulated talk. City men came to their neighborhood taverns daily, and "tavern haunting, tippling, and gaming," as Samuel Goodrich, a New England historian and publisher, remembered, "were the chief resources of men in the dead and dreary winter months" in the countryside.

City taverns catered to clienteles of different classes: sordid sailors' grog-shops near the waterfront were rife with brawling and prostitution; neighborhood taverns and liquor-selling groceries were visited by craftsmen and clerks; well-appointed and relatively decorous places were favored by substantial merchants. Taverns on busy highways often specialized in teamsters or stage passengers, while country inns took their patrons as they came.

Taverns accommodated women as travelers, but their barroom clienteles were almost exclusively male. Apart from the dockside dives frequented by prostitutes, or the liquor-selling groceries of poor city neighborhoods, women rarely drank in public.

Gambling was a substantial preoccupation for many male citizens of the early republic. Men played billiards at tavern tables for money stakes. They threw dice in "hazard," slamming the dice boxes down so hard and so often that tavern tables wore the characteristic scars of their play. Even more often Americans sat down to cards, playing brag, similar to modern-day poker, or an elaborate table game called faro. Outdoors they wagered with each other on horse races or bet on cock-fights and wrestling matches.

Drink permeated and propelled the social world of early-nineteenth-century America—first as an unquestioned presence and later as a serious and divisive problem. "Liquor at that time," recalled the builder and architect Elbridge Boyden, "was used as commonly as the food we ate." Before 1820 the vast majority of Americans considered alcohol an essential stimulant to exertion as well as a symbol of hospitality and fellowship. Like the Kentuckians with whom Daniel Drake grew up, they "regarded it as a duty to their families and visitors . . . to keep the bottle well replenished." Weddings, funerals, frolics, even a casual "gathering of two or three neighbors for an evening's social chat" required the obligatory "spirituous liquor"—rum, whiskey, or gin—"at all seasons and on all occasions."

Northern householders drank hard cider as their common table beverage, and all ages drank it freely. Dramming—taking a fortifying glass in the forenoon and again in the afternoon—was part of the daily regimen of many men. Clergymen took sustaining libations between services, lawyers before going to court, and physicians at their patients' bedsides. To raise a barn or get through a long day's haying without fortifying drink seemed a virtual impossibility. Slaves enjoyed hard drinking at festival times and at Saturday-night barbecues as much as any of their countrymen. But of all Americans they probably drank the least on a daily basis because their masters could usually control their access to liquor.

In Parma, Ohio, in the mid-1820s, Lyndon Freeman, a farmer, and his brothers were used to seeing men "in their cups" and passed them by without comment. But one dark and rainy night they discovered something far more shocking, "nothing less than a *woman beastly drunk . . .* with a flask of whiskey by her side." American women drank as well as men, but usually much less heavily. They were more likely to make themselves "tipsy" with hard cider and alcohol-containing patent medicines than to become inebriated with rum or whiskey. Temperance advocates in the late 1820s estimated that men consumed fifteen times the volume of distilled spirits that women did; this may have been a considerable exaggeration, but there was a great difference in drinking habits between the sexes. Americans traditionally found drunkenness tolerable and forgivable in men but deeply shameful in women.

By almost any standard, Americans drank not only nearly universally but in large quantities. Their yearly consumption at the time of the Revolution has been estimated at the equivalent of three and one-half gallons of pure two-hundred-proof alcohol for each person. After 1790 American men began to drink even more. By the late 1820s their imbibing had risen to an all-time high of almost four gallons per capita.

Along with drinking went fighting. Americans fought often and with great relish. York, Pennsylvania, for example, was a peaceable place as American communities went, but the Miller and Weaver families had a long-running quarrel. It had begun in 1800 when the Millers found young George Weaver stealing apples in their yard and punished him by "throwing him over the fence," injuring him painfully. Over the years hostilities broke out periodically. Lewis Miller remembered walking down the street as a teenaged boy and meeting Mrs. Weaver, who drenched him with the bucket of water she was carrying. He retaliated by "turning about and giving her a kick, laughing at her, this is for your politeness." Other York households had their quarrels too; in "a general fight on Beaver Street," Mistress Hess and Mistress Forsch tore each other's caps from their heads. Their husbands and then the neighbors interfered, and "all of them had a knock down."

When Peter Lung's wife, Abigail, refused "to get up and dig some potatoes" for supper from the yard of their small house, the Hartford, Connecticut, laborer recalled in his confession, he "kicked her on the side . . . then gave her a violent push" and went out to dig the potatoes himself. He returned and "again kicked her against the shoulder and neck." Both had been drinking, and loud arguments and blows within the Lung household, as in many others, were routine. But this time the outcome was not. Alice Lung was dead the next day, and Peter Lung was arrested, tried, and hanged for murder in 1815.

In the most isolated, least literate and commercialized parts of the United States, it was "by no means uncommon," wrote Isaac Weld, "to meet with those who have lost an eye in a combat, and there are men who pride themselves upon the dexterity with which they can scoop one out. This is called *gouging.*"

Slaves wrestled among themselves, sometimes fought one another bitterly over quarrels in the quarters, and even at times stood up to the vastly superior force of masters and overseers. They rarely, if ever, reduced themselves to the ferocity of eye gouging. White Southerners lived with a pervasive fear of the violent potential of their slaves, and the Nat Turner uprising in Virginia in 1831, when a party of slaves rebelled and killed whites before being overcome, gave rise to tighter and harsher controls. But in daily reality slaves had far more to fear from their masters.

Margaret Hall was no proponent of abolition and had little sympathy for black Americans. Yet in her travels south she confronted incidents of what she ironically called the "good treatment of slaves" that were impossible to ignore. At a country tavern in Georgia, she summoned the slave chambermaid, but "she could not come" because "the mistress had been whipping her and she was not fit to be seen. Next morning she made her appearance with her face marked in several places by the cuts of the cowskin and her neck handkerchief covered with spots of blood."

Southern stores were very much like Northern ones, Francis Kemble Butler observed, except that they stocked "negro-whips" and "mantraps" on their shelves. A few slaves were never beaten at all, and for most, whippings were not a daily or weekly occurrence. But they were, of all Americans, by far the most vulnerable to violence. All slaves had, as William Wells Brown, an ex-slave himself, said, often "heard the crack of the whip, and the screams of the slave" and knew that they were never more than a white man's or woman's whim away from a beating. With masters' unchecked power came worse than whipping: the mutilitating punishments of the old penal law including branding, ear cropping, and even occasionally castration and burning alive as penalties for severe offenses. In public places or along the road blacks were also subject to casual kicks, shoves, and cuffs, for which they could retaliate only at great peril. "Six or seven feet in length, made of cowhide, with a platted wire on the end of it," as Brown recalled it, the negrowhip, for sale in most stores and brandished by masters and overseers in the fields, stood for a pervasive climate of force and intimidation.

PUBLIC PUNISHMENT

The penal codes of the American states were far less blood-thirsty than those of England. Capital punishment was not often imposed on whites for crimes other than murder. Yet at the beginning of the nineteenth century many criminal offenses were punished by the public infliction of pain and suffering. "The whipping post and stocks stood on the green near the meetinghouse" in most of the towns of New England and near courthouses everywhere. In Massachusetts before 1805 a counterfeiter was liable to have an ear cut off, and a forger to have one cropped or partially amputated, after spending an hour in the pillory. A criminal convicted of manslaughter was set up on the gallows to have his forehead branded with the letter M. In most jurisdictions town officials flogged petty thieves as punishment for their crime. In New Haven, Connecticut, around 1810, Charles Fowler, a local historian, recalled seeing the "admiring students of [Yale] college" gathered around to watch petty criminals receive "five or ten lashes . . . with a rawhide whip."

Throughout the United States public hangings brought enormous crowds to the seats of justice and sometimes seemed like brutal festivals. Thousands of spectators arrived to pack the streets of courthouse towns. On the day of a hanging near Mount Holly, New Jersey, in the 1820s, the scene was that of a holiday: "around the place in every direction were the assembled multitudes—some in tents, and by-wagons, engaged in gambling and other vices of the sort, in open day." In order to accommodate the throngs, hangings were usually held not in the public square but on the outskirts of town. The gallows erected on a hill or set up at the bottom of a natural amphitheater allowed onlookers an unobstructed view. A reprieve or stay of execution might disappoint a crowd intent on witnessing the deadly drama and provoke a riot, as it did in Pembroke, New Hampshire, in 1834.

At a drunkard's funeral in Enfield, Massachusetts, in the 1830s—the man had strayed out of the road while walking home and fallen over a cliff, "his stiffened fingers still grasping the handle of the jug"—Rev. Sumner G. Clapp, the Congregationalist minister of Enfield, mounted a log by the woodpile and preached the town's first temperance sermon before a crowd full of hardened drinkers. In this way Clapp began a campaign to "civilize" the manners of his parishioners, and "before many years there was a great change in the town; the incorrigible were removed by death, and others took warning." Drinking declined sharply, and along with it went "a general reform in conduct."

Although it remained a powerful force in many parts of the United States, the American way of drunkenness began to lose ground as early as the mid-1820s. The powerful upsurge in liquor consumption had provoked a powerful reaction, an unprecedented attack on all forms of drink that gathered momentum in the Northeast. Some New England clergymen had been campaigning in their own communities as early as 1810, but their concerns took on organized impetus with the founding of the American Temperance Society in 1826. Energized in part by a concern for social order, in part by evangelical piety, temperance reformers popularized a radically new way of looking at alcohol. The "good creature" became "demon rum"; prominent physicians and writers on physiology, like Benjamin Rush, told Americans that alcohol, traditionally considered healthy and fortifying, was actually a physical and moral poison. National and state societies distributed antiliquor tracts, at first calling for moderation in drink but increasingly demanding total abstinence from alcohol.

To a surprising degree these aggressive temperance campaigns worked. By 1840 the consumption of alcohol had declined by more than two-thirds, from close to four gallons per person each year to less than one and one-half. Country storekeepers gave up the sale of spirits, local authorities limited the number of tavern licenses, and farmers even abandoned hard cider and cut down their apple orchards. The shift to temperance was a striking transformation in the everyday habits of an enormous number of Americans. "A great, though silent change," in Horace Greeley's words, had been "wrought in public sentiment."

But although the "great change" affected some Americans everywhere, it had a very uneven impact. Organized temperance reform was sharply delimited by geography. Temperance societies were enormously powerful in New England and western New York and numerous in eastern New York, New Jersey, and Pennsylvania. More than three fourths of all recorded temperance pledges came from these states. In the South and West, and in the laborers' and artisans' neighborhoods of the cities, the campaign against drink was much weaker. In many places drinking ways survived and even flourished, but as individuals and families came under the influence of militant evangelical piety, their "men of business and sobriety" increased gradually in number. As liquor grew "unfashionable in the country," Greeley noted, Americans who wanted to drink and carouse turned increasingly to the cities, "where no one's deeds or ways are observed or much regarded."

Closely linked as they were to drink, such diversions as gambling, racing, and blood sports also fell to the same forces of change. In the central Massachusetts region that George Davis, a lawyer in Sturbridge, knew well, until 1820 or so gaming had "continued to prevail, more and more extensively." After that "a blessed change had succeeded," overturning the scenes of high-stakes dice and card games that he knew in his young manhood. Impelled by a new perception of its "pernicious effects," local leaders gave it up and placed "men of respectable standing" firmly in opposition. Racecourses were abandoned and "planted to corn." Likewise, "bear-baiting, cock-fighting, and other cruel amusements" began to dwindle in the Northern countryside. Elsewhere the rude life of the tavern and "cruel amusements" remained widespread, but some of their excesses of "sin and shame" did diminish gradually.

Over the first four decades of the nineteenth century, the American people increasingly made churchgoing an obligatory ritual. The proportion of families affiliated with a local church or Methodist circuit rose dramatically, particularly after 1820, and there were fewer stretches of the wholly pagan, unchurched territory that travelers had noted around 1800. "Since 1830," maintained Emerson Davis in his retrospect of America, *The Half Century*, ". . . the friends of the Sabbath have been gaining ground. . . . In 1800, good men slumbered over the desecration of the Sabbath. They have since awoke. . . ." The number of Sunday mails declined, and the campaign to eliminate the delivery of mail on the Sabbath entirely grew stronger. "In the smaller cities and towns," wrote Mrs. Trollope in 1832, worship and "prayer meetings" had come to "take the place of almost all other amusements." There were still communities near the edge of settlement where a traveler would "rarely find either churches or chapels, prayer or preacher," but it was the working-class neighborhoods of America's larger cities that were increasingly the chief strongholds of "Sunday dissipation" and "Sabbath-breaking."

Whipping and the pillory, with their attentive audiences, began to disappear from the statute book, to be replaced by terms of imprisonment in another new American institution, the state penitentiary. Beginning with Pennsylvania's abolition of flogging in 1790 and Massachusetts's elimination of mutilating punishments in 1805, several American states gradually accepted John Hancock's view of 1796 that "mutilating or lacerating the body" was less an effective punishment than "an indignity to human nature." Connecticut's town constables whipped petty criminals for the last time in 1828.

Slaveholding states were far slower to change their provisions for public punishment. The whipping and mutilation of blacks may have become a little less ferocious over the decades, but the whip remained the essential instrument of punishment and discipline. "The secret of our success," thought a slave owner, looking back after emancipation, had been "the great motive power contained in that little instrument." Delaware achieved notoriety by keeping flogging on the books for whites and blacks alike through most of the twentieth century.

Although there were important stirrings of sentiment against capital punishment, all American states continued to execute convicted murderers before the mid-1840s. Public hangings never lost their drawing power. But a number of American public officials began to abandon the long-standing view of executions as instructive communal rituals. They saw the crowd's holiday mood and eager participation as sharing too much in the condemned killer's own brutality. Starting with Pennsylvania, New York, and Massachusetts in the mid-1830s, several state legislatures voted to take executions away from the crowd, out of the public realm. Sheriffs began to carry out death sentences behind the walls of the jailyard, before a small assembly of representative onlookers. Other states clung much longer to tradition and continued public executions into the twentieth century.

Early-nineteenth-century Americans were more licentious than we ordinarily imagine them to be.

"On the 20th day of July" in 1830, Harriet Winter, a young woman working as a domestic in Joseph Dunham's household in Brimfield, Massachusetts, "was gathering raspberries" in a field west of the house. "Near the close of day," Charles Phelps, a farm laborer then living in the town, "came to the field where she was," and in the gathering dusk they made love—and, Justice of the Peace Asa Lincoln added in his account, "it was the Sabbath." American communities did not usually document their inhabitants' amorous rendezvous, and Harriet's tryst with Charles was a commonplace event in early-nineteenth-century America. It escaped historical oblivion because she was unlucky, less in becoming pregnant than in Charles's refusal to marry her. Asa Lincoln did not approve of Sabbath evening indiscretions, but he was not pursuing Harriet for immorality. He was concerned instead with economic responsibility for the child. Thus he interrogated Harriet about the baby's father—while she was in labor, as was the long-customary practice—in order to force Charles to contribute to the maintenance of the child, who was going to be "born a bastard and chargeable to the town."

Some foreign travelers found that the Americans they met were reluctant to admit that such things happened in the United States. They were remarkably straitlaced about sexual matters in public and eager to insist upon the "purity" of their manners. But to take such protestations at face value, the unusually candid Englishman Frederick Marryat thought, would be "to suppose that human nature is not the same everywhere."

The well-organized birth and marriage records of a number of American communities reveal that in late-eighteenth-century America pregnancy was frequently the prelude to marriage. The proportion of brides who were pregnant at the time of their weddings had been rising since the late seventeenth century and peaked in the turbulent decades during and after the Revolution. In the 1780s and 1790s nearly one third of rural New England's brides were already with child. The frequency of sexual intercourse before marriage was surely higher, since some couples would have escaped early pregnancy. For many couples sexual relations were part of serious courtship. Premarital pregnancies in late-eighteenth-century Dedham, Massachusetts, observed the local historian Erastus Worthington in 1828, were occasioned by "the custom then prevalent of females admitting young men to their beds, who sought their company in marriage."

Pregnancies usually simply accelerated a marriage that would have taken place in any case, but community and parental pressure worked strongly to assure it. Most rural communities simply accepted the "early" pregnancies that marked so many marriages, although in Hingham, Massachusetts, tax records suggest that the families of well-to-do brides were considerably less generous to couples who had had "early babies" than to those who had avoided pregnancy.

"Bundling very much abounds," wrote the anonymous author of "A New Bundling Song," still circulating in Boston in 1812, "in many parts in country towns." Noah Webster's first *Dictionary of the American Language* defined it as the custom that allowed couples "to sleep on the same bed without undressing"—with, a later commentator added, "the shared understanding that innocent endearments should not be exceeded." Folklore and local tradition, from Maine south to New York, had American mothers tucking bundling couples into bed with special chastity-protecting garments for the young woman or a "bundling board" to separate them.

In actuality, if bundling had been intended to allow courting couples privacy and emotional intimacy but not sexual contact, it clearly failed. Couples may have begun with bundling, but as courtship advanced, they clearly pushed beyond its restraints, like the "bundling maid" in "A New Bundling Song" who would "sometimes say when she lies down/She can't be cumbered with a gown."

Young black men and women shared American whites' freedom in courtship and sexuality and sometimes exceeded it. Echoing the cultural traditions of West Africa, and reflecting the fact that their marriages were not given legal status and security, slave communities were somewhat more tolerant and accepting of sex before marriage.

Gradations of color and facial features among the slaves were testimony that "thousands," as the abolitionist and former slave Frederick Douglass wrote, were "ushered into the world annually, who, like myself, owe their existence to white fathers, and those fathers most frequently their own masters." Sex crossed the boundaries of race and servitude more often than slavery's defenders wanted to admit, if less frequently than the most outspoken abolitionists claimed. Slave women had little protection from whatever sexual demands masters or overseers might make, so that rapes, short liaisons, and long-term "concubinage" all were part of plantation life.

As Nathaniel Hawthorne stood talking with a group of men on the porch of a tavern in Augusta, Maine, in 1836, a young man "in a laborer's dress" came up and asked if anyone knew the whereabouts of Mary Ann Russell. "Do you want to use her?" asked one of the bystanders. Mary Ann was, in fact, the young laborer's wife, but she had left him and their child in Portland to become "one of a knot of whores." A few years earlier the young men of York, Pennsylvania, made up a party for "overturning and pulling to the ground" Eve Geese's "shameful house" of prostitution in Queen Street. The frightened women fled out the back door as the chimney collapsed around them; the apprentices and young journeymen many of whom had surely been previous customers—were treated by local officials "to wine, for the good work."

From medium-sized towns like Augusta and York to great cities, poor American women were sometimes pulled into a darker, harsher sexual world, one of vulnerability, exploitation, and commerce. Many prostitutes took up their trade out of poverty and domestic disaster. A young widow or a country girl arrived in the city and, thrown on her own resources, often faced desperate economic choices because most women's work paid too poorly to provide decent food, clothing, and shelter, while other women sought excitement and independence from their families.

As cities grew, and changes in transportation involved more men in long-distance travel, prostitution became more visible. Men of all ages, married and unmarried, from city lawyers to visiting country storekeepers to sailors on the docks, turned to brothels for sexual release, but most of the customers were young men, living away from home and unlikely to marry until their late twenties. Sexual commerce in New York City was elaborately graded by price and the economic status of clients, from the "parlor houses" situated not far from the city's best hotels on Broadway to the more numerous and moderately priced houses that drew artisans and clerks, and finally to the broken and dissipated women who haunted dockside grogshops in the Five Points neighborhood.

From New Orleans to Boston, city theaters were important sexual marketplaces. Men often bought tickets less to see the performance than to make assignations with the prostitutes, who sat by custom in the topmost gallery of seats. The women usually received free admission from theater managers, who claimed that they could not stay in business without the male theatergoers drawn by the "guilty third tier."

Most Americans—and the American common law—still did not regard abortion as a crime until the fetus had "quickened" or began to move perceptibly in the womb. Books of medical advice actually contained prescriptions for bringing on delayed menstrual periods, which would also produce an abortion if the woman happened to be pregnant. They suggested heavy doses of purgatives that created violent cramps, powerful douches, or extreme kinds of physical activity, like the "violent exercise, raising great weights . . . strokes on the belly . . . [and] falls" noted in William Buchan's *Domestic Medicine*, a manual read widely through the 1820s. Women's folklore echoed most of these prescriptions and added others, particularly the use of two American herbal preparations—savin, or the extract of juniper berries, and Seneca snakeroot—as abortion-producing drugs. They were dangerous procedures but sometimes effective.

Starting at the turn of the nineteenth century, the sexual lives of many Americans began to change, shaped by a growing insistence on control: reining in the passions in courtship, limiting family size, and even redefining male and female sexual desire.

Bundling was already on the wane in rural America before 1800; by the 1820s it was written about as a rare and antique custom. It had ceased, thought an elderly man from East Haddam, Connecticut, "as a consequence of education and refinement." Decade by decade the proportion of young women who had conceived a child before marriage declined. In most of the towns of New England the rate had dropped from nearly one pregnant bride in three to one in five or six by 1840; in some places prenuptial pregnancy dropped to 5 percent. For many young Americans this marked the acceptance of new limits on sexual behavior, imposed not by their parents or other authorities in their communities but by themselves.

These young men and women were not more closely supervised by their parents than earlier generations had been; in fact, they had more mobility and greater freedom. The couples that courted in the new style put a far greater emphasis on control of the passions. For some of them—young Northern merchants and professional men and their intended brides—revealing love letters have survived for the years after 1820. Their intimate correspondence reveals that they did not give up sexual expression but gave it new boundaries, reserving sexual intercourse for marriage. Many of them were marrying later than their parents, often living through long engagements while the husband-to-be strove to establish his place in the world. They chose not to risk a pregnancy that would precipitate them into an early marriage.

Many American husbands and wives were also breaking with tradition as they began to limit the size of their families. Clearly, married couples were renegotiating the terms of their sexual lives together, but they remained resolutely silent about how they did it. In the first two decades of the nineteenth century, they almost certainly set about avoiding childbirth through abstinence; coitus interruptus, or male withdrawal; and perhaps sometimes abortion. These contraceptive techniques had long been traditional in preindustrial Europe, although previously little used in America.

As they entered the 1830s, Americans had their first opportunity to learn, at least in print, about more effective or less self-denying forms of birth control. They could read reasonably inexpensive editions of the first works on contraception published in the United States: Robert Dale Owen's *Moral Physiology* of 1831 and Dr. Charles Knowlton's *The Fruits of Philosophy* of 1832. Both authors frankly described the full range of contraceptive techniques, although they solemnly rejected physical intervention in the sexual act and recommended only douching after intercourse and coitus interruptus. Official opinion, legal and religious, was deeply hostile. Knowlton, who had trained as a physician in rural Massachusetts, was prosecuted in three different counties for obscenity, convicted once, and imprisoned for three months.

But both works found substantial numbers of Americans eager to read them. By 1839 each book had gone through nine editions, putting a combined total of twenty to thirty thousand copies in circulation. An American physician could write in 1850 that contraception had "been of late years so much talked of." Greater knowledge about contraception surely played a part in the continuing decline of the American birthrate after 1830.

New ways of thinking about sexuality emerged that stressed control and channeling of the passions. Into the 1820s almost all Americans would have subscribed to the commonplace notion that sex, within proper social confines, was enjoyable and healthy and that prolonged sexual abstinence could be injurious to health. They also would have assumed that women had powerful sexual drives.

Starting with his "Lecture to Young Men on Chastity" in 1832, Sylvester Graham articulated very different counsels about health and sex. Sexual indulgence, he argued, was not only morally suspect but psychologically and physiologically risky. The sexual overstimulation involved in young men's lives produced anxiety and nervous disorders, "a shocking state of debility and excessive irritability." The remedy was diet, exercise, and a regular routine that pulled the mind away from animal lusts. Medical writings that discussed the evils of masturbation, or "solitary vice," began to appear. Popular books of advice, like William Alcott's *Young Man's Guide*, gave similar warnings. They tried to persuade young men that their health could be ruined, and their prospects for success darkened, by consorting with prostitutes or becoming sexually entangled before marriage.

A new belief about women's sexual nature appeared, one that elevated them above "carnal passion." Many American men and women came to believe during the nineteenth century that in their true and proper nature as mothers and guardians of the home, women were far less interested in sex than men were. Women who defined themselves as passionless were in a strong position to control or deny men's sexual demands either during courtship or in limiting their childbearing within marriage.

Graham went considerably farther than this, advising restraint not only in early life and courtship but in marriage itself. It was far healthier, he maintained, for couples to have sexual relations "very seldom."

Neither contraception nor the new style of courtship had become anything like universal by 1840. Prenuptial pregnancy rates had fallen, but they remained high enough to indicate that many couples simply continued in familiar ways. American husbands and wives in the cities and the Northern countryside were limiting the number of their children, but it was clear that those living on the farms of the West or in the slave quarters had not yet begun to. There is strong evidence that many American women felt far from passionless, although others restrained or renounced their sexuality. For many people in the United States, there had been a profound change. Reining in the passions had become part of everyday life.

"Everyone smokes and some chew in America," wrote Isaac Weld in 1795. Americans turned tobacco, a new and controversial stimulant at the time of colonial settlement, into a crucially important staple crop and made its heavy use a commonplace—and a never-ending source of surprise and indignation to visitors. Tobacco use spread in the United States because it was comparatively cheap, a homegrown product free from the heavy import duties levied on it by European governments. A number of slave rations described in plantation documents included "one hand of tobacco per month." Through the eighteenth century most American smokers used clay pipes, which are abundant in colonial archeological sites, although some men and women dipped snuff or inhaled powdered tobacco.

Where the smokers of early colonial America "drank" or gulped smoke through the short, thick stems of their seventeenth-century pipes, those of 1800 inhaled it more slowly and gradually; from the early seventeenth to the late eighteenth century, pipe stems became steadily longer and narrower, increasingly distancing smokers from their burning tobacco.

In the 1790s cigars, or "segars," were introduced from the Caribbean. Prosperous men widely took them up; they were the most expensive way to consume tobacco, and it was a sign of financial security to puff away on "long-nines" or "principe cigars at three cents each" while the poor used clay pipes and much cheaper "cut plug" tobacco. After 1800 in American streets, barrooms, stores, public conveyances, and even private homes it became nearly impossible to avoid tobacco chewers. Chewing extended tobacco use, particularly into workplaces; men who smoked pipes at home or in the tavern barroom could chew while working in barns or workshops where smoking carried the danger of fire.

"In all the public places of America," wrote Charles Dickens, multitudes of men engaged in "the odious practice of chewing and expectorating," a recreation practiced by all ranks of American society. Chewing stimulated salivation and gave rise to a public environment of frequent and copious spitting, where men every few minutes were "squirting a mouthful of saliva through the room."

Spittoons were provided in the more meticulous establishments, but men often ignored them. The floors of American public buildings were not pleasant to contemplate. A courtroom in New York City in 1833 was decorated by a "mass of abomination" contributed to by "judges, counsel, jury, witnesses, officers, and audience." The floor of the Virginia House of Burgesses in 1827 was "actually flooded with their horrible spitting," and even the aisle of a Connecticut meetinghouse was black with the "ejection after ejection, incessant from twenty mouths," of the men singing in the choir. In order to drink, an American man might remove his quid, put it in a pocket or hold it in his hand, take his glassful, and then restore it to his mouth. Women's dresses might even be in danger at fashionable balls. "One night as I was walking upstairs to valse," reported Margaret Hall of a dance in Washington in 1828, "my partner began clearing his throat. This I thought ominous. However, I said to myself, 'surely he will turn his head to the other side.' The gentleman, however, had no such thought but deliberately shot across me. I had not courage enough to examine whether the result landed in the flounce of my dress."

The segar and the quid were almost entirely male appurtenances, but as the nineteenth century began, many rural and lower-class urban women were smoking pipes or dipping snuff. During his boyhood in New Hampshire, Horace Greeley remembered, "it was often my filial duty to fill and light my mother's pipe."

After 1820 or so tobacco use among women in the North began to decline. Northern women remembered or depicted with pipe or snuffbox were almost all elderly. More and more Americans adopted a genteel standard that saw tobacco use and womanliness—delicate and nurturing—as antithetical, and young women avoided it as a pollutant. For them, tobacco use marked off male from female territory with increasing sharpness.

In the households of small Southern and Western farmers, however, smoking and snuff taking remained common. When women visited "among the country people" of North Carolina, Frances Kemble Butler reported in 1837, the "proffer of the snuffbox, and its passing from hand to hand, is the usual civility." By the late 1830s visiting New Englanders were profoundly shocked when they saw the women of Methodist congregations in Illinois, including nursing mothers, taking out their pipes for a smoke between worship services.

The Americans of 1820 would have been more recognizable to us in the informal and egalitarian way they treated one another. The traditional signs of deference before social superiors—the deep bow, the "courtesy," the doffed cap, lowered head, and averted eyes—had been a part of social relationships in colonial America. In the 1780s, wrote the American poetess Lydia Huntley Sigourney in 1824, there were still "individuals . . . in every grade of society" who had grown up "when a bow was not an offense to fashion nor . . . a relic of monarchy." But in the early nineteenth century such signals of subordination rapidly fell away. It was a natural consequence of the Revolution, she maintained, which, "in giving us liberty, obliterated almost every vestige of politeness of the 'old school.'"

Shaking hands became the accustomed American greeting between men, a gesture whose symmetry and mutuality signified equality. Frederick Marryat found in 1835 that it was "invariably the custom to shake hands" when he was introduced to Americans and that he could not carefully grade the acknowledgment he would give to new acquaintances according to their signs of wealth and breeding. He found instead that he had to "go on shaking hands here, there and everywhere, and with everybody." Americans were not blind to inequalities of economic and social power, but they less and less gave them overt physical expression. Bred in a society where such distinctions were far more clearly spelled out, Marryat was somewhat disoriented in the United States; "it is impossible to know who is who," he claimed, "in this land of equality."

Well-born British travelers encountered not just confusion but conflict when they failed to receive the signs of respect they expected. Margaret Hall's letters home during her Southern travels outlined a true comedy of manners. At every stage stop in the Carolinas, Georgia, and Alabama, she demanded that country tavernkeepers and their households give her deferential service and well-prepared meals; she received instead rancid bacon and "such an absence of all kindness of feeling, such unbending frigid heartlessness." But she and her family had a far greater share than they realized in creating this chilly reception. Squeezed between the pride and poise of the great planters and the social debasement of the slaves, small Southern farmers often displayed a prickly insolence, a considered lack of response, to those who too obviously considered themselves their betters. Greatly to their discomfort and incomprehension, the Halls were experiencing what a British traveler more sympathetic to American ways, Patrick Shirreff, called "the democratic rudeness which assumed or presumptuous superiority seldom fails to experience."

In the seventeenth century white American colonials were no taller than their European counterparts, but by the time of the Revolution they were close to their late-twentieth-century average height for men of slightly over five feet eight inches. The citizens of the early republic towered over most Europeans. Americans' early achievement of modern stature—by a full century and more—was a striking consequence of American abundance. Americans were taller because they were better nourished than the great majority of the world's peoples.

Yet not all Americans participated equally in the nation's abundance. Differences in stature between whites and blacks, and between city and country dwellers, echoed those between Europeans and Americans. Enslaved blacks were a full inch shorter than whites. But they remained a full inch taller than European peasants and laborers and were taller still than their fellow slaves eating the scanty diets afforded by the more savagely oppressive plantation system of the West Indies. And by 1820 those who lived in the expanding cities of the United States—even excluding immigrants, whose heights would have reflected European, not American, conditions—were noticeably shorter than the people of the countryside, suggesting an increasing concentration of poverty and poorer diets in urban places.

Across the United States almost all country households ate the two great American staples: corn and "the eternal pork," as one surfeited traveler called it, "which makes its appearance on every American table, high and low, rich and poor." Families in the cattle-raising, dairying country of New England, New York, and northern Ohio ate butter, cheese, and salted beef as well as pork and made their bread from wheat flour or rye and Indian corn. In Pennsylvania, as well as Maryland, Delaware, and Virginia, Americans ate the same breadstuffs as their Northern neighbors, but their consumption of cheese and beef declined every mile southward in favor of pork.

Farther to the south, and in the West, corn and corn-fed pork were truly "eternal"; where reliance on them reached its peak in the Southern uplands, they were still the only crops many small farmers raised. Most Southern and Western families built their diets around smoked and salted bacon, rather than the Northerners' salt pork, and, instead of wheat or rye bread, made cornpone or hoecake, a coarse, strong bread, and hominy, pounded Indian corn boiled together with milk.

Before 1800, game—venison, possum, raccoon, and wild fowl—was for many American households "a substantial portion of the supply of food at certain seasons of the year," although only on the frontier was it a regular part of the diet. In the West and South this continued to be true, but in the Northeast game became increasingly rare as forests gave way to open farmland, where wild animals could not live.

Through the first half of the eighteenth century, Americans had been primarily concerned with obtaining a sufficiency of meat and bread for their families; they paid relatively little attention to foodstuffs other than these two "staffs of life," but since that time the daily fare of many households had grown substantially more diverse.

Remembering his turn-of-the-century Kentucky boyhood, Daniel Drake could still see the mealtime scene at the house of a neighbor, "Old Billy," who "with his sons" would "frequently breakfast in common on mush and milk out of a huge buckeye bowl, each one dipping in a spoon." "Old Billy" and his family were less frontier savages than traditionalists; in the same decade Gov. Caleb Strong of Massachusetts stopped for the night with a country family who ate in the same way, where "each had a spoon and dipped from the same dish." These households ate as almost all American families once had, communally partaking of food from the same dish and passing around a single vessel to drink from. Such meals were often surprisingly haphazard affairs, with household members moving in and out, eating quickly and going on to other tasks.

But by 1800 they were already in a small and diminishing minority. Over the eighteenth century dining "in common" had given way to individualized yet social eating; as families acquired chairs and dining utensils, they were able to make mealtimes more important social occasions. Most Americans expected to eat individual portions of food at a table set with personal knives, forks, glasses, bowls, and plates. Anything that smacked of the old communal ways was increasingly likely to be treated as a sin against domestic decency. The clergyman Peter Cartwright was shocked at the table manners of a "backward" family who ate off a "wooden trencher," improvised forks with "sharp pieces of cane," and used a single knife, which they passed around the table.

"One and all, male and female," the observant Margaret Hall took note, even in New York's best society, ate "invariably and indefatigably with their knives." As a legacy of the fork's late arrival in the colonies, Americans were peculiar in using their "great lumbering, long, two-pronged forks," not to convey food to the mouth, as their English and French contemporaries did, but merely to keep their meat from slipping off the plate while cutting it. "Feeding yourself with your right hand, armed with a steel blade," was the prevalent American custom, acknowledged Eliza Farrar's elaborate *Young Lady's Friend* of 1836. She added that it was perfectly proper, despite English visitors' discomfort at the sight of a "prettily dressed, nice-looking young woman ladling rice pudding into her mouth with the point of a great knife" or a domestic helper "feeding an infant of seventeen months in the same way."

Mrs. Farrar acknowledged that there were stirrings of change among the sophisticated in the 1830s, conceding that some of her readers might now want "to imitate the French or English . . . and put every mouthful into your mouth with your fork." Later in the nineteenth century the American habit of eating with the knife completely lost its claims to gentility, and it became another relic of "primitive manners." Americans gradually learned to use forks more dexterously, although to this day they hold them in the wrong hand and "upside down" from an Englishman's point of view.

The old ways, so startlingly unfamiliar to the modern reader, gradually fell away. Americans changed their assumptions about what was proper, decent, and normal in everyday life in directions that would have greatly surprised most of the men and women of the early republic. Some aspects of their "primitive manners" succumbed to campaigns for temperance and gentility, while others evaporated with the later growth of mass merchandising and mass communications.

Important patterns of regional, class, and ethnic distinctiveness remain in American everyday life. But they are far less powerful, and less central to understanding American experience, than they once were. Through the rest of the nineteenth century and into the twentieth, the United States became ever more diverse, with new waves of Eastern and Southern European immigrants joining the older Americans of Northern European stock. Yet the new arrivals—and even more, their descendants—have experienced the attractiveness and reshaping power of a national culture formed by department stores, newspapers, radios, movies, and universal public education. America, the developing nation, developed into us. And perhaps our manners and morals, to some future observer, will seem as idiosyncratic and astonishing as this portrait of our earlier self.

QUESTIONS TO CONSIDER

1. Which social group had the most self-assurance in its bearing? Which two seemed the least inhibited?
2. What options did early Americans use to dispose of human waste?
3. Why did Americans not bathe very much? What changes permitted a gradual improvement in bathing practices?
4. How significant was alcohol in the lives of early Americans? Does this surprise you?
5. What factors contributed to the rise of respectability beginning in the 1820s?
6. What evidence does Larkin advance for his contention that Americans were not sexually strait-laced? What changes occurred in the early nineteenth century?
7. Which common practice of early America seems most alien to you? Why?

10

Women, Work, and Protest in the Early Lowell Mills*

Thomas Dublin

During the years 1820 to 1850 the United States began to move away from its near-total dependence on agriculture as its economic base and develop an industrial capacity that would rank first in the world by the time World War I began. Perhaps surprisingly, young women in the northeastern part of the nation provided a key element in the early industrializing process. Wooed from their New England homes by the promise of a measure of independence and the opportunity to set aside some money for marriage, they permitted a transition to industry that minimally disrupted men's economic pursuits. These women, roughly college-age in their makeup, provided a transitory labor force that seemed unlikely to be in the labor force long enough to become activists in resisting adverse labor conditions. But the sense of community they developed in company boarding houses, not unlike college dormitories for later generations, developed in them a surprising solidarity in the face of oppressive employers. Ultimately, Irish immigrants in the late 1840s provided management with a more docile labor force and this brief phase in women's history passed into memory.

Thomas Dublin, professor of history at the State University of New York at Binghamton, earned his doctorate at Columbia University.

*Reprinted by permission from *Labor History*, Winter 1975. Copyright 1975 by *Labor History*.

He specializes in early nineteenth century history, particularly women and their work; his most important book is *Women at Work: The Transformation of Work and Community in Lowell, Massachusetts, 1826–1860* (1979).

In the years before 1850 the textile mills of Lowell, Massachusetts, were a celebrated economic and cultural attraction. Foreign visitors invariably included them on their American tours. Interest was prompted by the massive scale of these mills, the astonishing productivity of the power-driven machinery, and the fact that women comprised most of the work-force. Visitors were struck by the newness of both mills and city as well as by the culture of the female operatives. The scene stood in sharp contrast to the gloomy mill towns of the English industrial revolution.

Lowell was, in fact, an impressive accomplishment. In 1820, there had been no city at all—only a dozen family farms along the Merrimack River in East Chelmsford. In 1821, however, a group of Boston capitalists purchased land and water rights along the river and a nearby canal, and began to build a major textile manufacturing center. Opening two years later, the first factory employed Yankee women recruited from the nearby countryside. Additional mills were constructed until, by 1840, ten textile corporations with thirty-two mills valued at more than ten million dollars lined the banks of the river and nearby canals. Adjacent to the mills were rows of company boarding houses and tenements which accommodated most of the eight thousand factory operatives.

As Lowell expanded, and became the nation's largest manufacturing center, the experiences of women operatives changed as well. The increasing number of firms in Lowell and in the other mill towns brought the pressure of competition. Overproduction became a problem and the prices of finished cloth decreased. The high profits of the early years declined and so, too, did conditions for the mill operatives. Wages were reduced and the pace of work within the mills was stepped up. Women operatives did not accept these changes without protest. In 1834 and 1836 they went on strike to protest wage cuts, and between 1843 and 1848 they mounted petition campaigns aimed at reducing the hours of labor in the mills.

These labor protests in early Lowell contribute to our understanding of the response of workers to the growth of industrial capitalism in the first half of the nineteenth century. They indicate the importance of values and attitudes dating back to an earlier period and also the transformation of these values in a new setting.

The major factor in the rise of a new consciousness among operatives in Lowell was the development of a close-knit community among women working in the mills. The structure of work and the nature of housing contributed to the growth of this community. The existence of community among women, in turn, was an important element in the repeated labor protests of the period.

The organization of this paper derives from the logic of the above argument. It will examine the basis of community in the experiences of women operatives and then the contribution that the community of women made to the labor protests in these years as well as the nature of the new consciousness expressed by these protests.

The preconditions for the labor unrest in Lowell before 1850 may be found in the study of the daily worklife of its operatives. In their everyday, relatively conflict-free lives, mill women created the mutual bonds which made possible united action in times of crisis. The existence of a tight-knit community among them was the most important element in determining the collective, as opposed to individual, nature of this response.

Before examining the basis of community among women operatives in early Lowell, it may be helpful to indicate in what sense "community" is being used. The women are considered a "community" because of the development of bonds of mutual dependence among them. In this period they came to depend upon one another and upon the larger group of operatives in very important ways. Their experiences were not simply similar or parallel to one another, but were inextricably intertwined. Furthermore, they were conscious of the existence of community, expressing it very clearly in their writings and in labor protests. "Community" for them had objective and subjective dimensions and both were important in their experience of women in the mills.

The mutual dependence among women in early Lowell was rooted in the structure of mill work itself. Newcomers to the mills were particularly dependent on their fellow operatives, but even experienced hands relied on one another for considerable support.

New operatives generally found their first experiences difficult, even harrowing, though they may have already done considerable handspinning and weaving in their own homes. The initiation of one of them is described in fiction in the *Lowell Offering:*

> The next morning she went into the Mill; and at first the sight of so many bands, and wheels, and springs in constant motion, was very frightful. She felt afraid to touch the loom, and she was almost sure she could never learn to weave . . . the shuttle flew out, and made a new bump on her head; and the first time she tried to spring the lathe, she broke out a quarter of the treads.

While other accounts present a somewhat less difficult picture, most indicate that women only became proficient and felt satisfaction in their work after several months in the mills.

The textile corporation made provisions to ease the adjustment of new operatives. Newcomers were not immediately expected to fit into the mill's regular work routine. They were at first assigned work as spare-hands and were paid a daily wage independent of the quantity of work they turned out. As a sparehand, the newcomer worked with an experienced hand who instructed her in the intricacies of the job. The sparehand spelled her partner for short stretches of time, and occasionally took the place of an absentee. One woman described the learning process in a letter reprinted in the *Offering*:

> Well, I went into the mill, and was put to learn with a very patient girl. . . . You cannot think how odd everything seems. . . . They set me to threading shuttles, and tying weaver's knots, and such things, and now I have improved so that I can take care of one loom. I could take care of two if only I had eyes in the back part of my head.

After the passage of some weeks or months, when she could handle the normal complement of machinery—two looms for weavers during the 1830s—and when a regular operative departed, leaving an opening, the sparehand moved into a regular job.

Through this system of job training, the textile corporations contributed to the development of community among female operatives. During the most difficult period in an operative's career, the first months in the mill, she relied upon other women workers for training and support. And for every sparehand whose adjustment to mill work was aided in this process, there was an experienced operative whose work was also affected. Women were relating to one another during the work process and not simply tending their machinery. Given the high rate of turnover in the mill workforce, a large proportion of women operatives worked in pairs. At the Hamilton Company in July 1836, for example, more than a fifth of all females on the Company payroll were sparehands. Consequently, over forty percent of the females employed there in this month worked with one another. Nor was this interaction surreptitious, carried out only when the overseer looked elsewhere; rather it was formally organized and sanctioned by the textile corporations themselves.

In addition to the integration of sparehands, informal sharing of work often went on among regular operatives. A woman would occasionally take off a half or full day from work either to enjoy a brief vacation or to recover from illness, and fellow operatives would each take an extra loom or side of spindles so that she might continue to earn wages during her absence. Women were generally paid on a piece rate basis, their wages being determined by the total output of the machinery they tended during the payroll period. With friends helping out during her absence, making sure that her loops kept running, an operative could earn almost a full wage even though she was not physically present. Such informal work-sharing was another way in which mutual dependence developed among women operatives during their working hours.

Living conditions also contributed to the development of community among female operatives. Most women working in the Lowell mills of these years were housed in company boarding houses. In July 1836, for example, more than 73 percent of females employed by the Hamilton Company resided in company housing adjacent to the mills. Almost three fourths of them, therefore, lived and worked with each other. Furthermore, the work schedule was such that women had little opportunity to interact with those not living in company dwellings. They worked, in these years, an average of 73 hours a week. Their work day ended at 7:00 or 7:30 P.M., and in the hours between supper and the 10:00 curfew imposed by management on residents of company boarding houses there was little time to spend with friends living "off the corporation."

Women in the boarding houses lived in close quarters, a factor that also played a role in the growth of community. A typical boarding house accommodated twenty-five young women, generally crowded four to eight in a bedroom. There was little possibility of privacy within the dwelling, and pressure to conform to group standards was very strong (as will be discussed). The community of operatives which developed in the mills, it follows, carried over into life at home as well.

The boarding house became a central institution in the lives of Lowell's female operatives in these years, but it was particularly important in the initial integration of newcomers into urban industrial life. Upon first leaving her rural home for work in Lowell, a woman entered a setting very different from anything she had previously known. One operative, writing in the *Offering*, described the feelings of a fictional character: "the first entrance into a factory boarding house seemed something dreadful. The room looked strange and comfortless, and the women cold and heartless; and when she sat down to the supper table, where among more than twenty girls, all but one were strangers, she could not eat a mouthful."

In the boarding house, the newcomer took the first steps in the process which transformed her from an "outsider" into an accepted member of the community of women operatives.

Recruitment of newcomers into the mills and their initial hiring was mediated through the boarding house system. Women generally did not travel to Lowell for the first time entirely on their own. They usually came because they knew someone—an older sister, cousin, or friend—who had already worked in Lowell. The scene described above was a lonely one—

but the newcomer did know at least one boarder among the twenty seated around the supper table. The Hamilton Company Register Books indicate that numerous pairs of operatives, having the same surname and coming from the same town in northern New England, lived in the same boarding houses. If the newcomer was not accompanied by a friend or relative, she was usually directed to "Number 20, Hamilton Company," or to a similar address of one of the other corporations where her acquaintance lived. Her first contact with fellow operatives generally came in the boarding houses and not in the mills. Given the personal nature of recruitment in this period, therefore, newcomers usually had the company and support of a friend or relative in their first adjustment to Lowell.

Like recruitment, the initial hiring was a personal process. Once settled in the boarding house a newcomer had to find a job. She would generally go to the mills with her friend or with the boarding house keeper who would introduce her to an overseer in one of the rooms. If he had an opening, she might start work immediately. More likely, the overseer would know of an opening elsewhere in the mill, or would suggest that something would probably develop within a few days. In one story in the *Offering*, a newcomer worked on some quilts for her house keeper, thereby earning her board while she waited for a job opening.

Upon entering the boarding house, the newcomer came under pressure to conform with the standards of the community of operatives. Stories in the *Offering* indicate that newcomers at first stood out from the group in terms of their speech and dress. Over time, they dropped the peculiar "twang" in their speech which so amused experienced hands. Similarly, they purchased clothing more in keeping with urban than rural styles. It was an unusual and strongwilled individual who could work and live among her fellow operatives and not conform, at least outwardly, to the customs and values of this larger community.

The boarding houses were the centers of social life for women operatives after their long days in the mills. There they ate their meals, rested, talked, sewed, wrote letters, read books and magazines. From among fellow workers and boarders they found friends who accompanied them to shops, to Lyceum lectures, to church and church sponsored events. On Sundays or holidays, they often took walks along the canals or out into the nearby countryside. The community of women operatives, in sum, developed in a setting where women worked and lived together, twenty-four hours a day.

Given the all-pervasiveness of this community, one would expect it to exert strong pressures on those who did not conform to group standards. Such appears to have been the case. The community influenced newcomers to adopt its patterns of speech and dress as described above.

In addition, it enforced an unwritten code of moral conduct. Henry Miles, a minister in Lowell, described the way in which the community pressured those who deviated from accepted moral conduct:

> A girl, suspected of immoralities, or serious improprieties, at once loses caste. Her fellow boarders will at once leave the house, if the keeper does not dismiss the offender. In self-protection, therefore, the patron is obliged to put the offender away. Nor will her former companions walk with her, or work with her; till at length, finding herself everywhere talked about, and pointed at, and shunned, she is obliged to relieve her fellow-operatives of a presence which they feel brings disgrace.

The power of the peer group described by Mills may seem extreme, but there is evidence in the writing of women operatives to corroborate his account. Such group pressure is illustrated by a story (in the *Offering*)—in which operatives in a company boarding house begin to harbor suspicions about a fellow boarder, Hannah, who received repeated evening visits from a man whom she does not introduce to the other residents. Two boarders declare that they will leave if she is allowed to remain in the household. The house keeper finally informed Hannah that she must either depart or not see the man again. She does not accept the ultimatum, but is promptly discharged after the overseer is informed, by one of the boarders, about her conduct. And, only one of Hannah's former friends continues to remain on cordial terms.

One should not conclude, however, that women always enforced a moral code agreeable to Lowell's clergy, or to the mill agents and overseers for that matter. After all, the kind of peer pressure imposed on Hannah could be brought to bear on women in 1834 and 1836 who on their own would not have protested wage cuts. It was much harder to go to work when one's roommates were marching about town, attending rallies, circulating strike petitions. Similarly, the ten-hour petitions of the 1840s were certainly aided by the fact of a tight-knit community of operatives living in a dense neighborhood of boarding houses. To the extent that women could not have completely private lives in the boarding houses, they probably had to conform to group norms, whether these involved speech, clothing, relations with men, or attitudes toward the ten-hour day. Group pressure to conform, so important to the community of women in early Lowell, played a significant role in the collective response of women to changing conditions in the mills.

In addition to the structure of work and housing in Lowell, a third factor, the homogeneity of the mill workforce, contributed to the development of community among female operatives. In this period the mill workforce was homogeneous in terms of sex, nativity, and age. Payroll and other records of the Hamilton Company reveal that more than 85 percent of those employed in July 1836 were women and that over 96 percent were native-born. Furthermore, over 80 percent of the female workforce was between the ages of 15 and 30 years old; and only 10 percent was under 15 or over 40.

Workforce homogeneity takes on particular significance in the context of work structure and the nature of worker housing. These three factors combined meant that women operatives had little interaction with men during their daily lives. Men and women did not perform the same work in the mills, and generally did not even labor in the same rooms. Men worked in the picking and initial carding processes, in the repair shop and on the watchforce, and filled all supervisory positions in the mills. Women held all sparehand and regular operative jobs in drawing, speeding, spinning, weaving, and dressing. A typical room in the mill employed eighty women tending machinery, with two men overseeing the work and two boys assisting them. Women had little contact with men other than their supervisors in the course of the working day. After work, women returned to their boarding houses, where once again there were few men. Women, then, worked and lived in a predominantly female setting.

Ethnically, the workforce was also homogeneous. Immigrants formed only 3.4 percent of those employed at Hamilton in July 1836. In addition, they comprised only 3 percent of residents in Hamilton company housing. The community of women operatives was composed of women of New England stock drawn from the hill-country farms surrounding Lowell. Consequently, when experienced hands made fun of the speech and dress of newcomers, it was understood that they, too, had been "rusty" or "rustic" upon first coming to Lowell. This common background was another element shared by women workers in early Lowell.

The work structure, the workers' housing, and workforce homogeneity were the major elements which contributed to the growth of community among Lowell's women operatives. To best understand the larger implications of community it is necessary to examine the labor protests of this period. For in these struggles, the new values and attitudes which developed in the community of women operatives are most visible.

In February 1834, 800 of Lowell's women operatives "turned-out"—went on strike—to protest a proposed reduction in their wages. They marched to numerous mills in an effort to induce others to join them; and, at an outdoor rally, they petitioned others to "discontinue their labors until terms of reconciliation are made." Their petition concluded:

Resolved, That we will not go back into the mills to work unless our wages are continued . . . as they have been.

Resolved, That none of us will go back, unless they receive us all as one.

Resolved, That if any have not money enough to carry them home, they shall be supplied.

The strike proved to be brief and failed to reverse the proposed wage reductions. Turning-out on a Friday, the striking women were paid their back wages on Saturday, and by the middle of the next week had returned to work or left town. Within a week of the turn-out, the mills were running near capacity.

This first strike in Lowell is important not because it failed or succeeded, but simply because it took place. In an era in which women had to overcome opposition simply to work in the mills, it is remarkable that they would further overstep the accepted middle-class bounds of female propriety by participating in a public protest. The agents of the textile mills certainly considered the turn-out unfeminine. William Austin, agent of the Lawrence Company, described the operatives' procession as an "amizonian [sic] display." He wrote further, in a letter to his company treasurer in Boston: "This afternoon we have paid off several of these Amazons & presume that they will leave town on Monday." The turn-out was particularly offensive to the agents because of the relationship they thought they had with their operatives. William Austin probably expressed the feelings of other agents when he wrote: "Notwithstanding the friendly and disinterested advice which has been on all proper occasions [sic] communicated to the girls of the Lawrence mills a spirit of evil omen . . . has prevailed, and overcome the judgment and discretion of too many, and this morning a general turn-out from most of the rooms has been the consequence."

Mill agents assumed an attitude of benevolent paternalism toward their female operatives, and found it particularly disturbing that the women paid such little heed to their advice. The strikers were not merely unfeminine, they were ungrateful as well.

Such attitudes notwithstanding, women chose to turn-out. They did so for two principal reasons. First, the wage cuts undermined the sense of dignity and social equality which was an important element in their Yankee heritage. Second, these wage cuts were seen as an attack on their economic independence.

Certainly a prime move for the strike was outrage at the social implications of the wage cuts. In a statement of principles accompanying the petition which was circulated among operatives, women expressed well the sense of themselves which prompted their protest of these wage cuts:

UNION IS POWER

Our present object is to have union and exertion, and we remain in possession of our unquestionable rights. We circulate this paper wishing to obtain the names of all who imbibe the spirit of our Patriotic Ancestors, who preferred privation to bondage, and parted with all that renders life desirable—and even life itself—to procure independence for their children. The oppressing hand of avarice would enslave us, and to gain their object, they gravely tell us of the pressure of the time, this we are already sensible of, and deplore it. If any are in want of assistance, the Ladies will be compassionate and assist them; but we prefer to have the disposing of our charities in our own hands; and as we are free, we would remain in possession of what kind Providence has bestowed upon us; and remain daughters of freemen still.

At several points in the proclamation the women drew on their Yankee heritage. Connecting their turn-out with the efforts of their "Patriotic Ancestors" to secure independence from England, they interpreted the wage cuts as an effort to "enslave" them—to deprive them of their independent status as "daughters of freemen."

Though very general and rhetorical, the statement of these women does suggest their sense of self, of their own worth and dignity. Elsewhere, they expressed the conviction that they were the social equals of the overseers, indeed of the mill owners themselves. These reductions made it clear that the operatives were subordinate to their employers, rather than equal partners in a contract binding on both parties. By turning-out the women emphatically denied that they were subordinates; but by returning to work the next week, they demonstrated that in economic terms they were no match for their corporate superiors.

In point of fact, these Yankee operatives were subordinate in early Lowell's social and economic order, but they never consciously accepted this status. Their refusal to do so became evident whenever the mill owners attempted to exercise the power they possessed. This fundamental contradiction between the objective status of operatives and their consciousness of it was at the root of the 1834 turn-out and of subsequent labor protests in Lowell before 1850. The corporations could build mills, create thousands of jobs, and recruit women to fill them. Nevertheless, they bought only the workers' labor power, and then only for as long as these workers chose to stay. Women could always return to their rural homes, and they had a sense of their own worth and dignity, factors limiting the actions of management.

Women operatives viewed the wage cuts as a threat to their economic independence. This independence had two related dimensions. First, the women were self-supporting while they worked in the mills and, consequently, were independent of their families back home. Second, they were able to save out of their monthly earnings and could then leave the mills for the old homestead whenever they so desired. In effect, they were not totally dependent upon mill work. Their independence was based largely on the high level of wages in the mills. They could support themselves and still save enough to return home periodically. The wage cuts threatened to deny them this outlet, substituting instead the prospect of total dependence on mill work. Small wonder, then, there was alarm that "the oppressing hand of avarice would enslave us." To be forced, out of economic necessity, to lifelong labor in the mills would have indeed seemed like slavery. The Yankee operatives spoke directly to the fear of dependency based on impoverishment when offering to assist any women workers who "have not money enough to carry them home." Wage reductions, however, offered only the *prospect* of a future dependence on mill employment. By striking, the women asserted their actual economic independence of the mills and their determination to remain "daughters of freemen still."

While the women's traditional conception of themselves as independent daughters of freemen played a major role in the turn-out, this factor acting alone would not necessarily have triggered the 1834 strike. It would have led women as individuals to quit work and return to their rural homes. But the turn-out was a collective protest. When it was announced that wage reductions were being considered, women began to hold meetings in the mills during meal breaks in order to assess tactical possibilities. Their turn-out began at one mill when the agent discharged a woman who had presided at such a meeting. Their procession through the streets passed by other mills, expressing a conscious effort to enlist as much support as possible for their cause. At a mass meeting, the women drew up a resolution which insisted that none be discharged for their participation in the turn-out. This strike, then, was a collective response to the proposed wage cuts—made possible because women had come to form a "community" of operatives in the mill, rather than simply a group of individual workers. The existence of such a tight-knit community turned individual opposition of the wage cuts into a collective protest.

In October 1836, women again went on strike. This second turn-out was similar to the first in several respects. Its immediate cause was also a wage reduction; marches and a large outdoor rally were organized; again, like the earlier protest, the basic goal was not achieved; the corporations refused to restore wages; and operatives either left Lowell or returned to work at the new rates.

Despite these surface similarities between the turn-outs, there were some real differences. One involved scale: over 1500 operatives turned out in 1836, compared to only 800 earlier. Moreover, the second strike lasted much longer than the first. In 1834 operatives stayed out for only a few days; in 1836, the mills ran far below capacity for several months. Two weeks after the second turn-out began, a mill agent reported that only a fifth of the strikers had returned to work: "The rest manifest *good 'spunk'* as they call it." Several days later he described the impact of the continuing strike on operations in his mills: "We must be feeble for months to come as probably not less than 250 of our former scanty supply of help have left town." These lines read in sharp contrast to the optimistic reports of agents following the turn-out in February 1834.

Differences between the two turn-outs were not limited to the increased scale and duration of the later one. Women displayed a much higher degree of organization in 1836 than earlier. To co-ordinate strike activities, they formed a Factory Girls' Association. According to one historian, membership in the short-lived association reached 2500 at its height. The larger organization among women was reflected in the tactics employed. Strikers, according to one mill agent, were able to halt production to a greater extent than numbers alone could explain; and, he complained, although some operatives were willing to work, "it has been impossible to give employment to many who remained." He attributed this difficulty to the strikers' tactics: "This was in many instances no doubt the result of calculation and contrivance. After the original turn-out they [the operatives] would assail a particular room—as for instance, all the warpers, or all the warp spinners, or all the speeder and stretcher girls, and this would close the mill as effectually as if all the girls in the mill had left."

Now giving more thought than they had in 1834 to the specific tactics of the turn-out, the women made a deliberate effort to shut down the mills in order to win their demands. They attempted to persuade less committed operatives, concentrating on those in crucial departments within the mill. Such tactics anticipated those of skilled mulespinners and loomfixers who went out on strike in the 1880s and 1890s.

In their organization of a Factory Girls' Association and in their efforts to shut down the mills, the female operatives revealed that they had been changed by their industrial experience. Increasingly, they acted not simply as "daughters of freemen" offended by the impositions of the textile corporations, but also as industrial workers intent on improving their position within the mills.

There was a decline in protest among women in the Lowell mills following these early strike defeats. During the 1837–1843 depression, textile corporations twice reduced wages without evoking a collective response from operatives. Because of the frequency of production cutbacks and lay-offs in these years, workers probably accepted the mill agents' contention that they had to reduce wages or close entirely. But with the return of prosperity and the expansion of production in the mid-1840s, there were renewed labor protests among women. Their actions paralleled those of working men and reflected fluctuations in the business cycle. Prosperity itself did not prompt turn-outs, but it evidently facilitated collective actions by women operatives.

In contrast to the protests of the previous decade, the struggles now were primarily political. Women did not turn-out in the 1840s; rather, they mounted annual petition campaigns calling on the State legislature to limit the hours of labor within the mills. These campaigns reached their height in 1845 and 1846, when 2000 and 5000 operatives respectively signed petitions. Unable to curb the wage cuts, or the speed-up and stretch-out imposed by mill owners, operatives sought to mitigate the consequences of these changes by reducing the length of the working day. Having been defeated earlier in economic struggles, they now sought to achieve their new goal through political action. The Ten Hour Movement, seen in these terms, was a logical outgrowth of the unsuccessful turn-outs of the previous decade. Like the earlier struggles, the Ten Hour Movement was an assertion of the dignity of operatives and an attempt to maintain that dignity under the changing conditions of industrial capitalism.

The growth of relatively permanent labor organizations and institutions among women was a distinguishing feature of the Ten Hour Movement of the 1840s. The Lowell Female Labor Reform Association was organized in 1845 by women operatives. It became Lowell's leading organization over the next three years, organizing the city's female operatives and helping to set up branches in other mill towns. The Association was affiliated with the New England Workingmen's Association and sent delegates to its meetings. It acted in concert with similar male groups, and yet maintained its own autonomy. Women elected their own officers, held their own meetings, testified before a State legislative committee, and published a series of "Factory Tracts" which exposed conditions within the mills and argued for the ten-hour day.

An important educational and organizing tool of the Lowell Female Labor Reform Association was the *Voice of Industry,* a labor weekly published in Lowell between 1845 and 1848 by the New England Workingmen's Association. Female operatives were involved in every aspect of its publication and used the *Voice* to further the Ten Hour Movement among women. Their Association owned the press on which the *Voice* was printed. Sarah Bagley, the Association president, was a member of the three-person publishing committee of the *Voice* and for a time served as editor. Other women were employed by the paper as traveling editors.

They wrote articles about the Ten Hour Movement in other mill towns, in an effort to give ten-hour supporters a sense of the large cause of which they were a part. Furthermore, they raised money for the *Voice* and increased its circulation by selling subscriptions to the paper in their travels about New England. Finally, women used the *Voice* to appeal directly to their fellow operatives. They edited a separate "Female Department," which published letters and articles by and about women in the mills.

Another aspect of the Ten Hour Movement which distinguished it from the earlier labor struggles in Lowell was that it involved both men and women. At the same time that women in Lowell formed the Female Labor Reform Association, a male mechanics' and laborers' association was also organized. Both groups worked to secure the passage of legislation setting ten hours as the length of the working day. Both groups circulated petitions to this end and when the legislative committee came to Lowell to hear testimony, both men and women testified in favor of the ten-hour day.

The two groups, then, worked together, and each made an important contribution to the movement in Lowell. Women had the numbers, comprising as they did over 80 percent of the mill workforce. Men, on the other hand, had the votes, and since the Ten Hour Movement was a political struggle, they played a crucial part. After the State committee reported unfavorably on the ten-hour petitions, the Female Labor Reform Association denounced the committee chairman, a State representative from Lowell, as a corporation "tool." Working for his defeat at the polls, they did so successfully and then passed the following postelection resolution: "*Resolved*, That the members of this Association tender their grateful acknowledgments to the voters of Lowell, for consigning William Schouler to the obscurity he so justly deserves." Women took a more prominent part in the Ten Hour Movement in Lowell than did men, but they obviously remained dependent on male voters and legislators for the ultimate success of their movement.

Although co-ordinating their efforts with those of working men, women operatives organized independently within the Ten Hour Movement. For instance, in 1845 two important petitions were sent from Lowell to the State legislature. Almost 90 percent of the signers of one petition were females, and more than two thirds of the signers of the second were males. Clearly the separation of men and women in their daily lives was reflected in the Ten Hour petitions of these years.

The way in which the Ten Hour Movement was carried from Lowell to other mill towns also illustrated the independent organizing of women within the larger movement. For example, at a spirited meeting in Manchester, New Hampshire, in December 1845—one presided over by Lowell operatives—more than a thousand workers, two thirds of them women, passed resolutions calling for the ten-hour day. Later, those in attendance divided along male-female lines, each meeting separately to set up parallel organizations. Sixty women joined the Manchester Female Labor Reform Association that evening, and by the following summer it claimed over three hundred members. Female operatives met in company boarding houses to involve new women in the movement. In their first year of organizing, Manchester workers obtained more than 4,000 signatures on ten-hour petitions. While men and women were both active in the movement, they worked through separate institutional structures from the outset.

The division of men and women within the Ten Hour Movement also reflected their separate daily lives in Lowell and in other mill towns. To repeat, they held different jobs in the mills and had little contact apart from the formal, structured overseer-operative relation. Outside the mill, we have noted, women tended to live in female boarding houses provided by the corporations and were isolated from men. Consequently, the experiences of women in "these early" mill towns were different from those of men, and in the course of their daily lives they came to form a close-knit community. It was logical that women's participation in the Ten Hour Movement mirrored this basic fact.

The women's Ten Hour Movement, like the earlier turnouts, was based in part on the participants' sense of their own worth and dignity as daughters of freemen. At the same time, however, it also indicated the growth of a new consciousness. It reflected a mounting feeling of community among women operatives and a realization that their interests and those of their employers were not identical, that they had to rely on themselves and not on corporate benevolence to achieve a reduction in the hours of labor. One woman, in an open letter to a State legislator, expressed this rejection of middle-class paternalism: "Bad as is the condition of so many women, it would be much worse if they had nothing but your boasted protection to rely upon; but they have at last learnt the lesson which a bitter experience teaches, that not to those who style themselves as 'natural protectors' are they to look for the needful help, but to the strong and resolute of their own sex." Such an attitude, underlying the self-organizing of women in the ten-hour petition campaigns, was clearly the product of the industrial experience in Lowell.

Both the early turn-outs and the Ten Hour Movement were, as noted above, in large measure dependent upon the existence of a close-knit community of women operatives. Such a community was based on the work structure, the nature of worker housing, and workforce homogeneity. Women were drawn together by the initial job training of newcomers; by the informal work sharing among experienced hands; by living in company boarding houses; by sharing religious, educational, and social activities in their leisure hours. Working and living in a new and alien setting, they came to rely upon one another for friendship and support. Understandably, a community feeling developed among them.

This evolving community as well as the common cultural traditions which Yankee women carried into Lowell were major elements that governed their response to changing mill conditions. The preindustrial tradition of independence and self-respect made them particularly sensitive to management labor policies. The sense of community enabled them to transform their individual opposition to wage cuts and to the increasing pace of work into public protest. In these labor struggles women operatives expressed a new consciousness of their rights both as workers and as women. Such a consciousness, like the community of women itself, was one product of Lowell's industrial revolution.

The experiences of Lowell women before 1850 present a fascinating picture of the contradictory impact of industrial capitalism. Repeated labor protests reveal that female operatives felt the demands of mill employment to be oppressive. At the same time, however, the mills provided women with work outside of the home and family, thereby offering them an unprecedented [opportunity]. That they came to challenge employer paternalism was a direct consequence of the increasing opportunities offered them in these years. The Lowell mills both exploited and liberated women in ways unknown to the preindustrial political economy.

QUESTIONS TO CONSIDER

1. What factors made Lowell such a cultural attraction in the 1820–1850 period?
2. What three factors contributed to the strong sense of community among the mill girls?
3. What motivated the women to strike in 1834?
4. How did the 1836 strike differ from that of 1834?
5. What new approach did women take to improve conditions in 1845–1846? How successful was this new approach?
6. How was the Lowell experience a two-sided one for women?

11

The Mountain Man
as Jacksonian Man*

William Goetzmann

William Goetzmann (1930–) received his Ph.D. in American Studies from Yale University in 1957. He directs the American Studies program at the University of Texas and specializes in American cultural
history and the history of the American West. He won a Pulitzer Prize
in 1966 for his *Exploration and Empire: The Explorer and Scientist in
the Winning of the American West.* Among his other books is *The
Mountain Man* (1978), a fuller treatment of the subject of this 1963
article.

Goetzmann argues that the conventional image of the uncivi-
lized mountain man seeking to escape encroaching civilization is
wide of the mark. Instead, the mountain man was a typical Jacksonian man pursuing traditional conservative goals. Despite his alleged disregard for civilization, he consciously promoted American acquisition and development of the West to ensure the future
he envisioned for the region, a future strikingly similar to that pursued by other Jacksonian "venturous conservatives."

How does this article affect your perception of the independent, self-directed figure Jefferson idealized (as presented in
David Potter's article)? Was Jefferson's or deTocqueville's portrait
of the American character more accurate in depicting the mountain man? If the mountain man was not the ultimate independent,

*Reprinted by permission of William Goetzmann from *American Quarterly*, volume 15,
pages 402–415. Copyright © 1963 by the American Studies Association.

self-directed man, who was? In Volume II, David Brion Davis will consider the cowboy, another candidate, and see how he fits the stereotype.

One of the most often studied and least understood figures in American history has been the Mountain Man. Remote, so it would seem, as Neanderthal, and according to some almost as inarticulate, the Mountain Man exists as a figure of American mythology rather than history. As such he has presented at least two vivid stereotypes to the public imagination. From the first he has been the very symbol for the romantic banditti of the forest, freed of the artificial restrictions of civilization—a picturesque wanderer in the wilderness whose very life is a constant and direct association with Nature.

> "There is perhaps, no class of men on the face of the earth," said Captain Bonneville (and through him Washington Irving), "who lead a life of more continued exertion, peril, and excitement, and who are more enamoured of their occupations, than the free trappers of the west. No toil, no danger, no privation can turn the trapper from his pursuit. His passionate excitement at times resembles a mania. In vain may the most vigilant and cruel savages beset his path; in vain may rocks, and precipices, and wintry torrents oppose his progress; let but a single track of a beaver meet his eye, and he forgets all dangers and defies all difficulties. At times, he may be seen with his traps on his shoulder, buffeting his way across rapid streams amidst floating blocks of ice: at other times, he is to be found with his traps on his back clambering the most rugged mountains, scaling or descending the most frightening precipices, searching by routes inaccessible to the horse, and never before trodden by white man, for springs and lakes unknown to his comrades, and where he may meet with his favorite game. Such is the mountaineer, the hardy trapper of the west; and such as we have slightly sketched it, is the wild, Robin Hood kind of life, with all its strange and motley populace, now existing in full vigor among the Rocky mountains."

To Irving in the nineteenth century, the Mountain Man was Robin Hood, a European literary convention. By the twentieth century the image was still literary and romantic but somewhat less precise. According to Bernard De Voto, "For a few years Odysseus Jed Smith and Siegfried Carson and the wing-shod Fitzpatrick actually drew breath in this province of fable," and Jim Beckwourth "went among the Rockies as Theseus dared the wine-dark seas. Skirting the rise of a hill, he saw the willows stirring; he charged down upon them, while despairing Blackfeet sang the death-song—and lo, to the clear music of a horn, Roland had met the pagan hordes. . . ."

On the other hand, to perhaps more discerning eyes in his own day and down through the years, the Mountain Man presented another image—one that was far less exalted. Set off from the ordinary man by his costume of greasy buckskins, coonskin cap and Indian finery, not to mention the distinctive odor that went with bear grease and the habitual failure to bathe between one yearly rendezvous and the next, the Mountain Man seemed a forlorn and pathetic primitive out of the past. "They are stared at as though they were bears," wrote Rudolph F. Kurz, a Swiss artist who traveled the Upper Missouri.

The Mountain Man, so it was said, was out of touch with conventional civilization and hence not quite acceptable. Instead in his own time and even more today he has been viewed as a purely hedonistic character who lived for the year's end rendezvous where he got gloriously drunk on diluted rotgut company alcohol, gave his beaver away for wildly inflated company trade goods and crawled off into the underbrush for a delirious orgy with some unenthusiastic Indian squaw. In this view the romantic rendezvous was nothing more than a modern company picnic, the object of which was to keep the employees docile, happy and ready for the coming year's task.

Pacified, satisfied, cheated, impoverished, and probably mortified the next day, the Mountain Man, be he free trapper or not, went back to his dangerous work when the rendezvous was over. He was thus to many shrewd observers not a hero at all but a docile and obedient slave of the company. By a stretch of the imagination he might have seemed heroic, but because of the contrast between his daring deeds and his degraded status he seemed one of the saddest heroes in all history. Out of date before his time was up, he was a wild free spirit who after all was not free. He was instead an adventurer who was bringing about his own destruction even as he succeeded in his quest to search out the beaver in all of the secret places of the mountain West. A dependent of the London dandy and his foppish taste in hats, the Mountain Man was Caliban. He was a member of a picturesque lower class fast vanishing from the face of America. Like the Mohican Indian and quaint old Leatherstocking he was a vanishing breed, forlorn and permanently classbound in spite of all his heroics.

Both of these stereotypes embody, as do most effective stereotypes, more than a measure of reality. The Mountain Man traveled far out ahead of the march of conventional civilization, and the job he did required him to be as tough, primitive and close to nature as an Indian. Moreover, it was an out-of-doors life of the hunt and the chase that he often grew to like. By the same token because he spent much of his time in primitive isolation in the mountains, he very often proved to be a poor businessman ignorant of current prices and sharp company practices. Even if aware of his disadvantageous position he could do nothing to free himself until he had made his stake.

The fact is, however, that many Mountain men lived for the chance to exchange their dangerous mountain careers for an advantageous start in civilized life. If one examines their lives and their stated aspirations one discovers that the Mountain Men, for all their eccentricities, were astonishingly similar to the common men of their time-plain republican citizens of the Jacksonian era.

Jacksonian Man, according to Richard Hofstadter, "was an expectant capitalist, a hardworking ambitious person for whom enterprise was a kind of religion." He was "the master mechanic who aspired to open his own shop, the planter, or farmer who speculated in land, the lawyer who hoped to be a judge, the local politician who wanted to go to Congress, the grocer who would be a merchant. . . ." To this list one might well add, the trapper who hoped some day, if he hit it lucky and avoided the scalping knife, to be one or all of these, or perhaps better still, a landed gentleman of wealth and prestige.

"Everywhere," writes Hofstadter, the Jacksonian expectant capitalist "found conditions that encouraged him to extend himself." And there were many like William Ashley or Thomas James who out of encouragement or desperation looked away to the Rocky Mountains, teeming with beaver and other hidden resources, and saw a path to economic success and rapid upward mobility. In short, when he went out West and became a Mountain Man the Jacksonian Man did so as a prospector. He too was an expectant capitalist.

Marvin Meyers has added a further characterization of Jacksonian Man. He was, according to Meyers, the "venturous conservative," the man who desired relative freedom from restraint so that he might risk his life and his fortune, if not his sacred honor, on what appeared to be a long-term, continent-wide boom. Yet at the same time he wished to pyramid his fortune within the limits of the familiar American social and economic system, and likewise to derive his status therefrom. Wherever he went, and especially on the frontier, Jacksonian Man did not wish to change the system. He merely wished to throw it open as much as possible to opportunity, with the hope that by so doing he could place himself at the top instead of at the bottom of the conventional social and economic ladder. "They love change," wrote Tocqueville, "but they dread revolutions." Instead of a new world the Jacksonian Man wished to restore the old where the greatest man was the independent man—yeoman or mechanic, trader or ranchero—the man who basked in comfort and sturdy security under his own "vine and fig tree."

The structure of the Rocky Mountain fur trade itself, the life stories of the trappers and on rare occasions their stated or implied aspirations all make it clear that if he was not precisely the Meyers–Hofstadter Jacksonian Man, the Mountain Man was most certainly his cousin once removed, and a clearly recognizable member of the family.

It is a truism, of course, to state that the Rocky Mountain fur trade was a business, though writers in the Mountain Man's day since have sometimes made it seem more like a sporting event. The Mountain Man himself often put such an ambiguous face on what he was doing.

"Westward! Ho!" wrote Warren Ferris, an American Fur Company trapper. "It is the sixteenth of the second month A.D. 1830, and I have joined a trapping, trading, hunting expedition to the Rocky Mountains. Why, I scarcely know, for the motives that induced me to this step were of a mixed complexion,—something like the pepper and salt population of this city of St. Louis. Curiosity, a love of wild adventure, and perhaps also a hope of profit,—for times *are* hard, and my best coat has a sort of sheepish hang-dog hesitation to encounter fashionable folk—combined to make me look upon the project with an eye of favor. The party consists of some thirty men, mostly Canadian; but a few there are, like myself, from various parts of the Union. Each has some plausible excuse for joining, and the aggregate of disinterestedness would delight the most ghostly saint in the Roman calendar. Engage for money! no, not they;—health, and the strong desire of seeing strange lands, of beholding nature in the savage grandeur of her primeval state,—these are the only arguments that *could* have persuaded such independent and high-minded young fellows to adventure with the American Fur Company in a trip to the mountain wilds of the great west."

Ambiguous though the Mountain Man's approach to it may have been, it is abundantly clear that the Rocky Mountain fur trade was indeed a *business*, and not an invariably individualistic enterprise at that. The unit of operation was the company, usually a partnership for the sake of capital, risk and year-round efficiency. Examples of the company are The Missouri Fur Company, Gantt and Blackwell, Stone and Bostwick, Bean and Sinclair, and most famous of all, the Rocky Mountain Fur Company and its successors, Smith Jackson, and Sublette, Sublette & Campbell, and Sublette, Fitzpatrick, Bridger, Gervais and Fraeb. These were the average company units in the Rocky Mountain trade and much of the story of their existence in analogous to Jackson's war on the "Monster Bank" for they were all forced to contend against John Jacob Astor's "Monster Monopoly," the American Fur Co., which was controlled and financed by eastern capitalists.

Perhaps the most interesting aspect of the independent fur companies was their fluid structure of leadership. There was indeed, "a baton in every knapsack" or more accurately, perhaps, in every "possibles" bag. William Ashley, owner of a gun powder factory and Andrew Henry, a former Lisa lieutenant, and lead miner, founded the Rocky Mountain Fur Company. After a few years of overwhelming success, first Henry, and then Ashley, retired, and they were succeeded by their lieutenants, Jedediah Smith, David Jackson and William Sublette, three of the "enterprising young men" who had answered Ashley's advertisement in the St. Louis *Gazette and Public Advertiser* in 1823. When Smith and Jackson moved on to more attractive endeavors, first William Sublette and Robert Campbell, then Tom "Broken Hand" Fitzpatrick, James "Old Gabe" Bridger, Henry Fraeb, Milton "Thunderbolt" Sublette and Jean Baptiste Gervais moved up to fill their entrepreneurial role.

In another example Etienne Provost was successively an employee of Auguste Chouteau, partner with LeClair and leader of his own Green River brigade, and servant of American Fur. Sylvestre Pattie became a Santa Fe trader, then an independent trapper, then manager of the Santa Rita (New Mexico) Copper Mines and ultimately leader of an independent trapping venture into the Gila River country of the far Southwest—a venture that ended in disaster when he was thrown into a Mexican prison in California and there left to die. Most significant is the fact that few of the trappers declined the responsibility of entrepreneurial leadership when it was offered them. On the contrary, the usual practice was to indenture oneself to an established company for a period of time, during which it was possible to acquire the limited capital in the way of traps, rifles, trade goods, etc., that was needed to become independent and a potential brigade leader. Referring to his arrangement with the old Missouri Fur Company in 1809, Thomas James wrote,

> We Americans were all private adventurers, each on his own hook, and were led into the enterprise by the promises of the Company, who agreed to subsist us to the trapping grounds, we helping to navigate the boats, and on our arrival there they were to furnish us each with a rifle and sufficient ammunition, six good beaver traps and also four men of their hired French, to be under our individual commands for a period of three years.
>
> By the terms of the contract each of us was to divide one-fourth of the profits of our joint labor with the four men thus to be appointed to us.

James himself retired when he could from the upper Missouri trade and eventually became an unsuccessful storekeeper in Harrisonville, Illinois.

In addition to the fact of rapid entrepreneurial succession within the structure of the independent fur companies, a study of 446 Mountain Men (perhaps 45 percent of the total engaged in this pursuit between 1805 and 1845) indicates that their life-patterns could be extremely varied. One hundred seventeen Mountain Men definitely turned to occupations other than trapping subsequent to their entering the mountain trade. Of this number, 39 followed more than one pursuit. As such they often worked at as many as four or five different callings.

Moreover, beyond the 117 definite cases of alternative callings, 32 others were found to have indeterminate occupations that were almost certainly not connected with the fur trade, making a total of 149 out of 154 men for whom some occupational data exists who had turned away from the trapping fraternity before 1845. Of the remaining men in the study, 110 men yielded nothing to investigation beyond the fact that they had once been trappers, 182 can be listed as killed in the line of duty and only 5 men out of the total stayed with the great out-of-doors life of the free trapper that according to the myth they were all supposed to love.

The list of alternative callings pursued by the trappers is also revealing. Twenty-one became ranchers, fifteen farmers, seventeen traders (at stationary trading posts), eight miners, seven politicians, six distillers, five each storekeepers and army scouts, four United States Indian agents, three carpenters, two each bankers, drovers and hatters and at least one pursued each of the following occupations: sheepherder, postman, miller, medium, ice dealer, real estate speculator, newspaper editor, lawyer, lumberman, superintendent of schools, tailor, blacksmith, and supercargo of trading schooner. Moreover, many of these same individuals pursued secondary occupations such as that of hotel keeper, gambler, soldier, health resort proprietor, coal mine owner, tanner, sea captain, horse thief and opera house impresario.

From this it seems clear that, statistically at least, the Mountain Man was hardly the simple-minded primitive that mythology has made him out to be. Indeed it appears that whenever he had the chance, he exchanged the joys of the rendezvous and the wilderness life for the more civilized excitement of "getting ahead." In many cases he achieved this aim, and on a frontier where able men were scarce he very often became a pillar of the community, and even of the nation. From the beginning, as Ashley's famous advertisement implied, the Mountain Men were men of "enterprise" who risked their lives for something more than pure romance and a misanthropic desire to evade civilization. The picturesqueness and quaintness were largely the creation of what was the literary mentality of an age of artistic romanticism. For every "Cannibal Phil" or Robert Meldrum or "Peg-Leg" Smith there was a Sarchel Wolfskill (vintner), a George Yount (rancher) and a William Sublette (banker–politician).

Two further facts emerge in part from this data. First, it is clear that

Table 11.1

Total Number of Cases	446
Persons whose other occupations are known	117
Persons whose other occupations are probable	32
Persons with more than one other occupation	39
Persons who stayed on as trappers	5
Persons whose status is unknown	110
Persons killed in the fur trade	182

though the Jeffersonian agrarian dream of "Arcadia" bulked large in the Mountain Man's choice of occupations, it by no means obscured the whole range of "mechanical" or mercantile pursuits that offered the chance for success on the frontier. Indeed, if it suggests anything a statistical view of the Mountain Man's "other life" suggests that almost from the beginning the Far Western frontier took on the decided aspect of an urban or semi-urban "industrial" civilization. Secondly, though it is not immediately apparent from the above statistics, a closer look indicates that a surprising number of the Mountain Men succeeded at their "other" tasks to the extent that they became regionally and even nationally prominent.

William H. Ashley became Congressman from Missouri and a spokesman for the West, Charles Bent an ill-fated though famed governor of New Mexico. "Doc" Newell was a prominent figure in the organization of Oregon Territory. Elbridge Gerry, William McGaa, and John Simpson Smith were the founders and incorporators of Denver. Lucien Maxwell held the largest land grant in the whole history of the United States.

Joshua Pilcher was a famous superintendent of Indian affairs. William Sublette, pursuing a hard money policy, saved the Bank of Missouri in the panic of 1837 and went on to be Democratic elector for "young hickory" James K. Polk in 1844. Benjamin Wilson was elected first mayor of Los Angeles. James Clyman and his Napa Valley estate were famous in California as were the ranches of George Yount and J. J. Warner, while Sarchel Wolfskill was a co-founder of the modern California wine industry. James Waters built the first opera house in Southern California, and Kit Carson, in his later years a silver miner, received the supreme tribute of finding a dime novel dedicated to his exploits in plunder captured from marauding Apache Indians who had recently attacked and massacred a wagon train.

Many of the Mountain Men achieved fame and national status through works that they published themselves, or, as in the case of Carson, through works that immortalized correctly, or as was more usual, in-

Table 11.2   List of Occupations

A. Primary

1. Farmer	15	17. Blacksmith	1
2. Rancher	21	18. Tailor	1
3. Politician	7	19. Supercargo	1
4. Sheepherder	1	20. Superintendent of Schools	1
5. Scout (for govt.)	5	21. Lumberman	2
6. Trader	17	22. Newspaper Editor	1
7. Miner	8	23. Carpenter	3
8. Postman	1	24. Cattle Buyer	1
9. Distiller	6	25. Clockmaker	1
10. Miller	1	26. Saloon Keeper	1
11. Storekeeper	5	27. Baker	1
12. Medium	1	28. Fruit Grower	1
13. Banker	2	29. Vintner	1
14. Drover	2	30. Ice Dealer	1
15. Hatter	2	31. Real Estate Speculator	1
16. Indian Agent	4	32. Lawyer	1

B. Secondary

1. Trader	4	12. Lumberman	2
2. Transportation	2	13. Gambler	3
3. Scout	5	14. Blacksmith	1
4. Hotel Keeper	1	15. Soldier	1
5. Miner	2	16. Spa Keeper	1
6. Farmer	5	17. Coal Mine Operator	1
7. Politician	3	18. Tanner	1
8. Rancher	5	19. Opera House Impresario	1
9. Storekeeper	4	20. Sea Captain	1
10. Miller	3	21. Carpenter	1
11. Real Estate	3	22. Horse Thief	1

correctly, their exploits. Here one need only mention Kit Carson's *Autobiography* and his favorable treatment at the hands of Jessie Benton Fremont, T. D. Bonner's *Life and Adventures of James Beckwourth,* Francis Fuller Victor's *River of the West* (about Joe Meek), James Ohio Pattie's *Personal Narrative,* Thomas James' *Three Years Among the Indians and Mexicans,* H. L. Conard's *Uncle Dick Wooton,* David Coyner's *The Lost Trappers* (about Ezekial Williams), Irving's portrait of Joseph Reddeford Walker in *The Adventures of Captain Bonneville,* Zenas Leonard's *Narrative,* Peg-Leg Smith's "as told to" exploits in *Hutchings' California Magazine,* Stephen Meek's *Autobiography,* Warren Ferris' letters to the Buffalo, New York, *Western Literary Messenger,* John Hatcher's yarns in Lewis H. Garrard's *Wah to Yah and the Taos Trail* and perhaps most interesting of all, trapper John Brown's pseudoscientific *Mediumistic Experiences*, to realize the extent and range of the Mountain Man's communication with the outside world in his own day. Not only was he a typical man of his time, he was often a conspicuous success and not bashful about communicating the fact in somewhat exaggerated terms to his fellow countrymen.

Direct evidence of the Mountain Men's motives is scarce, but it is clear their intentions were complex.

"Tell them that I have no heirs and that I hope to make a fortune," wrote Louis Vasquez ("Old Vaskiss" to Bernard De Voto) in 1834 from "Fort Convenience" somewhere in the Rockies. Later as he set out on one last expedition in 1842 he added somewhat melodramatically, "I leave to make money or die." And finally Colonel A. G. Brackett, who visited Fort Bridger (jointly owned by Bridger and Vasquez), described him as "a Mexican, who put on a great deal of style, and used to ride about the country in a coach and four."

"It is, that I may be able to help those who stand in need, that I face every danger," wrote Jedediah Smith from the Wind River Mountains in 1829, "most of all, it is for this, that I deprive myself of the privilege of Society and the satisfaction of the Converse of My Friends! but I shall count all this pleasure, if I am allowed by the Alwise Ruler the privilege of Joining my Friends. . . ."

And he added, "Let it be the greatest pleasure that we can enjoy, the height of our ambition, now, when our Parents are in the decline of Life, to smooth the Pillow of their age, and as much as in us lies, take from them all cause of Trouble." So spoke Jedediah Smith of his hopes and ambitions upon pursuing the fur trade. No sooner had he left the mountains, however, than he was killed by Plains Indians before he could settle down in business with his brothers as he had intended. Noble and ignoble were the motives of the Mountain Men. Colonel John Shaw, starting across the southern plains and into the Rockies in search of gold; Thomas James, desperate to recoup his failing fortunes; the Little Rock *Gazette* of 1829 "confidently" believing "that this enterprise affords a prospect of great profit to all who may engage in it"; the St. Louis *Enquirer* in 1822 labeling the Rocky Mountains "the Shining Mountains," and innocently declaring, "A hunter pursuing his game found the silver mines of Potosi, and many others have been discovered by the like accidents, and there is no reason to suppose that other valuable discoveries may not be made"; Ashley calling clearly and unmistakably for men of "enterprise," all added up to the fact that the Mountain Man when he went West was a complex character. But in his complexity was a clearly discernible pattern—the pattern of Jacksonian Man in search of respectability and success in terms recognized by the society he had left behind. His goal was, of course, the pursuit of happiness. But happiness, contrary to Rousseauistic expectations, was not found in the wilderness; it was an integral product of society and civilization.

If the Mountain Man was indeed Jacksonian Man, then there are at least three senses in which this concept has importance. First, more clearly than anything else a statistical and occupational view of the various callings of the Mountain Man tentatively indicates the incredible rate and the surprising *nature* of social and economic change in the West. In little more than two decades most of the surviving enterprising men had left the fur trade for more lucrative and presumably more useful occupations. And by their choice of occupations it is clear that in the Far West a whole step in the settlement process had been virtually skipped. They may have dreamed of "Arcadia," but when they turned to the task of settling the West as fast as possible, the former Mountain Men and perhaps others like them brought with them all the aspects of an "industrial," mercantile and quasiurban society. The opera house went up almost simultaneously with the ranch, and the Bank of Missouri was secured before the land was properly put into hay.

Secondly, as explorers—men who searched out the hidden places in the western wilderness—the Mountain Men as Jacksonian Men looked with a flexible eye upon the new land. Unlike the Hudson's Bay explorer who looked only for beaver and immediate profit, the Mountain Man looked to the future and the development of the West, not as a vast game preserve, but as a land like the one he had back home.

> "Much of this vast waste of territory belongs to the Republic of the United States," wrote Zenas Leonard from San Francisco Bay in 1833. "What a theme to contemplate its settlement and civilization. Will the jurisdiction of the federal government ever succeed in civilizing the thousands of savages now roaming over these plains, and her hardy freeborn population here plant their homes, build their towns and cities, and say here shall the arts and sciences of civilization take root and flourish? Yes, here, even in this remote part of the Great West before many years will these hills and valleys be greeted with the enlivening sound of the workman's hammer, and the merry whistle of the ploughboy . . . we have good reason to suppose that the territory *west* of the mountains will some day be equally as important to the nation as that on the east."

In 1830 in a famous letter to John H. Eaton, the Secretary of War, Jedediah S. Smith, David E. Jackson, and William L. Sublette aired their views on the possibilities of the West. Smith made clear that a wagon road route suitable for settlers existed all the way to Oregon, and Sublette dramatized the point when he brought ten wagons and two dearborns and even a milch cow over the mountains as far as the Wind River rendezvous. Their report made abundantly clear that in their opinion the future of the West lay with settlers rather than trappers. Indeed they were worried that the English at Fort Vancouver might grasp this fact before the American government. In short, as explorers and trappers theirs was a broad-ranging, flexible, settler-oriented, public view of the Far West.

Tied in with this and of the greatest significance is a third and final point. Not only did they *see* a settler's future in the West, but at least some of the Mountain Men were most eager to see to it that such a future was *guaranteed* by the institutions of the United States Government which must be brought West and extended over all the wild new land to protect the settler in the enjoyment of his own "vine and fig tree." The Mexican Government, unstable, and blown by whim or caprice, could not secure the future, and the British Government, at least in North America, was under the heel of monopoly. France was frivolous and decadent. Russia was a sinister and backward despotism. Only the free institutions of Jacksonian America would make the West safe for enterprise. So strongly did he feel about this that in 1841 the Mountain Man Moses "Black" Harris sent a letter to one Thornton Grimsley offering him the command of 700 men, of which he was one, who were eager to "join the standard of their country, and make a clean sweep of what is called the Origon [*sic*] Territory; that is clear it of British and Indians." Outraged not only at British encroachments, he was also prepared to "march through to California" as well. It may well have been this spirit that settled the Oregon question and brought on the Mexican War.

Settlement, security, stability, enterprise, free enterprise, a government of laws which, in the words of Jackson himself, confines "itself to equal *protection*, and as Heaven does its rains, showers its favors alike on the high and the low, the rich and the poor," all of these shaped the Mountain Man's vision of the West and his role in its development. It was called Manifest Destiny. But long before John L. O'Sullivan nicely turned the phrase in the *Democratic Review*, the Mountain Man as Jacksonian Man— a "venturous conservative"—was out in the west doing his utmost to lend the Almighty a helping hand. James Clyman perhaps put it most simply:

> *Here lies the bones of old Black Harris*
> *who often traveled beyond the far west*
> *and for the freedom of Equal rights*
> *He crossed the snowy mountain Hights*
> *Especially with a Belly full.*

QUESTIONS TO CONSIDER

1. What modern parallel does Goetzmann suggest for the year-end rendezvous? What does this image do to the picture of trapper as a heroic, free man?
2. What is Goetzmann's thesis?
3. What does Goetzmann conclude about the mountain man's occupational mobility? How successful were these men in other occupational pursuits?
4. What does Goetzmann conclude were the goals of the (Jacksonian) mountain man?
5. Does Goetzmann's mountain man better fit the Jeffersonian, independent, self-directed ideal or deTocqueville's conforming materialist model? Why?
6. Summarize the essence of Goetzmann's article.

12

Slaves in Biracial
Protestant Churches*

John B. Boles

Slavery has perhaps had a greater impact on the American character than any other one element. Not only did it reduce most
African-Americans to the status of property until 1865, but it produced a legacy of racism that has touched all areas of American society right down to the present. It scarred white oppressors
as well as the black oppressed. It split the nation in a terrible civil
war that cost more American lives than all other wars put together.

Yet in recent years we have come to understand that the life of
the slave included some redeeming characteristics. Slave families
were far stronger and more durable than was long believed. And
in this article, we learn that the religious life of the slaves not only
provided a rich experience for them, but that it provided a rare example of cooperation and harmony between the races in the antebellum South.

John Boles earned his Ph.D. from the University of Virginia in 1969.
He is a professor of history at Rice University, specializing in the history of the South, slavery, and American religion, three areas that
come together in this article. Some of the material also appears in
his book *Black Southerners, 1619–1869.*

*Reprinted from *Varieties of Southern Religious Experience,* ed. by Samuel S. Hill (1988), by
permission of Louisiana State University Press.

Religion was the heart and soul of the Afro-American's human triumph over chattel slavery. Religion provided a system of ideas and practices that gave directions for living; it marked with symbols and ceremonies significant events in an individual's life; it provided hope, fulfillment, and a special kind of freedom for people mired in chattel bondage. Although the importance and centrality of the slaves' religion recently has been recognized, the precise origin, nature, and function of their faith are still issues under active debate.

Black Christianity found many ways of expressing itself, but for most slaves throughout the antebellum period the normative worship experience was a joint worship service attended by both blacks and whites. African components persisted in the slave culture's naming practices, kinship systems, musical instruments, body language, folktales and other oral traditions, and carving, pottery, quilting, and basketmaking styles. The imprint of Africa lingered also in religion. In fact, certain aspects of African religious thought may have predisposed slaves to accept the evangelical Protestantism they were exposed to after the mideighteenth century. But the emerging Afro-American Christianity was greatly influenced by white practices and by black participation in southern churches—so much so that it is possible to speak of a biracial religious community in the Old South. Complete equality and true justice never existed, but black and white met more equally under the steeple than anywhere else in southern society. That relationship is the focus of this essay, which surveys a broad and complex topic that ranges across two continents and three centuries.

The West Africa from which most slaves came contained hundreds of different cultural systems and an awesome variety of religious practices. But there were several underlying common assumptions and, even more important, some striking similarities to the kinds of Protestant evangelicalism Africans encountered in the American South. Meaningful generalizations, even though they risk oversimplification, can be made. For the West African the world was infused with spiritual forces. Nature gods and ancestral gods gave a special value to one's kinship group and the physical environs of one's village. Every event—from cataclysmic natural disasters to minor personal misfortunes—had its roots, it was believed, in the realm of the spiritual. African societies in the seventeenth and eighteenth centuries appear to have been completely nonsecular; religion was all-encompassing, an aspect of every detail of life, an influence on every occurrence. Most Africans had a conception of time in which the present and the past were almost fused into one. Ancestors were almost literally still present. But the future was extremely foreshortened, hardly conceivable except in the most limited, day-after-tomorrow sense. In a triune conception of the supernatural, ancestral spirits and nature spirits were the most common supernatural beings; they were normally deemed responsible for the happenstances of life and supplicated. Yet, superior to these two types of gods reigned an omnipotent, omniscient god who could be appealed to when all else had failed.

Ordinarily, in African societies the gods spoke to persons by sending a spirit, and possession—often frenzied—was the human evidence of communication with the supernatural. Throughout West Africa, people considered themselves an organic part of the cosmos, but water had a special role, a mystical, symbolic one. Streams, rivers, lakes, and springs were often "aquatic temples" where various nature or ancestral spirits dwelled. Springs gushing from the center of the earth were often thought to be symbolic of rebirth, still water represented creation, and water in general suggested life, fertility, and hope. Religious ceremonies often took place beside or even in water, were usually public, involved the community, and frequently were marked by participatory congregational singing. The religious ceremony bestowed and reinvigorated a sense of belonging by providing the individual with a sense of fellowship with contemporaries, ancestors, and the natural environment. Through spiritual possession, one encountered the supernatural essence of the universe.

Given the nature of American slavery, the specifics of African religions—the ritual specialists, the religious language, and the ritual paraphernalia—could not be transported intact to the American South. But the philosophical essence of the system was transplanted and slowly transformed. In the seventeenth century, slaves were too few and too intermixed with whites to be able to maintain much more than a haunting memory of Old World practices. On scattered occasions blacks were baptized as Christians, but the language barrier and the planters' lingering uncertainty about the continued slave status of a baptized bondsman minimized the Christianization of blacks. Also, there were few actively Christian whites in the South in the seventeenth century. By the third quarter of the eighteenth century, however, Baptist, Methodist, and Presbyterian evangelicals had established themselves and had begun the process of forming churches, recruiting ministers, and popular evangelizing that would eventually turn the Old South into a hothouse of religious orthodoxy and personal piety. The upsurge of African importations, the beginning of net population growth for American-born slaves, and the birth of Afro-American culture coincided with the commencement of the southern evangelical movement. These coincidental developments were to have a major impact on the evolution of Afro-American Christianity in the Old South.

In 1774 a young Princeton-educated tutor to the family of Councillor Robert Carter encountered an aged African-born slave, Daddy Gumby, on a Virginia plantation. The slave clearly had accepted Calvinistic teachings, as evidenced by his statement that "God yonder in Heaven Master will burn *Lyars* with *Fire* & *Brimstone!* . . . Men are wicked." When the tutor, Philip Vickers Fithian, said it was too hot to attend church, the old slave admonished him: "Too hot to serve the Lord! Why I that am so old & worn out go on foot." Clearly, some Africans who had mastered the English language had also adopted the Christian world view, and for every African like Daddy Gumby who did so, there must have been also several American-born slaves who found comfort and purpose in Christianity. All three of the southern evangelical denominations that would soon be dominant in the region welcomed black worshipers and actively preached to bondspeople. Many planters were still skeptical of the utility and wisdom of converting the slaves. But the growing popular denominations, consisting primarily of non-slave-owning yeoman farmers, believed all were equal in the eyes of God. The early Baptists and Methodists, especially, often criticized slavery and felt driven to spread the gospel to all God's creatures. Most church services were joint services—and remained so throughout the antebellum period—but there were other factors besides the churches' welcoming black members that made evangelical Christianity attractive to increasing numbers of slaves.

If ever there was a situation in which Africans might feel that the lesser gods had proven unequal to the task and that as a consequence their omnipotent god was the one to be relied on, then capture, the middle passage, and enslavement in the New World was it. Increasingly, after the mideighteenth century both newly imported and already acculturated slaves came into contact with fervent evangelicals who preached of a benevolent, all-powerful God who reached out to the lost and forlorn and provided deliverance. It was easy to identify the supreme African god with the Christian's God. The idea was especially compatible with African views when the Christian God was proffered by ministers (and congregational members) whose zeal and spirit-infused exhortations bore a comforting resemblance to African possession. And the African concept of ancestral gods, nature gods, and an omnipotent creator god was transferable to the Christian Trinity of God the Father, God the Son, and God the Holy Spirit.

As the slave population increased and slave families became ever more common, blacks grew more concerned with cultural values and religious services. After all, not only were their lives now substantially more stable, but they were having children. Families became, if not quite the norm, an often realizable goal. With families came a desire to cement relationships ceremonially, to legitimate and maintain cultural values. Parents are always more concerned than young singles to preserve religious traditions. At the same general time that demographic forces were pushing slaves in the direction of family formation and creation of their own culture, Protestantism was penetrating the plantation South. The willingness of the evangelical churches to accept blacks as members and, by the use of such terms of address as brother and sister, to include them in fellowship gave slaves a sense of belonging and group identity that again resonated with African memories. The Baptist practice of immersion may well have recalled African water rites, whereas the emotional intensity, the vigorous congregational singing, and the joyful sense of spiritual release common to the Methodists as well as the Baptists appealed to the African sensitivity. New World realities and Old World recollections formed the matrix out of which Afro-American Christianity emerged.

In the 1770s and 1780s, as pioneer churches were organized, there were black members participating in the very acts of incorporation. The absolute number of black church members was small at first (and before the nineteenth century total church membership was only a tiny fraction of the population). But slaves were attending churches, taking communion, being baptized and confirmed, listening to sermons, singing hymns, and gradually accepting the Christian world view. The Great Revival at the beginning of the nineteenth century established the mode of revival piety that came to characterize the antebellum South. At the very peak of the revival, during the climactic Cane Ridge camp meeting of 1801, there was "a Black assembly, hearing the exhortations of the Blacks; some of which appeared to be convicted and others converted." Thereafter, in steady, unspectacular fashion, the numbers of slaves worshiping in joint congregations grew, despite the fact that before the 1840s planters sporadically declared their unease about the potentially revolutionary implications of the gospel.

After the mid-1840s, when the three major denominations had splintered away from the national organizations and appeared safe on the issue of abolition, planters became even more supportive of efforts to Christianize the slaves, in part because they thought religion would make them better slaves. But there were reasons unrelated to plantation efficiency for sponsoring the preaching of the gospel to the blacks. Ministers advocated missionary activities both to rebut abolitionist charges that slaveholders left their bondspeople in heathenish conditions and out of genuine desires to enlarge God's Kingdom. Guilt and the urge to evangelize were both factors, their relative importance differing from person to person and at various times. During the final generation of the Old South, several hundred white missionaries preached regularly to slave congregations in the regions where the black population was high. In addition, by the eve of the

Civil War perhaps as many as a quarter of all slaves were members of churches, principally in areas where average slaveholdings were small. But one should resist the temptation to interpret the resulting slave Christianity simply as an example of successful social control exerted by whites over blacks.

Slaves avidly accepted Christianity and made it their own because it served their purposes so well. Slaves understood that, as the white ministers often said and as the Bible proclaimed, in the eyes of God all are equal, slave and free alike. Likewise, salvation was available to everyone who had faith in Christ. In addition, slaves could identify with Jesus, particularly in his role as the suffering servant. With salvation came the promise of a better life after the earthly travail was finished, but just as important, the Christian faith provided a moral purpose for day-by-day living. As children of God, black men and women felt that their lives were not meaningless or of little worth. And because God was just, many slaves expected recompense in the end for the injustice of their present lives in bondage. The concept of the Chosen People was widely adopted by the slaves as descriptive of their own situation: for like the people of Israel they were enslaved, mistreated, and downtrodden, and if they kept faith with God, they could look forward to eventual triumph. The effect was to provide a healthy dose of self-respect for the slave community. Their identification with the people of Israel gave a certain sense of moral grandeur, even a feeling of moral superiority vis-à-vis haughty masters, to the slaves struggling to maintain their essential humanity amidst an institution that classified them as mere property. In the churches black men and women found persuasive reason to live as morally responsible adults, discovered arenas for the practice of black leadership, and enjoyed a status far closer to equality with whites than anywhere else in southern society. No wonder the church was the dominant institutional force in the lives of so many black southerners throughout the antebellum period and into our own time.

Historians have sufficiently recognized neither the role of the slaves in the southern churches nor the role of those churches in the lives of the slaves. From the inception of institutional church life, particularly among the soon-dominant Baptists and Methodists, slaves were active church members. Of course, the percentage of black members varied according to their percentage in the local population, but in every region blacks and whites worshiped together. Blacks commonly represented 20 to 40 percent of the congregation of Baptist churches; often they were the majority. Generally, blacks sat segregated at the rear of the church, in the balcony, or in a lean-to addition to the church. Blacks and whites heard the same sermons, took communion at the same service, were baptized or confirmed together, and were buried in the same cemeteries. Black delegates attended district association and quarterly meetings down to the Civil War. On occasion, when the white members built a new church building, the blacks were given the old building and allowed virtual autonomy over matters in the adjunct church. A white committee would be appointed to supervise the black congregation, which might be called, for example, the Stamping Ground African Baptist Church to distinguish it from the parent, white Stamping Ground Baptist Church. But such supervision appears to have been nominal. The slaves so separated were less the victims of segregation than the beneficiaries of whites' recognition that bondspeople had special needs and special interests best served by their own leaders. In the far more common biracial churches, black deacons and elders sometimes served alongside whites, and it was not unusual, when no white minister was available, for the whole congregation to listen with approval to a black preacher. In fact, sometimes biracial congregations requested certain black preachers. Across the South, especially talented black preachers gained great fame as pulpit orators, and whites agreed that black ministers such as John Jasper and Andrew Marshall had unrivaled power to move a congregation.

In its economic, political, and social realm the Old South was a deferential, hierarchical society. But distinctions of class and race counted for surprisingly less in the religious realm. Such relative democracy before God did not remove distinctions in what was called the "civil" world, but it helped reduce conflict there. There was more nearly a biracial community in the antebellum Protestant churches than in the society as a whole. Standards for admission to and dismissal from churches were essentially the same for both races. A measure of spiritual equality was accorded blacks even in the language of address: "Brother" and "Sister" were affixed to their given names, as with white comembers. Church clerks would write back to slaves' home churches to obtain letters of dismissal for slaves recently sold away, and when a letter arrived attesting to the slave's good standing, he or she would be admitted to the new church. The process of joining or removing from a church was the same for slave and free. A person made a profession of his faith and either was baptized or submitted evidence of his prior baptism at another church. The relationship of the church to slavery was filled with irony and contradiction. Even while churches had slave members and accorded them relative equality in the spiritual realm, the churches were always careful to recognize the realities of the slave society of which they were a part. Churches generally sought slaveowners' permission—and obtained it—before accepting slave members. Church minutes contain numerous letters like the following, entered in the Chestnut Grove (Virginia) Baptist Church books on the second Sunday of July, 1862.

> Rev Mr. Briggs
> My man servant Hubbard wishes to attach himself to your church; you can admit him if you think proper
> J. A. Michie

> Rev. Mr. Briggs:
> Harvard and Nelson have my permission to join the Baptist Church at Earlysville, and I pray that the Holy Spirit may guide and direct them through life—and that they may finally be saved in heaven.
> June 23rd 1862 Joshua Jackson

The fact that the owners were called upon to grant permission indicates the pervasiveness of the master-slave relationship. But as these letters also suggest, slaves had significant autonomy, and some slave owners had genuine moral concern for the souls of their bondspeople. Like all human institutions, slavery was enormously complex and as varied as the persons involved.

An even more impressive example of how slaves entered into the life and spirit of the churches, and vice versa, is provided in the way the churches functioned as moral courts. The three dominant evangelical churches took seriously and tried to put into practice Jesus' directives as outlined in Matthew 18:15. Different denominations had differing procedures. A Baptist church, for example, would meet at least once a month on Saturday or Sunday afternoon in a "business" session in which the major business was the moral supervision of its members. Each member was expected "with love and charity" to watch over other members and counsel them to change if they had been seen to transgress some moral law. When there was a dispute or no quick confession was forthcoming, charges would be brought against the offending party at the business session. Most transgressions consisted of such human failings as drunkenness, profanity, breaking the Sabbath, fornication, adultery, stealing, and lying. Charges were made, witnesses heard, and testimony taken, and the defendant was judged either innocent or guilty. If judged guilty, the person either confessed and promised reformation or was excommunicated. Such activity was a significant part of religious life and responsibility in the Old South, and slaves participated in the whole process voluntarily and, to a surprising degree, as virtually the equals of whites. Bondspeople clearly took pride in their name and good character; it was one thing masters could not take away from them.

Blacks were held by whites—and apparently by other Christian slaves—to substantially the same moral standards as whites were. Testimony was taken from and about slaves in the same way it was for white communicants. When whites brought charges against a black member, the accused was not automatically assumed to be guilty. Rather, the case was decided on its merits. Baptist church minute books in Mississippi reveal several occasions on which charges by whites against slave members were dismissed and the slave deemed innocent. In like fashion, slaves bore testimony against whites, and the whites then underwent moral examination. All this happened in a society in which slaves could not testify against whites in civil courts. In 1819 one William West was denied a letter of dismissal from the Hephzibah Baptist Church in East Feliciana Parish, Louisiana, because the church had concluded he had unjustly whipped a "black brother of the church." Three years later another white member, D. Edds, was excommunicated after charges that he had abused one of his slaves were substantiated by examination. The church records show that masters frequently brought charges against slaves for lying, stealing, and even running away, but in every case slaves were accorded at least a reasonable semblance of due process trial and often were judged innocent. That masters would utilize the church in an attempt to maintain plantation discipline is not surprising, but that they accepted the authority of the church—where black testimony was given—suggests a social complexity not always appreciated by historians.

Moreover, slaves brought charges against one another, defended themselves, and in general stood before their fellow members as free moral agents. Clearly, whites and blacks accepted the same moral code, identifying the same sins to be overcome. The churches' position on black adultery is highly significant. In a society in which slave marriages were not legally recognized and could be ended at the master's convenience, evangelical churches held slaves strictly accountable for adultery. Hence, in the eyes of many southern churchgoers, the slave marriage was sacred and its commitments firm (though slaves who had been sold and separated against their will could remarry). None of this indicates that the South was not racist, for in subtle ways whites were always in the ascendant position, and blacks were literally and figuratively at the back of the church. Nevertheless, what is more remarkable is the degree to which there existed a biracial religious community in the Old South.

Historians have been too prone to emphasize the differences between white and black religion in the Old South, contrasting joyful, emotionally demonstrative black services with stereotypical images of arid, lifeless white services. But most white southerners, including Baptists and Methodists, enjoyed fervent worship with spirited preaching and participatory singing. Predominantly white rural churches were more like the lively black services than the Episcopal ceremony or the more sophisticated urban churches. As the antebellum period drew to a close, all of the white denominations were moving toward trained ministers, more sedate worship, and shorter services, while black Christianity remained truer to the early revivalistic style. Even so, commonalities in belief, sermon structure, and worship style persisted. More than a century after the Civil War, remnants of these shared practices were visible in the clear affinity between Baptist presidential candidate Jimmy Carter and black church members in 1976.

Talented slaves rose to positions of leadership in the churches, serving often as elders and deacons and occasionally as preachers. In all regions from the 1770s through the Civil War there were black ministers who preached to black and mixed audiences. The absence of educational standards and the looseness of ecclesiastical organizations made it easier for blacks to become Baptist preachers and no doubt enhanced the popularity of that denomination for slaves. At some times in some states it was illegal for slaves to become preachers, but white church authorities bent the laws and permitted slave "exhorters" to preach and "testify." Although it was also illegal to teach slaves to read, literate bondspeople existed in all areas of the South. Often they had been taught by God-fearing masters or mistresses so they could read the Bible, though occasionally white children or other literate slaves were their tutors. When black preachers spoke to mixed congregations, they trod softly lest the gospel theme of liberation raise the hackles of the whites. But when unsupervised, most black ministers apparently preached of the freedom provided by redemption. No doubt the described "freedom from sin" and "spiritual liberty" often came near to being a double-entendre for freedom from slavery, at least to suspicious whites, especially after insurrection scares. But it would be a mistake to interpret slave religion simply as either an opiate for passive slaves or a training ground for rebel activists. This conclusion becomes increasingly evident when one considers the variety of institutional forms that slave religion took.

The overwhelming majority of slave worshipers practiced their faith with whites in the mainline Protestant churches, but in most good-sized southern towns and cities there were independent black churches under the control of free black leaders. Many of these churches benefited from white patrons. Saint James African Episcopal Church in Baltimore is a good example of such an autonomous church. Occasionally—as in Richmond and Louisville—the major black Baptist church was the largest congregation in town. Although only free blacks held the leadership positions in such churches, since the church charters discriminated against slaves, bondspeople found in the all-black churches a meaningful and uplifting kind of worship. White visitors often noted the decorum, the eloquent sermon, and the marvelous singing that characterized the black temples of worship. The theology preached was little different from that in biracial churches, though by the 1830s the old camp-meeting kind of fervor was practically absent from the urban white churches. Except for the fact that services were usually longer and more overtly emotional, the theology, ritual, and organization of the black churches closely resembled those of the white churches. Independent black churches added much to the cultural life of urban blacks, providing a sense of order and direction, an opportunity to practice leadership skills, a variety of self-help organizations, and—most important—visible proof to all blacks, slave and free, that they could govern important aspects of their lives. Sometimes, as when the black church was a mission church funded by a predominantly white denomination, a white minister officiated. But the usual pattern in these influential citadels of black cultural life was for total black leadership, a secular as well as religious leadership that continued well into the post-bellum period.

An insufficiently understood and greatly exaggerated aspect of slave religion is the so-called underground church, the invisible institution of covert worship services held deep in the woods or secretly in slave cabins and urban cellars. Certainly the religious lives of slaves extended beyond the church structures, beyond the formal services where whites were present. Devout bondspeople in the privacy of their quarters surely had prayer meetings, sang hymns and spirituals of their own composition, and pondered the dilemmas of trying to do right in a world that did them so wrong. Weather permitting and master permitting, slaves on Sunday afternoons often met together for songs and preaching to supplement what they had heard in the morning worship hours. In these informal settings, black preachers could preach with less constraint. This could mean that they exhorted their listeners to rebel, but it probably more often simply freed the slave ministers to preach the gospel with greater ebullience, enlivening their messages with colorful imagery and weaving into their texts stories of Old Testament heroes and New Testament miracles that magnified the awesome power of God and love of Christ. Black ministers proclaimed the terrors of hell and the joys of heaven with a concreteness of detailed description that few whites could match. In the manner of the rich African oral tradition, the spoken word moved people and transmitted the heart of their culture from one generation to the next, entertaining them in the process. With consummate oratorical skills Afro-American preachers utilized an African medium to spread and maintain a Euro-American message. As might be expected, black Christians magnified the role and importance of the preacher. Nowhere were their verbal skills given more license than in the Sunday afternoon and nighttime meetings where they were not inhibited by the presence of whites. Here black preachers developed their characteristic and distinctive homiletic style.

On other occasions—as perhaps when a master prohibited slaves from attending church or when the white minister at church showed scant respect for the blacks' true religious feelings by preaching little but self-serving doctrines, such as "Slaves, obey your master"—slaves sought in their own special brush-arbor service to explore and proclaim the full gospel message of repentance and joy. Extant testimony by slaves shows their dissatisfaction with ministers who foreshortened the Christian message. Maria, one of Mary Boykin Chesnut's slaves, had real affection for one white minister who "preaches to black and white just the same. There ain't but one Gospel for all," she said. But she despised another minister who "goes for low-life things—hurting people's feelings. Don't you tell lies—don't you steal. . . . Before God," she insisted, "we are as white as he is. And in the pulpit he has no need to make us feel we are servants." In situations in which slaves were repeatedly subject to such truncated preaching, they slipped away, held secret services (sometimes turning a pot upside down in the belief that it would capture the sounds of their ceremonies and not betray their presence), relied on their own leaders, and created their own secret churches largely invisible to prying whites. The very attempt to do this, of course, indicates how false was the belief by some earlier scholars that slaves had no role models or cultural norms other than those provided by their masters.

In two small and isolated geographical regions, the sea islands of Georgia and South Carolina and the sugar-producing areas of New Orleans and rural Louisiana, where the ratio of blacks to whites was extremely high, African (or, in Louisiana, Caribbean) admixtures were strong enough to give slave religious services a decidedly un-European cast, as exemplified in the frenzied shouts of the sea islands and the voodoolike practices of south Louisiana. But with these two exceptions, perhaps in no other aspect of black cultural life had the values and practices of whites so deeply penetrated as in religious services. After all, black folklore, dance, art, basketry, and other practices flourished during those hours from sundown to sunup, when white supervision was least, and most readily identifiable Africanisms occurred in those areas of slave life whites found of marginal importance. Of what concern was it to a planter what kinds of stories slaves told in evenings on their cabin stoops or what kinds of motifs they wove into their baskets or sewed into their quilts? In this cultural twilight zone, which apparently had no effect on the plantation work routines or on the society's racial etiquette, blacks carved out a surprising and significant degree of autonomy. From this beachhead of cultural self-determination slaves resisted dehumanization and expanded control or at least influence over aspects of their life ranging from food supply to clothing styles.

With religion it was different. Whites did care what blacks believed, in part because the whites felt the truths of the gospel were too important to be left to "untutored" and "superstitious" slaves, in part because the masters correctly sensed the potentially liberating and even revolutionary implications of several scriptural doctrines. Whites worshiped with blacks and listened to the same sermons. Apparently slaves sat through the entire worship service, hearing the same theology the whites heard; only at the conclusion of the service, when the minister turned his special attention to the slaves in the gallery or back rows and addressed them in a short homily that was an addendum to the main sermon, did slaves have to endure the message of social control. Exhortations for slaves to obey their master and repeated admonitions not to lie or steal made religion seem safe to whites and also made many slaves doubt the intentions of the preacher. But the substance and the heart of the sermon was understood by the bondspeople, and that message of life-affirming joy, a message that obliterated one's this-worldly status and placed supreme value on steadfast faith, was more revolutionary than planters ever suspected.

Christianity taught that, in the eyes of God, slaves were the equals of their masters; it taught slaves that their souls were precious. It provided a context wherein slaves along with their masters struggled against the evil forces within themselves. Christianity was life-affirming for slaves as well as whites; it infused individuals of both races with joy and confidence. Strong emotions and fervent belief characterized the worship services of the free people as well as of the enslaved. In a social institution that defined them as no more than property, slaves found within the church powerful reassurance of their humanity. Within the church, one's earthly status was of less avail than one's spiritual status, and armed with faith, slaves discovered a profound guarantee of their worth as persons. Passivity and cynicism alike were overcome as bondspeople struggled to purify their lives through the discipline offered by the church. Slaves recognized the harmful effects of lying, stealing, violence against one another, drunkenness, and promiscuity, especially when fellow slaves were hurt. Consequently, they labeled such practices sinful, and when conversion promised to help them reform their lives, they, like all evangelicals, spoke of being freed from sin. Eloquent black preachers and devout laymen gave testimony to slaves' sense of responsibility, providing role models of enduring strength. The prototype of the Chosen People kept alive faith in a final retribution, and Jesus, as a personal friend and savior, offered daily encouragement to lives filled with suffering and toil. Religious slaves often felt themselves morally superior to their master, and the whites' disproportionate wealth and power had no effect on such self-confidence. Experiencing hope, joy, and purpose in their faith, Christian slaves found more than a will simply to survive physically. They survived as a people who amidst chattel slavery could find within themselves the power to love and care, the strength to forgive, and the patience to endure with their souls unshattered.

Psychologically, most slaves inwardly repudiated slavery and persevered remarkably intact. Certainly there were some whose sense of worth was gnawed away by the constant abuse, and these became virtual Sambos—spiritless, unresisting, and conforming to the white's desires. Other bondspeople displaced their anger at the institution of slavery onto those weaker than themselves and mistreated their spouses, their children, or the farm animals. Slaves occasionally fought among themselves, taking out their anger in blows against available enemies. Some committed suicide or lashed out blindly against offending whites and were killed as a consequence. Yet, the remarkable fact is not the expected social pathology, but the degree to which slaves succeeded in maintaining their families, their honor, and their sense of individual worth. As Thomas Wentworth Higginson recalled when he looked back on his wartime experience among black soldiers: "We abolitionists had underrated the suffering produced by slavery among the negroes, but had overrated the demoralization. Or rather, we did not know how the religious temperament of the negroes had checked the demoralization." Perhaps more than any other factor, Christianity in several forms—the biracial church, the independent black church, and the so-called invisible church—provided slaves with a purpose and a perspective with which to overcome slavery psychologically and spiritually and survive as humans.

As some critics have charged, in one sense much slave religion was otherworldly and escapist. Partly because their life in this world was frequently broken by separation and hardship and partly because the African heritage of an extremely foreshortened view of the world made the expansive Christian view of the hereafter exhilarating, slaves in their songs and sermons often reveled in blissful descriptions of heaven. Such raptures were to some extent compensatory. But elements of the descriptions—the portrayal of heaven as a place where all God's children have shoes, for example, and where there is no more work and where families and loved ones are united never to be torn apart again—were telling comments on life in this world. Moreover, the clear implication that slaves were destined for, and deserved, "a home in glory land" reveals a profound rejection of images of degradation and worthlessness. Belief by slaves that in the end they would occupy seats in heaven spoke volumes about their sense of God's justice, and their sense of eternal reward again raised the uplifting theme of identification with the Chosen People. Such beliefs no doubt worked against suicidal assaults against bondage, but these beliefs also immeasurably armed slaves for a more profound, inner repudiation of the bonds of slavery.

There is also some truth in another view, that slave religion was primarily a staging ground for black revolt. Surely black Christians saw the contradiction between the gospel's view of equality and freedom and the preacher's injunction that slaves must obey their masters. Throughout the history of Christianity, oppressed peoples have been inspired by the teachings of Jesus to attack their oppressors and repudiate their earthly rulers. No one can deny that Christianity raises the possibility of rebellion for the sake of conscience, and slave owners certainly were aware of that. Church participation, moreover, gave slaves a chance to develop leadership skills, to communicate with one another, and to cultivate the sense of common purpose and of injustice that could stimulate insurrection. For some slaves in particular situations, religion did motivate and facilitate rebellion. Most slave revolts in the United States, both those that were only planned and those actually undertaken, had a religious dimension, from the Stono revolt in 1739 to Nat Turner's rebellion in 1831. There was a fateful ambiguity at the heart of the slave's response to Christianity; the fervent rebel and the passive, long-suffering servant were equally authentic expressions of black religion. But in the Old South the overwhelming majority of slaves internalized rebellion, for they recognized the imbalance of power that made armed insurrection sheer futility.

Submission was, in many instances, merely a conscious decision, a way of coping with the exigencies of life in a slave society. Submission was not total but partial and controlled; it reflected the limited possibilities for overt action and the kind of sublimated moral rebellion permissible. For the huge majority of slaves, their folk Christianity provided them both a spiritual release and a spiritual victory. They could inwardly repudiate the system and thus steel themselves to survive it. This more subtle, more profound type of spiritual freedom made their Christianity the most significant aspect of slave culture and effectively defused much of the potential for insurrection. Repeatedly the narratives tell of slaves' having their souls "freed." One aged ex-slave remarked that she had often heard her mother say: "'I am so glad I am free.' I did not know then what she was talking about. I thought she meant freedom from slavery." It was precisely this belief that one was in the ultimate sense "free" that allowed countless slaves to persevere. In ways masters never suspected, the Christianity of blacks mitigated against slave uprisings and supported the essential humanity of a people defined as property.

The Civil War and emancipation brought many changes to southern blacks. Northern churchmen saw the South, with its four million freedpeople, as a fertile mission field. Northern churches—the Methodist Episcopal Church, the African Methodist Episcopal Church, the African Methodist Episcopal Church Zion, the Presbyterian Church, the Baptist Church, and the Reformed Episcopal Church—rushed to establish southern branches. Tens of thousands of ex-slaves withdrew from their former biracial churches and joined these new all-black churches. (Some white missionaries and scattered white northerners who had recently settled in the South were also members, but in the South churches affiliated with northern denominations became overwhelmingly dominated by blacks.) After the initial, formative stage, when northern missionaries were founding the churches, freedmen who had been slave preachers and exhorters led the new denominations. These men and their fervent congregations were part of the harvest of slave Christianity.

Across the South many thousands of freedpeople also withdrew from their former biracial churches and formed black versions of the southern denominations. The National Baptist Convention and the Colored Methodist Episcopal Church were the two largest of these new denominations. In all the black churches the theology, the ritual, and the organization were very similar to those of the white churches from which their membership was drawn. The numbers and devotion of the black worshipers and the adeptness of their ministers suggested the vitality of slave Christianity under the auspices of the parent southern churches. Even though slave members had not been accorded complete equality, they had practiced leadership roles, nurtured their sense of self-worth, and grown in faith. More a testimony to the humanity of the slaves than to their slaveowners' intentions, black participation in antebellum southern churches had been a critical proving ground for slave survival skills and cultural growth. The burgeoning of black churches after the Civil War points back to the centrality of Christianity in the slave community.

It should be pointed out that the blacks withdrew from the churches; they were not initially excluded. Many whites tried to persuade the freedpeople not to separate, both because they feared losing control over them and because they doubted the ability of blacks to preach the gospel "pure and undefiled." Still others genuinely hated to see a racial division in the church. But freedpeople had chafed under white control—even under well-intentioned white paternalism—for too long. Black faith was strong, black leaders were capable, and the black need for self-direction and autonomy was manifest. Consequently, southern churches became significantly more segregated after the Civil War, and the move away from joint worship was black-instigated. Despite the similarities in theology and organization, the two races have continued down separate denominational paths ever since. The differences between white and black Christianity—especially the expressed emotion, sermon style, and music—were greater in 1960 than they had been in 1860. Contemporary differences have obscured historical similarities. But that is only another one of the ironies of southern history.

QUESTIONS TO CONSIDER

1. Why was religion important for slaves?
2. What factors in the late eighteenth century combined to stimulate major changes in slave religion?
3. What evangelical practices tapped into memories of African religions?
4. What doctrines of Christianity made it appealing to slaves?
5. What practices of the biracial churches are most surprising to you? Why?
6. What was the "underground church?" How and why did it function?
7. How did Christianity serve slaves both as other-worldly escapism and as a stimulus to revolt?
8. Why did separate black churches emerge after the Civil War?

13

The Winning of the West Reconsidered*

Brian W. Dippie

If slavery was not the most important factor shaping the American character, for many decades historians and mythmakers alike offered an alternative nomination: the West. The mythic region symbolized for many the dreams and distinctives of Americanism. But the West has faded over the past generation as the embodiment of the American character. Where once it was the favorite setting for movies, television shows, novelists, and painters, it has slipped well behind space and the modern city as a popular venue for adventure. In part, this decline reflects the undermining of Frederick Jackson Turner's frontier thesis. Turner argued that the frontier had shaped the American character, stimulating individualism, self-reliance, practicality, optimism, and a democratic spirit. Since the 1950s, Turner's ideas have been the object of continual attack by historians. In this selection, Brian Dippie traces the challenges to Turner's hegemony and suggests that rather than the critics developing a new western history, they have fragmented the field into an unmanageable collection of disputants. The loss of the central myth of the West as the foundation of American values has sabotaged the common heritage on which writers built stories to entertain us.

Brian W. Dippie is a professor of history at the University of Victo-

*Reprinted by permission of the Woodrow Wilson International Center for Scholars from *The Wilson Quarterly,* summer 1990.

ria in British Columbia. He earned his Ph.D. at the University of Texas
in 1970 and has written a number of books on the West, reflecting
his special interest in the region.

We are now within easy striking distance of 100 years since Frederick Jackson Turner, following the lead of the Superintendent of the Census, proclaimed the end of the frontier and, with it, "the closing of a great historic moment": "The peculiarity of American institutions is, the fact that they have been compelled to adapt themselves to the changes of an expanding people—to the changes involved in crossing a continent, in winning a wilderness, and in developing at each area of this progress out of the primitive economic and political conditions of the frontier into the complexity of city life."

Then, in 1890, it was all over.

Turner, a young historian at the University of Wisconsin, delivered his paper on "The Significance of the Frontier in American History" at the 1893 meeting of the American Historical Association in Chicago. The setting gave point to his observations. Chicago was then playing host to a gargantuan fair, the World's Columbian Exposition, commemorating the 400th anniversary of the discovery of the New World. The session at which Turner spoke met on the Exposition grounds, where buildings coated in plaster of Paris formed a White City, symbolizing civilization's dominion over what not long before had been a wilderness on the shore of Lake Michigan. Chicago's magical growth was, in microcosm, the story of America. Four centuries after Columbus's landfall, a century since white settlers began occupying the interior of the continent, there was no frontier left, no vast reserve of "free land" to the west.

Turner's timing was acute, the psychological moment perfect to find symbolic meaning in recent events. The rise of the Ghost Dance movement, with its vision of a rejuvenated Indian America, the arrest and killing of Sioux leader Sitting Bull on December 15, 1890, the culminating tragedy at Wounded Knee two weeks later—all attested that the "winning of the West" was no longer a process but a *fait accompli.* Indian wars, a fact of American life since the first English colony was planted at Jamestown, were finished. There was no longer an Indian domain to contest; it had disappeared, along with the Jeffersonian vision of an agrarian democracy resting on an abundance of cheap land.

Whatever else farmer discontent represented in the 1890s, it manifested an awareness of the new urban-industrial order. America's twentieth-century future was reaffirmed in Chicago the year after the Exposition, when labor unrest erupted into violence and troops that had served on distant frontiers "taming" Indians were shipped in to tame Chicago's unemployed instead.

When Turner read his paper, then, portents were everywhere. Near the Exposition grounds, Buffalo Bill's Wild West show was offering the public its immensely popular version of the frontier experience. Sitting Bull's horse and the cabin from which the chief was led to his death were both on display. Frederic Remington, the artist most responsible for the public's perceptions of life in the West, was on hand to tour the Exposition's midway and to take in Buffalo Bill's show; a year later he was back in Chicago to cheer George Armstrong Custer's old unit, the "gallant Seventh," against, as he put it, "the malodorous crowd of anarchistic foreign trash."

It did not take a prophet to discern a pattern in all this, but Turner reached beyond the obvious. Frontiering, he argued, was not merely a colorful phase of American history. It had actually shaped the American character. On the frontier, environment prevailed over inherited culture. The frontier promoted individualism, self-reliance, practicality, optimism, and a democratic spirit that rejected hereditary constraints. In Turner's reading of U.S. history, the significance of the frontier was simply enormous. To understand American history, one had to understand western history. Whatever distinguished Americans as a people, Turner believed, could be attributed to the cumulative experience of westering: "What the Mediterranean Sea was to the Greeks, breaking the bond of custom, offering new experiences, calling out new institutions and activities, that, and more, the ever retreating frontier has been to the United States."

Turner's audience in Chicago received these ideas with polite indifference. In time, however, the frontier thesis gained influential adherents. For almost half a century, it served as the master explanation of American development. Problems of fact and interpretation were acknowledged. But Turner's essay offered a coherent, self-flattering vision of the American past, and it seemed prophetic in anticipating American involvement abroad. It would be "rash," Turner wrote, to "assert that the expansive character of American life has now entirely ceased. . . . [T]he American energy will continually demand a wider field for its exercise." Cuba and the Philippines soon proved him right. Like any good historical explanation, the frontier thesis seemed to account for past *and* future. Finally, its sweeping imagery and elegiac tone nicely matched the nostalgic mood, which, during the twentieth century, would make the mythic Wild West a global phenomenon.

The inadequacy of the frontier thesis did not become plain until the 1940s, after the complex industrial civilization it sought to explain had suffered through the Great Depression and risen to become a world power. But if American history was only temporarily under Turner's shadow, western history has never quite emerged.

Begin with the basics: time and place. Turner's West was a fluid concept, an advancing frontier line and a retreating area of free land. If one instead defined the West as a geographical entity—that old standby "the trans-Mississippi West," for example—then over half of western American history proper has transpired since Turner's 1890 cutoff date. What the Louisiana Purchase inaugurated in 1803 is an ongoing story of growth and change. The boundaries of this geographic West are usually set at the 49th parallel to the north, the Mexican border to the south, the Mississippi to the east, and the Pacific Ocean to the west, though historians have found each of these too arbitrary. Some see these boundaries as too inclusive to be meaningful, others as too restrictive. Historians of the fur trade might want to embrace all of North America, historians of the borderlands all of Mexico, students of outlawry the Old Southwest, and students of the Indian wars the Old Northwest.

Then there is the matter of time. Turner's frontier West ended with the nineteenth century. To effect a revolution in western history one need simply move forward into the twentieth. Immediately, most of the familiar signposts are missing: fur trade and exploration, Indian wars and Manifest Destiny (overland migration, war with Mexico, Mormonism, the slavery expansion controversy), gold rushes and railroad building, vigilantism and six-gun violence, trail drives and the open-range cattle industry, the farmers' frontier and the Populist revolt. Beyond 1900, a different West emerges, a hard-scrabble land rich in scenery and resources, perhaps, but thinly populated for the most part, chronically short of capital and reliant on government aid (such as cheap water and access to federal lands), a cultural backwater whose primary appeal nationally is as the setting for a romantic historical myth. Writing in a bittersweet key about the creation of these myths in *The Mythic West in Twentieth-Century America* (1986), historian Robert G. Athearn began by recalling his own boyhood sojourn at his grandfather's Montana ranch: "To me, the wilderness just couldn't hold a candle to indoor plumbing. Of course, I was just a kid, an unformed man whose regard for the freedom of the untouched country was yet nascent. I had not yet developed a sense of romance or the appreciation of idealized landscapes. I never before had felt suppressed or imprisoned. Not until I was locked into the Missouri River breaks and banished from the world, so to speak."

A romantic myth that is untrue for the present is probably untrue for the past as well. But redefining western history's subject-matter, twentieth-century perspective encourages a reassessment of the nineteenth century. That process began in 1955, when Earl Pomeroy of the University of Oregon published a breakthrough essay, "Toward a Reorientation of Western History: Continuity and Environment." Not only did it pull together many scholars' dissatisfactions with the frontier thesis; it offered a persuasive alternative.

The crux of Pomeroy's revision was in the word "continuity." "America was Europe's 'West' before it was America," a pair of literary critics once observed. Frontiering was a global phenomenon, as old as the idea of the West, which was freighted with significance even for the ancient Greeks. More than a direction or a place, the West was a cultural ideal signifying quest and the prospect of fulfillment in some elusive Elysium. To the west, then, myths ran their course, and America was simply a new stage for an old dream.

Charging the Turnerians with a "radical environmental bias," Pomeroy argued that inherited culture had strongly persisted in the West. Indeed, cultural continuity, imitation in everything from state constitutions to architectural styles, a deep conservatism only intensified by the process of moving away from established centers, and a constant search for respectability and acceptance—these, not individualism, inventiveness, and an untrammeled democratic spirit, were the real characteristics of the West. "Conservatism, inheritance, and continuity bulked at least as large in the history of the West as radicalism and environment," Pomeroy wrote. "The westerner has been fundamentally [an] imitator rather than [an] innovator. . . . He was often the most ardent of conformists."

For the popular image of the West as pathbreaker for the nation, Pomeroy substituted the West as a kind of colonial dependency, an area dominated by eastern values, eastern capital, eastern technology, eastern politics. To understand American development, one need no longer look west; but to understand western development, one *had* to look east. That was the essence of Earl Pomeroy's reorientation.

To historians born during the twentieth century, Pomeroy's version of the western past seems much nearer the mark than Turner's. Moreover, Pomeroy reinvigorated western history by suggesting subjects outside the frontier thesis that merited investigation—frontier justice, constitution-making, and politics and parties. His call was answered, most notably, by Yale's Howard Lamar, who sought to rectify the historical neglect of the later territorial period with *Dakota Territory, 1861–1889* (1956) and *The Far Southwest, 1846–1912: A Territorial History* (1966). In the latter, Lamar showed that the various cultures imported into the Southwest remained remarkably impervious to what Turner had regarded as the homogenizing influence of the frontier environment. "Throughout the territorial period New Mexico remained stubbornly and overwhelmingly

Spanish-American in culture, tradition-directed in habits, and Roman Catholic in religion. Indeed, Anglo-American citizens remained the minority ethnic group in New Mexico until 1928. Colorado, on the other hand, was essentially an American frontier mining society, which retained close business and social connections with the American East. The settlers of Utah, though partly native American in origin, felt so persecuted because of their firm belief in the Mormon religion—and the accompanying doctrine of polygamous marriage—that they deliberately developed their own unique social and political systems. . . . The diverse pioneer settlers of Arizona Territory, hailing from Mexican Sonora, the Confederate South, the American Northeast, and Mormon Utah, formed a conglomerate American frontier society not quite like any of the other three."

Another staple of revisionist western history is economic studies emphasizing the West's dependence on eastern investment capital. In his 1955 essay, Pomeroy wrote that the economic history even of "the pre-agricultural frontiers" would come to rest "on the cold facts of investment capital." However, he said, "we still know the homesteader better than the landlord, the railroad builder better than the railroad operator. The trapper, the prospector, and the cowboy, moving picturesquely over a background of clean air and great distances, hold us more than the tycoons and corporations that dominated them."

The revisionists had their work cut out. They showed, in William H. Goetzmann's memorable phrase, that even the trappers, those legendary embodiments of wanderlust, were Jacksonian men, expectant capitalists out to make their fortune. In *Bill Sublette, Mountain Man* (1959), John E. Sunder detailed the career of one of the most famous beaver trappers of the early nineteenth-century. Sublette frequently relied on eastern capital or credit to keep his dreams alive, and was almost as familiar with the business hotels of New York, Philadelphia, and Washington as he was with the backwoods.

According to legend, cowboys were second-generation mountain men, fiddle-footed wanderers with guns on their hips. Their status as what we now refer to as seasonal agrarian workers might be obscured by romance, but, Lewis Atherton noted in *The Cattle Kings* (1961), cowboys were simply hired hands who lived with the environment while their employers, the ranchers, were businessmen out to dominate it. "The cowboy's life involved so much drudgery and loneliness and so little in the way of satisfaction that he drank and caroused to excess on his infrequent visits to the shoddy little cowtowns that dotted the West. . . . Most of his physical dangers scarcely bordered on the heroic, necessary as they were in caring for other men's cattle, and they served primarily to retire him from cowpunching." Atherton shared the disparaging view of Bruce Sibert, a rancher in the Dakotas during the 1890s: "Only the few good ones got into the cow business and made good." For those who did become ranchers in "the cow business," Gene M. Gressley observed in *Bankers and Cattlemen* (1966), profit was the motive, capitalization a major problem. Again, eastern money figured prominently.

Nowhere was eastern domination more evident than on the mining frontier. Gold rushes thoroughly disrupted the stately progression of Turner's frontier line, making a shambles of his East-West advance and the stages of social evolution preceding urban civilization. As Richard Wade asserted in *The Urban Frontier* (1959), his history of early Pittsburgh, Cincinnati, Lexington, Louisville, and St. Louis, "The towns were the spearheads of the frontier."

Mining was a case in point. "On the mining frontier the camp—the germ of the city—appeared almost simultaneously with the opening of the region," Duane A. Smith wrote in *Rocky Mountain Mining Camps: The Urban Frontier* (1967). In California, the flood of gold-hungry Forty-Niners created an overnight urban civilization with eastern values. In his history of the Far West, *The Pacific Slope* (1965), Pomeroy noted that in 1860 California had a population three times that of Oregon, Washington, Idaho, Utah, and Nevada combined, and an economy thoroughly integrated into that of the Atlantic Seaboard. A network of eastern merchants and investigators supplied the California miners through West Coast middlemen. As miners dug deeper into the ground, overhead soared, and the need for capital with it. Thus, the network even stretched across the Atlantic. British investors contributed so heavily that they made the Far West part of Britain's "invisible empire," and provided the leadership to draw out more cautious American investors as well, Clark C. Spence explained in *British Investments and the American Mining Frontier, 1860–1901* (1958). It was not long before the fabled individual prospector and his trusty mule were eclipsed.

In advocating a reorientation of western history, Pomeroy had suggested various paths historians might follow to discover East-West continuities. The study of frontier justice would open into an examination of western legal history. Inquiry into frontier religion, literacy, education, and architecture would establish the westerners' cultural conservatism. Likewise, scrutiny of the U.S. Army in the West would show it to be only intermittently a fighting force but continuously a visible manifestation of the federal government and its role in promoting western development. Forest G. Hill's *Roads, Rails, and Waterways: The Army Engineers and Early Transportation* (1957) and Goetzmann's *Army Explorations in the American West, 1803–1863* (1959) responded to the challenge. Goetzmann went on to redirect the history of western exploration from the exploits of hardy individuals to a collective, nationalistic enterprise in which the federal government played a decisive part, the theme of his Pulitzer Prize-winning *Exploration and Empire: The Explorer and the Scientist in the Winning of the American West* (1966). Other histories showed that western communities routinely exaggerated the Indian threat in order to enjoy the benefits—payrolls, improved transportation and communication facilities, even a livelier social life—that an army presence brought. The link between East and West, metropolis and hinterland, federal government and frontier citizen, was everywhere a fact of western life. Even today, the federal government owns vast areas of the West.

By submerging regional in national concerns, "colonial" histories make western history, as such, of limited significance. Regional history is based on the assumption that there are meaningful differences between local and national developments. The South's claim to distinctiveness, historian C. Vann Woodward has argued, arose from its unique past, marked by the un-American experience of guilt arising from slavery, military defeat, and occupation. History, more than any other factor, accounted for southern uniqueness. But Pomeroy's argument robbed the West of its distinctiveness, making it simply an appendage of the East that was neither exceptional nor especially consequential in the history of the nation.

Opposition to that point of view was not long in coming, and it has usually worked some variation on the exceptionalist premise. Gerald D. Nash, the first historian to attempt a synthesis of twentieth century Western history, rejects Turner's 1890 cutoff date and agrees with Pomeroy that colonialism remained a fact of western life well into the twentieth century. But Nash argues that World War II liberated the West from its political, economic, and cultural dependency on the East. The year 1945 becomes a new dividing line in western history, signifying the moment not when the frontier passed into oblivion but when the West passed out of colonialism to become "a pace-setter for the nation."

Yet only by focusing on the Sun Belt, and especially on Southern California, is Nash able to make much of a case for the West as a twentieth-century pace-setter. One must be cautious in making parts of the West synonymous with the whole and, out of regional pride, discarding too readily the unflattering fact of western dependency.

Such caution characterizes Patricia Nelson Limerick's provocative new synthesis, *The Legacy of Conquest: The Unbroken Past of the American West* (1987). Limerick is skeptical about the talk of the New West, arguing instead for a continuity in western history uninterrupted by any turning points. In her mind, it is this continuity—not links to the East, but the defining western experience "of a place undergoing conquest and never fully escaping its consequences"—that validates a regional approach.

A legacy of conquest, of course, is consonant with Pomeroy's colonial thesis. But Limerick in effect views the East-West relationship from a western perspective rather than a national one. "With its continuity restored," she writes, "western American history carries considerable significance for American history as a whole. Conquest forms the historical bedrock of the whole nation, and the American West is a preeminent case study in conquest and its consequences."

"Celebrating one's past, one's tradition, one's heritage," she concludes, "is a bit like hosting a party: one wants to control the guest list tightly. . . . To celebrate the western past with an open invitation is a considerable risk: The brutal massacres come back along with the cheerful barn raisings, the shysters come back with the saints, contracts broken come back with contracts fulfilled."

Limerick calls her introduction "Closing the Frontier and Opening Western History," as if summoning her fellow historians to put away the toys of childhood and get on with the sterner duties of adulthood. Western historians today regularly berate themselves for failing to keep up with trends in the discipline, for glorying in narrative at the expense of analysis, for favoring the colorful and peripheral to the neglect of the ordinary and substantial. Hard riding makes for easy reading. The very qualities that explained the public's love affair with the West also explained western history's decline in academic circles.

Over the years, suggestions for revitalizing western history have been pretty conventional: Find out where everyone else is going and follow. Learn to quantify. Adopt social-science methodologies. Alter the very nature of historical inquiry and expression or fade into academic oblivion, western historians were warned. But the most extravagant claims for the new social history, for example, have been recanted, and dire predictions about the early demise of "old-fashioned" history have failed to come true. It is apparent now that the advocates of new history too often adopted the strategy of Melville's lightning-rod salesman and sold fear rather than necessity. To date, the net effect of the new history revolution has been new topics rather than a consistent new direction for western history, fragmentation rather than synthesis.

Turner's thesis is now notorious for excluding women and everyone whose skin was dark or whose language was not English. Indians were obstacles handy for demarking the frontier line and eliciting pioneer traits in the white men who would overcome them; women apparently stayed in the East until the land was tidied up and made presentable; Mexicans and other ethnics never existed.

Women have been a favorite topic of the new history. Studies of army wives and daughters, women teachers, women on the overland trails, farm women, prostitutes, divorcees, widows, and urban women have forever altered the sentimental stereotypes of sunbonneted pioneer mothers and soiled doves with hearts of gold.

Pomeroy's argument for cultural continuity has been echoed in discussions of one key issue: Did the move West liberate women from conventional sex roles or not? John Mack Faragher concludes *Women and Men on the Overland Trail* (1979) with a flat negative: "The move West called upon people not to change but to transfer old sexual roles to a new but altogether familiar environment." While confessing that she had hoped to find otherwise, Julie Roy Jeffrey, in *Frontier Women: The Trans-Mississippi West, 1840–1880* (1979), is forced to agree with Faragher: "The frontier experience served to reinforce many conventional familial and cultural ideas. . . . The concept of woman as lady, the heart of domestic ideology, survived."

Jeffrey did detect some changes in women's roles. Prostitutes, for instance, were treated as individuals in the West rather than simply as a pariah class. Polly Welts Kaufman in *Women Teachers on the Frontier* (1984) also strains against the limitations implied by the colonial interpretation, noting that the 250 women who went west to teach for the National Board of Popular Education before the Civil War decided to do so largely out of a desire for independence and control over their lives. Kaufman concedes, however, that teaching was among the few occupations that met "society's expectations for women." Liberation plays an even larger part in Paula Petrik's *No Step Backward: Woman and Family on the Rocky Mountain Mining Frontier, Helena, Montana, 1865–1900* (1987). The move west, Petrik maintained, did change things for some women, at least during the frontier period.

Another prominent strain of western historical scholarship takes the western myth itself as its subject. Americans have loved the Wild West myth with an abiding, though some say waning, passion. It has circled the globe in its appeal. To its critics, however, the myth is an invitation to the wrong set of values. It embodies an essentially conservative ethos— rugged individualism, stern justice, indifference or hostility to women and ethnics, exploitation of the environment, development at any cost. But it also embodies the American dream, and has served as the polestar for generations of immigrants who sought a greater measure of human happiness in a land of unrivaled wealth and opportunity.

It should come as no surprise, then, that the popular image of the Wild West is largely the work of outsiders meeting outside needs. There seems no escaping eastern domination. Pomeroy himself traced an aspect of this cultural imperialism in his imaginative *In Search of the Golden West: The Tourist in Western America* (1957). The West, he found, became whatever the eastern tourist wanted it to be: "[F]or 60 or 70 years . . . tourists had to be reassured, and westerners felt that they had to assure them, that the West was no longer wild and woolly—until fashions changed and it was time to convince them that it was as wild as it ever had been."

How wild was it to begin with? There is an established tradition in western history of separating fiction from fact to get at the truth behind the frontier's most storied individuals and episodes. Don Russell's *The Lives and Legends of Buffalo Bill* (1960), Joseph G. Rosa's *They Called Him Wild Bill: The Life and Adventures of James Butler Hickok* (1964, rev. 1974), William A. Settle, Jr.'s *Jesse James Was His Name; or, Fact and Fiction Concerning the Careers of the Notorious James Brothers of Missouri* (1966), Robert K. De Arment's *But Masterson: The Man and the Legend* (1979), and Jack Burrows's *John Ringo: The Gunfighter Who Never Was* (1987) are good examples of this approach to biography.

Cultural historians find the legends more arresting—and revealing—than the facts. Strip Billy the Kid of his myth and little of historical consequence remains. Even the number of his victims does not hold up under scrutiny. But the mythic Billy the Kid is full of interest, as Stephen Tatum explains in *Inventing Billy the Kid: Visions of the Outlaw in America* (1982). During the first 40 years after his death at the hands of Pat Garrett in 1881, writers (including Garrett himself in his *The Authentic Life of Billy, the Kid*) portrayed the Kid as the villain in "a romance story dramatizing civilization's triumph over a stubborn, resistant, and savage wilderness."

For roughly the next 30 years, however, Billy was portrayed in a more positive light. Disillusioned by the power of gangsters and the weakness and corruption of government, the Kid's "creators"—including the composer Aaron Copland, who wrote the score for the 1938 ballet, *Billy the Kid*—conjured up a new image. Because society is "unable to defend itself or recognize the evil within its own ranks," Tatum writes, "the outsider like the Kid enters the scene to save the day and restore a society of common people being threatened by evil bankers and their henchmen. Yet no matter how noble his actions, in this era the Kid is not integrated into society at story's end."

But after 1955, Tatum continues, inventions of the Kid "typically omit the romance framework of civilization's progress or foundation, and instead present a dehumanizing society at odds with an authentic individual's personal code." No longer is there much hope that the hero can transform the world; the Kid "appears in works that dramatize the individual at odds with society, a civil law unrelated to moral law, and violence hardly legitimated or regenerative." This culminated in the purely meaningless cinematic violence of Sam Peckinpah's famous *Pat Garrett and Billy the Kid* (1973). Today, the Kid awaits new myth-makers.

Since cultural values shift over time, myths, in order to remain relevant, shift their meanings as well. If the major challenge facing western history is to relate past to present in a meaningful way, the mythic approach has much to offer. It accounts for continuity *and* change. George Armstrong Custer is dead, his Last Stand long over. Why then do so many people continue to refight it? Why can they still see it in their minds? Why are passions still aroused by the man? We may dismiss Custer as a minor figure historically, but he was once a national hero, a martyr to cause and country, held up as a model for America's youth. His defenders still think him a paragon, if not a saint, and he has been compared to Jesus. His detractors regard him as a racist villain, fit symbol for America's mistreatment of its native peoples. In 1988, a Sioux activist likened him to Adolf Hitler and argued that the Custer Battlefield National Monument was as welcome in Indian country as a Hitler monument would be in Israel.

Myths have consequences, and Richard Slotkin's *Regeneration Through Violence: The Mythology of the American Frontier, 1600–1860* (1973) and *The Fatal Environment: The Myth of the Frontier in the Age of Industrialization, 1800–1890* (1985) are the most ambitious attempts yet to trace patterns of frontier mythology, from Cotton Mather through Walt Whitman and Theodore Roosevelt. So deeply has the language of the frontier myth been woven into our popular culture, he writes, "that it still colors the way we count our wealth and estimate our prospects, the way we deal with nature and with the nations so that the Myth can still tell us what to look for when we look at the stars."

Works like Slotkin's assume something Turner labored to prove: American exceptionalism. On the other hand, they encourage a reexamination of the qualities supposedly fostered by frontiering and which, according to Turner, combined to form the American character.

The character-forming western myth is marked by some notable omissions. "Where are the women in this tradition?" asked Helen Winter Stauffer and Susan J. Rosowski in *Women and Western American Literature* (1982). It is a question that cuts to the heart of a male myth steeped in escapist fantasies. The myth does include Indians, but simply as part of the savage Nature that the white pioneer was expected to subdue, a test of the sort that meets any quester after Elysium. The native *fact* offers its own rebuttal: The white man's occupation of America was an armed invasion, nothing more, nothing less.

When one moves from individuals and events and omissions to the qualities or traits revered in western myth, it is apparent that the myth generates its own critiques, its own counter-images.

Rugged individualists taming a raw wilderness? Roderick Nash's *Wilderness and the American Mind* (1967, rev. 1982) and Lee Clark Mitchell's *Witnesses to a Vanishing America: The Nineteenth-Century Response* (1981) show that frontiering and its apotheosis of axe and plow created a contrary reaction, a conservationist outlook that deplored the wastefulness inherent in pioneering and opened the way to resource management and federal controls.

Buoyant optimism and the mastery of material things? The lunacy of such hopeful frontier slogans as "Rain follows the plow" was revealed during the 1930s, when the interior of the continent turned into a dust bowl, spurring a massive internal migration that exposed the hollow promise of western opportunity. The California Dream? Ask the Okies.

Cowboy freedom in a spacious land where all were equal? Ask the multitude of western wage-earners who found the pay low, conditions hard, strife endemic, upward mobility limited, and independence illusory. Or ask any racial minority struggling to get ahead in the West.

Six-gun justice and self-reliance? The horrifying rate of contemporary violence would seem rebuttal enough to such a cherished tradition, but in *The Cattle Towns* (1968), Robert Dykstra shoots down the Hollywood version of Dodge City and its ilk.

Abundant natural resources ensuring all a chance to prosper? The antimyth points to the depletion and spoliation of a rich heritage, a destructive "Myth of Superabundance," and the rise of resource monopolization and agribusiness, the creation of a boom-and-bust economy, and a continuing reliance on the federal government. More colonialism, and precious little individual opportunity. Myth, after all, is myth.

For the historian, the western myth offers a skewed but revealing national portrait, a study not in what was but in what once seemed desirable. To the extent that it was always false, we have a measure of the distance between expectation and reality in western and American history. To the extent that it now seems unbecoming, we have a measure of the distance between the values of yesterday and today. The myth and the antimyth are keys to the western past and the western present that can also unlock the American past and the American present.

QUESTIONS TO CONSIDER

1. How did Frederick Jackson Turner say that the frontier had shaped the American character?
2. What are the standard boundaries of the "West?"
3. How did Earl Pomeroy challenge Turner's ideas in 1955?

4. How did mining reflect Pomeroy's challenge to Turnerian orthodoxy?
5. What are the theses of Gerald Nash and Patricia Limerick about Western development?
6. What group was most obviously neglected by Turner's view of the West? What do recent studies suggest about the impact of the move west on that group?
7. What major myths about the West have developed their own counter-myths?

14

The Know-Nothings*

Thomas Horrocks

Thomas Horrocks here raises a topic from the darker side of the American character. Nativism, the fear of and resistance to ideas and peoples different from the American norm, is an emotional movement that ebbs and flows with the passing of years. The antebellum period saw its most powerful direct expression in the American Party, but it would crest again in the 1920s and enjoy considerable success through the passage of the National Origins Act in 1924, cutting the flow of nontraditional immigrants to a trickle.

American historians of the past generation have increasingly tended to view politics and the political parties as functions of ethno-cultural factors more than economic or ideological beliefs. While the Democrats were historically the party most open to non-Anglo immigrants, the Federalists and then the Whigs attracted persons of English extraction and Puritan religious roots—in other words, establishment Americans. When the Whigs split over the slavery issue after the 1852 election, Northern Whigs joined with antislavery Democrats to organize the Republican Party. Southern Whigs were adrift. In 1856 they coalesced as the American Party, or Know-Nothings, then faded. In 1860 they comprised the bulk of the Constitutional Union Party. When the Democrats also split over

*Reprinted by permission of Cowles Magazines, Inc., publisher of *American History Illustrated*, January 1983.

slavery in 1860, they paved the way for victory for Lincoln and the Republicans, and the Civil War ensued.

After Reconstruction, the Southern Whigs continued to be in a quandary. They could not rejoin their ideological soulmates, the Republicans, for that party was anathema in the South because of its role in the war and its aftermath. They lacked sufficient strength to succeed alone. And so, almost by default, they drifted into the Democratic Party in the south, and for a century they contributed to the ideological conservatism and tendency toward nativism of Southern Democrats. Thus, the post-1938 congressional alliance between Republicans and Southern Democrats represents not an aberration, but, in essence, a reestablishment of the old Whigs.

In the 1983 article, Horrocks explains how antiforeignism, mixed with longstanding anti-Catholicism, combined to produce the American Party, a negative idea wrapping itself in the guise of patriotism, or "true" Americanism. These feelings still lurk in the American character today, generally below the surface, but sometimes erupting in ugly incidents of bigotry.

On the evening of June 22, 1856, former President Millard Fillmore arrived in New York City from a triumphant European tour. A rousing welcome, complete with fireworks and cannon-fire, greeted the former chief executive as his ship, the *Atlantic*, docked.

The several thousand spectators who waited on the pier were there not so much to welcome home their ex-president as to greet their presidential candidate. Fillmore, who had served in the Executive Mansion as a member of the Whig party, was now running for that high office again under the banner of a different party. He was the standard bearer for the American party, popularly known as the "Know-Nothings."

In the bitter presidential campaign of 1856, Fillmore and the Know-Nothings stressed Union over sectional politics. Unionism, however, was not the issue that elevated the Know-Nothings into a position of political prominence. They owed their extraordinary ascent to nativism, an issue equally as explosive as that of slavery in the decades prior to the Civil War.

The Know-Nothing party came into existence in response to the growing influence of both the Catholic church and the immigrant in American life. The political form that nativism embraced in mid-nineteenth-century America was a culmination of more than two centuries of hostility between Protestants and Roman Catholics.

The roots of this hostile relationship reach back to the Protestant Reformation. The first colonists who sailed to America in the seventeenth century carried with their luggage an intense distrust of Roman Catholicism. This attitude, transported from England and the Continent, pervaded all levels of colonial life. A perfect example of this fact is that, as late as 1700, Catholics were denied full civil and religious rights in all of the colonies except Rhode Island.

This sentiment toward Roman Catholicism rested on a belief held by many Protestants that the Church of Rome was closely linked with monarchism and reaction. During the period of the Early Republic many Americans regarded Catholicism as the antithesis of their democratic ideals. However, during those early years Roman Catholics made up a small part of the population.

But the Catholic church started to exhibit signs of rapid expansion during the 1830s. In the next two decades, five million immigrants, many of them Catholics from Germany and Ireland, sailed to America.

Inspired by an expanding membership, the Catholic hierarchy shed its timid and retiring image, and adopted a more confident and aggressive attitude. Catholic bishops throughout the country, led by Archbishop John Hughes of New York, began to demand legislation favorable to the Church. Catholic church leaders called for the elimination of Bible reading in the public schools, and the division of public school funds to aid a parochial school system. Many Protestants reacted with alarm, believing these demands to be a direct attack on two cherished American institutions, the Bible and the public school system.

In response to the active Catholic position, nativist organizations first started to appear in the 1830s and continued to multiply during the next two decades. Newspapers, pamphlets, and books, all warning of the perils of Catholicism, poured out from the presses into the hands of a receptive public. Whether in a sermon from the pulpit or a speech from the podium, nativist leaders alerted Americans of the imminent Papal plot to subvert the country.

The fervor that accompanied the nativist movement sometimes resulted in violence and destruction. Convent burning and bloody riots occurred in various cities. Mob violence in Philadelphia in 1844 left thirteen dead and over fifty wounded. Although nativist leaders contributed much to this uncontrolled emotion, the Catholic church was not totally blameless. Church leaders committed various blunders in their response to nativist accusations.

One such blunder occurred in November 1850, when Archbishop Hughes delivered a fiery speech to a crowd in Saint Patrick's Cathedral in New York City. The archbishop, known for his oratorical skills and his penchant for controversy, made use of the former and proceeded to become enmeshed in the latter. Responding to the charge that the Church planned to convert America, the archbishop declared that it was true and that "everybody should know it." This error on the part of an eminent Church leader contributed greatly to Protestant hysteria.

Soon all immigrants became a target of nativism, mainly because so many were Catholic. Many American Protestants regarded Catholic immigrants as the soldiers of the Vatican's plot to subvert the country. They also identified foreigners in general as the source of America's many social ills, blaming pauperism, a rising crime rate, and public drunkenness on the foreign element. More importantly, Americans believed the immigrants were taking jobs away from native-born workers and were corrupting the political process by voting in large blocs under the influence of crafty politicians.

By 1840 the nativist movement attracted a large following, especially from the ranks of the working class. Armed with a growing contingent of supporters, nativist leaders called upon politicians to address their concerns. Nativist leaders wanted legislation that would protect the Bible and the public school system. They also demanded a more strict naturalization process and stronger temperance laws.

The Democratic party, for the most part, turned a deaf ear to the nativists. From the beginning the party had vigorously courted the immigrant by representing itself as the voice of the "common man." The Democrats cultivated a strong alliance with foreigners in the large cities of the Northeast, where they tended to settle. The party was not about to alienate vital support by adopting the nativist program.

The Whig party, though more sympathetic toward nativism than were the Democrats, rarely acted on behalf of the nativists. At that time the Whigs were a moribund party. This was no more apparent than in the big cities of the Northeast, where the Whigs were losing the contest for the immigrant voter. Nevertheless, some party members still favored recruiting foreign-born voters. Thus, the party failed to take a decisive stand on the controversial issue of nativism.

Nativist leaders found little satisfaction in the meager response from the two major parties. Those Americans who zealously sought restrictions on the Catholic church and the immigrant had to look outside the two-party system for political redress. Their search resulted in the Know-Nothing party.

The Know-Nothings originated in New York City, which had been the scene of intense political involvement by Catholic leaders as well as a city hard hit by immigration. By 1840 New York had become the center of organized nativism. Secret societies such as the Order of United Americans (O.U.A.) and the Order of the Star Spangled Banner were created by citizens who feared the spread of Catholicism and the infiltration of the foreign-born.

The Order of the Star Spangled Banner was founded in 1850 by a thirty-four-year-old New York City businessman, Charles B. Allen. Emphasizing secrecy, members referred to themselves as the "Sires of '76" to conceal their true identity. "I know nothing" was their usual reply when questioned about their activities. Horace Greeley, editor of the *New York Tribune,* referred to them as the Know-Nothings, thus bestowing upon the Order its popular name.

The O.U.A., another secret nativist society established in 1844, played an influential role in the growth of the Know-Nothings. In 1852 members of the O.U.A. took over control of the party. The Know-Nothings then came under the direction of James W. Barker, a dry goods merchant who possessed a talent for organization. Under Barker's leadership the Know-Nothings became a vibrant political machine. By 1853 they had lodges throughout New York, with branches in New Jersey, Connecticut, Maryland, and Ohio.

Naturally the goals of the party reflected the nativist philosophy of its members. The Know-Nothings aimed "to resist the insidious policy of the Church of Rome" and to elect "none but native-born Protestant citizens" to public office. The party also pledged itself to protect the civil and religious rights of all Americans and to defend the Constitution.

The Know-Nothings pursued all of their goals under the rituals of secrecy. Diverse methods of communications, such as passwords, signs, grips, and signals of distress, were employed to conceal party operations. Meetings were called by distributing heart-shaped pieces of white paper. Red pieces sent to the members signaled danger.

By 1853 the Know-Nothings were secretly backing their own candidates for political office, or those of other parties, usually conservative Whigs. Because of the secrecy of their actions, Know-Nothing candidates astonished political observers when they were elected. Candidates who believed they were running unopposed and felt assured of victory found themselves on the losing end against an unknown opponent. All that the Democrats and Whigs could do was to watch helplessly as the Know-Nothings achieved success after success.

And successes there were! In the spring elections of 1854 the Know-Nothings recorded dramatic victories in Massachusetts, Delaware, and Pennsylvania. In Massachusetts the Know-Nothings not only elected a governor, but gained control of every state office as well. In the state legislature the Know-Nothings possessed every seat but two. In 1854 the party sent about seventy-five congressmen to Washington.

More surprising victories followed in 1855. By the end of that year the Know-Nothings controlled all the northeastern states except Vermont and Maine. The party also dominated the state governments of California and Tennessee. In many middle-Atlantic and southern states the Know-Nothings had replaced the Whigs as the major Democratic opposition.

The Know-Nothings quickly became the rage of the day. "Know-Nothing Candy," "Know-Nothing Tea," and "Know-Nothing Toothpicks" were popular items on store shelves. The party's name marked the sides of stagecoaches and omnibuses to attract riders. Nativist books appeared bearing the monogram "K.N." on their covers. The *North Carolina Weekly Standard* even printed a Know-Nothing menu for those possessing nativist tastes.

Though the Know-Nothings rose to political power because of the overwhelming popularity of nativism, the slavery issue quickly overshadowed the grievances against foreigners. The controversy over slavery was not new to the American political landscape. Twice before, in 1820 and in 1850, the issue had precipitated national crises, but compromise averted possible confrontation between North and South. With the passage of the Kansas-Nebraska Act in 1854, the avenue of compromise was forever closed.

The Kansas-Nebraska bill, based on the idea of popular sovereignty, allowed the question of slavery in those two territories to be decided by the settlers themselves. Until their decision, slavery would be legal in both territories because the Kansas-Nebraska Act repealed the Missouri Compromise of 1820. (The Missouri Compromise, held sacred by northern opponents of slavery, prohibited southern slaveholders from taking their slaves into any region above 36°30'.)

The passage of the Kansas-Nebraska Act opened the old wounds of sectionalism. Northerners greeted the act with outrage. Opponents of slavery, seeing land once reserved for freedom now open to slaveholding, gathered their forces in an attempt to stop the spread of an institution they considered abominable. The Kansas-Nebraska Act, along with the violence and bloodshed that followed in the wake of its passage, had a profound effect on the Democratic and Whig parties, as well as the Know-Nothings.

Democratic Senator Stephen A. Douglas of Illinois had sponsored the Kansas-Nebraska Act. As a result, many Northern Democrats left the party, feeling that it had fallen under the influence of a Southern slavocracy. These Democrats, together with antislavery Whigs, joined a coalition to fight the expansion of slavery. This coalition became the Republican party.

The disarray of the two-party system left many politicians without a political home. Conservative Whigs, seeing a dim future within their crumbling organization, believed that the Know-Nothing party would best serve their interests. Finding sectional politics distasteful, conservative Whigs turned to the Know-Nothing platform of conservatism, patriotism, and devotion to the Constitution. They also found the Know-Nothings' popularity with the American voter much to their liking.

A group of conservative Whigs, close associates of former President Fillmore, gained control of the Know-Nothing party, which had originally drawn its leaders from the ranks of the young and the working class. These men, attracted to the party by its newness and its concern for the people, were to a large extent politically inexperienced. Consequently, the Whigs had little trouble moving into positions of control within the party.

Once there, the Whigs proceeded to turn the Know-Nothings into an anti-Democratic organization that all men of the conservative Whig persuasion would find appealing. On the issue of slavery, the new Know-Nothing leaders adhered to the standard conservative Whig philosophy: compromise sectional politics. However, the most important change brought about by the new party leaders concerned nativism. The issue that furnished the Know-Nothings with their greatest political victories was now deemphasized to broaden the party's popular appeal, but the shift in emphasis disillusioned ardent Know-Nothing supporters.

With their vision fixed on the 1856 presidential election, the new Know-Nothing strategists now searched for a candidate who would be compatible with their conservative program. To his powerful friends and advisors in the party, Fillmore seemed to be the obvious choice. Fillmore had hopes of reviving the lifeless Whig party, but he soon realized the futility of such an undertaking. Although not a true nativist, he came to see the Know-Nothing party as an excellent vehicle for Whigs like himself to pursue their political goals.

Philadelphia hosted the Know-Nothing nominating convention, which opened on February 22, 1856. Several days before the opening session, party leaders arrived in the city to draft the party platform. The finished document emphasized Unionism and called for restraints on foreigners. In the meantime, the Know-Nothings had changed their name to the American party and lifted their veil of secrecy.

Twenty-seven states sent delegates to the convention. Know-Nothing leaders tried to evade the issue of slavery, but with the south's peculiar institution dominating national politics, the delegates could not escape its divisive effects. Almost immediately, they became involved in a heated debate over the issue. Northern delegates offered a resolution stating that no candidate should be nominated who did not favor the prohibition of slavery north of latitude 36°30'. The Fillmorites in control of the proceedings wanted no part of such a controversial plank; thus the resolution was tabled. As a result, a majority of the Northern delegates walked out of the convention.

Now basically a southern affair, the Know-Nothing convention nominated Fillmore and Andrew Jackson Donelson of Tennessee as their presidential and vice-presidential candidates. The Republican party nominated the glamorous "Pathfinder of the West," John C. Frémont, with the slogan "Free Speech, Free Soil and Frémont." In denouncing the Kansas-Nebraska Act, the Republicans called for the prohibition of slavery in any new territories. The Democrats, on the other hand, drafted a platform that defended Douglas's doctrine of popular sovereignty. They elected James Buchanan of Pennsylvania, who was minister to England under President Franklin Pierce, as their standard bearer.

Fillmore's advisors, having sent their candidate on a tour of Europe to escape the bitter debate over the Kansas-Nebraska issue, planned a gala reception for the former president's return. The political extravaganza was to mark the beginning of what the Know-Nothings hoped would be a successful campaign. However, when Fillmore walked off the *Atlantic*, his party was politically wounded. The Northern delegates who bolted the party backed the Republican candidate, thus denying the Know-Nothings vital Northern support.

Traveling from New York City to his hometown of Buffalo, Fillmore made twenty-seven public addresses. Throughout all of his speeches, the Know-Nothing candidate condemned the sectional policies of his two rivals and continually stressed the need of preserving the Union. Nativists who listened to Fillmore speak were disappointed because the ex-president seldom referred to their concerns.

Fillmore only mentioned the word "Catholic" once. In a speech to a crowd in Rome, New York, he spoke of his recent visit to another city of the same name and of his meeting with the Pope. The candidate assured his audience that he "had not become a Roman Catholic—far from it." Gone forever were the vitriolic anti-Catholic attacks of previous Know-Nothing campaigns. In fact, the lack of nativism in Fillmore's campaign led the Church hierarchy to believe that the Know-Nothings no longer posed a threat to American Catholics.

The Know-Nothings' attempt to evade the slavery issue and their downplay of nativism left them with an emotionless, ineffective platform. Nor did the party take real advantage of flaunting Unionism to the American public. In Fillmore, the Know-Nothings possessed a candidate of restraint and dignity, but these traits were of no value in an emotional campaign marked by bitterness.

Any hopes the Know-Nothings had of electing a president dissipated swiftly as the campaign progressed. When it became clear that Fillmore had no chance of winning, many conservative Whigs deserted the Know-Nothing fold.

Fearing that a Republican victory would dangerously heighten the sectional crisis, many influential Whigs swallowed their anti-Democratic feelings and voted for Buchanan. Among this group were Fletcher Webster and James B. Clay, sons of the former Whig heroes, and Rufus Choate, who believed that it was the Whigs' duty "to defeat and dissolve the new geographical, [Republican] party."

In November 1856, James Buchanan was elected president, defeating Frémont by one-half million votes and Fillmore by a million. The only state that Fillmore carried was Maryland. The Know-Nothing candidate received a surprising forty-four percent of the Southern vote.

Upon inspection, the election was much closer than the numbers indicate. Had only about eight thousand voters in Kentucky, Louisiana, and Tennessee cast their lot with Fillmore, those states would have gone to the ex-president and would have sent the election to the House of Representatives, where a Know-Nothing victory would not have been impossible.

The Know-Nothing party suffered a rapid decline after 1856. The party ceased to exist on the national level the next year when its national council held its final meeting. From 1857 through 1860 the Know-Nothings survived only at state and local levels. In the North, Know-Nothing supporters generally migrated into the ranks of the Republican party. In the South, many of the remaining Know-Nothings tended to be vigorously anti-Democratic, supporting the Constitutional Union party in 1860.

The party's legislative record was a dismal failure. Even at the state level, where the party had once won its greatest victories, the Know-Nothings failed to win concrete gains in their nativist campaign. To a great extent their poor record can be attributed to political inexperience. Many Know-Nothing office holders performed ineffectively because they did not understand the process of legislative initiative. Moreover, when the issue of slavery came to dominate debate in Congress, the Know-Nothings lost whatever chance they might have had for a successful program.

By the time Abraham Lincoln became president, the Know-Nothings had passed from the American political scene. Millard Fillmore was in retirement, no longer harboring political aspirations. Newspapers were no longer printing Know-Nothing menus, and "Know-Nothing Candy," "Know-Nothing Tea," and "Know-Nothing Toothpicks" gathered dust on the shelves of stores that catered to an eager clientele whose tastes turned to newer fads.

QUESTIONS TO CONSIDER

1. Define nativism.
2. What was the core of Know-Nothing belief?
3. Why was anti-Catholicism so powerful in the United States?
4. Where was the source of the Know-Nothing movement? How did the name develop?
5. What happened to the Know-Nothing movement?

15

The Glorious
and the Terrible*

Allan Nevins

Allan Nevins (1890–1971), a longtime Columbia University professor, stands in the first rank of twentieth-century historians. His writing is well-balanced, judicious, thorough, conscientious, and, as this article demonstrates, very readable. A biographer of Grover Cleveland, Hamilton Fish, and John D. Rockefeller, Nevins earned his greatest acclaim with his eight-volume *Ordeal of the Union,* a detailed study of the nation between 1846 and 1865.

In this article, written for *Saturday Review* on the centennial of the Civil War, Nevins takes issue with historians for overplaying the pageantry and splendor of the war at the expense of the slaughter and destruction we all know to be a part of it. Civil War general William Tecumseh Sherman allegedly originated the cliche "war is hell," but his wisdom has been sadly neglected by historians in favor of "the floating banners, the high-ringing cheers, the humors of the camp, the ardors of the charge," and the romance of it all. Nevins makes the terrible side of the war come vividly alive, not least in his depiction of the hatred engendered by the conflict, a hatred that survived to poison succeeding generations.

In an age for which total war might very well mean the end of the human race, Nevins offers a needed corrective to those who see war as a way to toughen up a nation gone soft. That macho

*Reprinted by permission of Omni Publications, New York, publisher of the *Saturday Review,* September 2, 1961.

strain within the national character has ebbed and flowed in popularity, with Theodore Roosevelt its most famous proponent. In the years following 1961, the United States fought an undeclared war in Vietnam whose horrors were brought home vividly to the populace via the television news. Thoroughly unglamorous, the Vietnam War may have painfully accomplished what Nevins sought to do.

Every great war has two sides, the glorious and the terrible. The glorious is perpetuated in multitudinous pictures, poems, novels, statues: in Meissonier's canvasses of Friedland and Austerlitz, Byron's stanzas on Waterloo and Tennyson's on the Light and Heavy brigades, St. Gaudens's Sherman riding forward victory-crowned, Freeman's "Lee." The terrible is given us in a much slighter body of memorabilia: Jacques Callot's gruesome etchings of the Thirty Years War, Goya's paintings of French atrocities in Spain, Zola's "The Debacle," Walt Whitman's hospital sketches, and the thousand-page novels that drearily emerged from the Second World War.

The two aspects do exist side by side. Every student of war comes upon hundreds of veracious descriptions of its pomp and pageantry, innumerable tales of devotion and heroism. They exalt the spirit. Yet every such student falls back from his exaltation upon a sombre remembrance of the butchery, the bereavement, and the long bequest of poverty, exhaustion, and despair. In observing the centenary of the Civil War, every sensible man should keep in mind that the conflict was a terrible reproach to American civilization and a source of poison and debilities still to be felt.

If it were not true that its debits far outweighed its credits, we might conclude that the republic would profit by a civil war in every generation, and that we should have commemorated Bull Run last July by again setting Yankee boys and Southern boys to killing each other. The mind recoils from the thought. But as the Civil War histories, novels, and motion pictures continue to pour forth, we shall be fortunate if we escape two very erroneous views.

The first view is that the war can somehow be detached from its context and studied as if it stood alone, without reference to causes or effects. War in fact, as Clausewitz long ago insisted, does not stand apart from and opposed to peace. It is simply a transfer of the normal inescapable conflicts of men from the realm of adjustment to that of violence. It represents not a complete transformation of national policy, but a continuance of policy by sanguinary means. That is, it cannot be understood without regarding both its causes and its results. Our Civil War, as Walt Whitman insisted, grew peculiarly out of national character. The other erroneous view is that the Civil War was, in the phrase of that graphic military historian Bruce Catton, a "Glory Road."

"Consider it not so deeply," Lady Macbeth says to her husband, stricken by the thought of red-handed murder; and "Consider it not so deeply," people instinctively say to those who remind them of war's inhuman massacre. Who wishes to while away an idle hour by looking at the harrowing pictures in the "Medical and Surgical History" of the war? It is a trick of human memories to forget, little by little, what is painful, and remember what is pleasant, and that tendency appertains to the folk memory as well. One of the finest descriptive pieces of the war was written by the true-hearted Theodore Winthrop, novelist and poet, just after his regiment crossed the Potomac on a spring night in 1861 to encamp on the Virginia side. It is rapturous in its depiction of the golden moon lighting a path over the river, the merry files of soldiers, the white tents being pitched in the dewy dawn. But ere long Winthrop was slain at Big Bethel in an engagement too blundering, shabby and piteous for any pen. We remember the happy march but forget the death.

Or take two contrasting scenes later in the war, of the same day—the day of Malvern Hill, July 1, 1862. That battle of Lee and McClellan reached its climax in the gathering dusk of a lustrous summer evening, no breath of wind stirring the air. The Union army had placed its ranks and its artillery on the slope of a great hill, a natural amphitheatre, which the Southerners assaulted. Participants never forgot the magnificence of the spectacle. From the Confederate and Union guns stately columns of black smoke towered high in the blue sky. The crash of musketry and deeper thud of artillery; the thunder of gunboat mortars from the James River, their shells curving in fiery golden lines; the cavalry on either flank, galloping to attack; the foaming horses flying from point to point with aides carrying dispatches; the steady advance of the Confederate columns and the unyielding resistance of the dense Union lines; then as darkness gathered, the varicolored signal lights flashing back and forth their messages—all this made an unforgettable panorama.

Both novelist and poet almost instinctively turn to the heroic aspects and picturesque incidents of war. Lowell's *Commemoration Ode,* one of the half-dozen finest pieces of literature born from the conflict, necessarily eulogizes the heroes; Mary Johnston's *The Long Roll,* perhaps the best Southern war novel, celebrates the ardors, not the anguishes, of Stonewall Jackson's foot-cavalry; St. Gaudens's monument on Boston Common to Robert Gould Shaw and his black infantry—the men whose dauntless hearts beat a charge right up the red rampart's slippery swell—shows the fighters, not the fallen. The historian assists in falsifying the picture. Cold, objective, he assumes that both the glorious and horrible sides exist, and need no special emphasis. He thus tends to equate the two, although the pains and penalties of war far outweigh its gleams of grandeur.

Then, too, a problem of expression impedes the realistic writer. It is not difficult to describe the pageantry of Pickett's charge. But when we come to the costs, what can we say except that the casualties were 3000 killed, 5000 wounded? It is impossible to describe the agony of even one soldier dying of a gangrened wound, or the heartache of one mother losing her first born; what of 10,000 such soldiers and mothers? Moreover, most historians, like the novelists and poets, have an instinctive preference for the bright side of the coin. Henry Steele Commager's otherwise fine introduction to his valuable compilation *The Blue and The Gray* has much to say about gallantry and bravery, but nothing about the squalor, the stench, and the agony.

If we protest against the prettification of the Civil War, the thoughtless glorification of what was essentially a temporary breakdown of American civilization, we must do so with an acknowledgment that it did call forth many manifestations of an admirable spirit. The pomp and circumstance, the parade and pageantry, we may dismiss as essentially empty. The valor of the host of young men who streamed to the colors we may deeply admire, but as valor we may fortunately take it for granted, for most men are brave. The patriotic ardor displayed in the first months of the war may also be taken for granted. What was highly impressive was the serious, sustained conviction, the long-enduring dedication, of countless thousands on both sides for their chosen cause. This went far beyond the transient enthusiasms of Sumter and Bull Run; far beyond ordinary battlefield courage. Lecky was correct in writing: "That which invests war with a certain grandeur is the heroic self-sacrifice which it elicits." All life is in a real sense a conflict between good and evil, in which every man or woman plays a part. A host of young Americans felt that they were enlisted in this larger struggle, and regarded their service to the North or South as part of a lifetime service to the right.

Those who seek examples of this dedication can find them scattered throughout the war records. Lincoln specially admired his young friend Elmer Ellsworth, who had endured poverty and hardship with monastic devotion to train himself for service; Lee specially admired John Pelham, the daring artillerist. Both gave their lives. Some fine illustrations of the consecrated spirit can be found in the two volumes of the *Harvard Memorial Biographies* edited by Thomas Wentworth Higginson just after the war. The ninety-eight Harvard dead were no better than the farm lads from Iowa or Alabama, the clerks from New Orleans or New York, but some of them had special gifts of self-expression. Hearken, for example, to Colonel Peter A. Porter, who wrote in his last will and testament:

> I can say, with truth, that I have entered on the course of danger with no am-
> bitious aspirations, nor with the idea that I am fitted, by nature, or experi-

ence, to be of any important service to the government; but in obedience to the call of duty, demanding every citizen to contribute what he could, in means, labor, or life, to sustain the government of his country—a sacrifice made the more willingly by me when I consider how singularly benefitted I have been, by the institutions of the land. . . .

As we distinguish between the shining glory of the war—this readiness of countless thousands to die for an enduring moral conviction—and the false or unimportant glories, so we must distinguish between the major and the lesser debits of the conflict. Some evils and mischiefs which seemed tremendous at the time have grown less in the perspective of years; some which at first appeared small now loom large.

It was one of the bloodiest of all wars; the total deaths in the Union and Confederate armies have been computed at about 620,000; and one of the facts which appalls any careful student is the enormous amount of suffering on the field and in the hospitals. The evidence of this, while not within the view of general readers, is incontrovertible. Armies the world over in 1860 were *worse* provided with medical and surgical facilities than in Napoleon's day. The United States, after its long peace, began the war with practically no medical service whatever. Surgical application of the ideas of Pasteur and Lister lay in the future. Almost every abdominal wound meant death. Any severe laceration of a limb entailed amputation, with a good chance of mortal gangrene or erysipelas. The North systematically prevented shipments of drugs and surgical instruments to the south, a measure which did not shorten the conflict by a day, but cost the Southern troops untold agony. Had it not been for the Sanitary Commission, a body privately organized and supported, Northern armies would have duplicated the experience of British forces in the Crimea; yet Secretary of War Stanton at first deliberately impeded the Commission's work.

The story of battle after battle was the same. Night descended on a field ringing with cries of agony: Water! Water! Help!—if in winter, Blankets! Cover! All too frequently no help whatever was forthcoming. After some great conflicts the wounded lay for days, and sometimes a week, without rescue. Shiloh was fought on a Sunday and Monday. Rain set in on Sunday night, and the cold April drizzle continued through Tuesday night. On Tuesday morning nine-tenths of the wounded still lay where they fell; many had been there forty-eight hours without attention; numbers had died of shock or exhaustion; some had even drowned as the rain filled depressions from which they could not crawl. Every house in the area was converted into a hospital, where the floors were covered with wretches heavily wounded, sometimes with arms or legs torn off, who after the first bandages, got no nursing, medical care, or even nourishment.

"The first day or two," wrote a newspaper reporter, "the air was filled with groans, sobs, and frenzied curses, but now the sufferers are quiet; not from cessation of pain, but mere exhaustion." Yet at this time the war was a year old.

Still more poignant versions of the same story might be given. Lee and Pope fought Second Manassas on the last Friday and Saturday in August, 1862, so near Washington that groups standing on housetops in the capital heard the rumble of artillery. The battleground, five miles long and three wide, was thickly strewn with dead and wounded. Pope retreated in confusion; many in Washington feared the city might be taken. In these circumstances, as late as the following Wednesday one member of the inadequate body of surgeons estimated that 2000 wounded had received no attention. Many had not tasted food for four days; some were dying of hunger and thirst. A reporter for the Washington *Republican* wrote on Thursday that some dying men could yet be saved by prompt help. And on Friday, a week after the battle began, a correspondent of the New York *Tribune* told of heart-rending scenes as the doctors searched among heaps of putrefying dead men for men yet clinging to life—men who, when anyone approached, would cry "Doctor, come to *me*; you look like a kind man; for God's sake come to *me*."

Anyone who is tempted to think of Gettysburg only in terms of its heroic episodes, its color and drama, should turn to the pages in *Battles and Leaders* in which General John D. Imboden describes the transport of the Confederate wounded, after their defeat, back into Maryland. He was ordered to ride to the head of the long wagon column as, in darkness and storm, it moved south:

> For four hours I hurried forward on my way to the front, and in all that time I was never out of hearing of the groans and cries of the wounded and dying. Scarcely one in a hundred had received adequate surgical aid, owing to the demands on the hard-working surgeons from still worse cases that had to be left behind. Many of the wounded in their wagons had been without food for thirty-six hours. Their torn and bloody clothing, matted and hardened, was rasping the tender, inflamed, and still oozing wounds. Very few of the wagons had even a layer of straw in them, and all were without springs. The road was rough and rocky from the heavy washings of the preceding day. The jolting was enough to have killed strong men, if long exposed to it. From nearly every wagon as the teams trotted on, urged by whip and shout, came such cries and shrieks as these:
> "My God! Why can't I die?"
> "My God! Will no one have mercy and kill me?"
> "Stop! Oh, for God's sake stop just for one minute; take me out and leave me to die on the roadside."
> Occasionally a wagon would be passed from which only low, deep

moans could be heard. No help could be rendered to any of the sufferers. No heed could be given to any of their appeals. Mercy and duty to the many forbade the loss of a moment in the vain efforts then and there to comply with the prayers of the few. On! On! We must move on. The storm continued and the darkness was appalling. There was no time even to fill a canteen with water for a dying man; for, except the drivers and the guards, all were wounded and utterly helpless in that vast procession of misery. During this one night I realized more of the horrors of war than I had in all the preceding two years.

After such a description, we can understand why a radical Northern Senator, looking across the battlefield of the Wilderness as fighting ended, told Hugh McCulloch that if in 1861 he had been given one glimpse of the agonies he there beheld, he would have said to the South: "Erring sisters, go in peace." John Esten Cooke was right in his elegy for Pelham; the living were brave and noble, but the dead were the bravest of all.

Yet *this* was far from being the ugliest side of the war. Nor was the suffering in the huge prison camps, South and North, part of the worst side of war; the suffering which MacKinlay Kantor describes in his novel and to which Benet briefly adverts in *John Brown's Body:*

> *The triple stockade of Andersonville the damned,*
> *Where men corrupted like flies in their own dung*
> *And the gangrened sick were black with smoke and their filth.*

What maims the bodies of men is less significant that what mains their spirit.

One ugly aspect of the Civil War too generally ignored is the devastation, more and more systematic, that accompanied it. For three reasons too little has been said of this devastation; the facts were kept out of official reports, the tale is too painful, and the recital easily becomes monotonous. Yet by 1862 the war in the South had become one of general depredation; by 1863, of wanton destruction; and by 1864, of an organized devastation which in terms of property anticipated the worst chapters of the two world wars. Georgia and the Shenandoah suffered in 1864 almost precisely as Belgium and Serbia suffered in 1914—the executions omitted. It was barbaric, and the only excuse to be made is that war is barbarism.

The turning point in the attitude of Northern military men was reached when General John Pope on July 18, 1862, issued from Washington headquarters a set of Draconian general orders. Order No. 5 directed that the army should subsist as far as practicable upon the country, giving vouchers for supplies seized. Order No. 7 decreed the summary execution of persons caught firing upon Union troops from houses. Order No. 11 (five days later) required officers to arrest immediately all disloyal males within reach, to make them take the oath of allegiance or go South, and to shoot all who violated their oath or who returned from the Confederacy. The order for living on the country, widely publicized East and West, changed the attitude of troops, and inspired private looting as well as public seizures of property. Pope was soon ousted, but the moral effect of his orders persisted.

Though most of the facts were excluded from official reports, their sum total, insofar as one shrewd observer could arrive at it, may be found in John T. Trowbridge's graphic volume written in 1866, *A Picture of the Desolated States.* In his preface Trowbridge speaks of the Union forces not as our heroic armies but our destroying armies. Even this practiced reporter is less graphic, however, than the people who suffered under the onslaught and wrote while their emotions, like their property, still burned. Hear a lady of Louisiana tell what occurred when N. P. Banks's army passed:

> I was watching from my window the apparently orderly march of the first Yankees that appeared in view and passed up the road, when, suddenly, as if by magic, the whole plantation was covered with men, like bees from an overthrown hive; and, as far as my vision extended, an inextricable medley of men and animals met my eye. In one place, excited troopers were firing into the flock of sheep; in another, officers and men were in pursuit of the boys' ponies, and in another, a crowd were in excited chase of the work animals. The kitchen was soon filled with some, carrying off the cooking utensils and the provisions of the day; the yard with others, pursuing the poultry. . . . They penetrated under the house, into the outbuildings and into the garden, stripping it in a moment of all its vegetables. . . . This continued during the day . . . and amid a bewildering sound of oaths and imprecations. . . . When the army had passed, we were left destitute.

Sherman believed in total war; that is, in waging war not only against the Southern armies, but the Southern people. His theory was that every man, woman, and child was "armed and at war." He wrote his wife in the summer of 1862 that the North might fall into bankruptcy, "but if they can hold on the war will soon assume a turn to extermination, not of soldiers alone, but the people." He denied, in effect, that Southerners had a right to resist invasion. When Union steamers were fired on near Randolph, Mississippi, in the fall of 1862, he destroyed Randolph, and a little later had all houses, farms, and cornfields devastated for fifteen miles along the banks.

When he drove his red plowshare across Georgia and the Carolinas, his object was to leave only scorched earth behind. He had already written of his Western operation: "Not a man is to be seen; nothing but women with houses plundered, fields open to the cattle and horses, pickets lounging on every porch, and desolation sown broadcast; servants all gone, and women and children bred in luxury . . . begging . . . for soldiers' rations." His aim was that which Phil Sheridan avowed: to leave them nothing but their eyes to weep with.

The final devastation of half the South was horrible to behold, and it was distressing to think that these savage losses had been inflicted by Americans upon fellow Americans. Yet this was far from being the worst aspect of the conflict, or the least easily reparable. Damages on which we can fix the dollar sign are important not in themselves, but as they become translated into cultural and spiritual losses; into the intellectual retardation caused by poverty, for example. The physical recovery of the South was rapid. As it was primarily an agricultural section, a few good crops at fair prices did much to restore it; and the swiftness with which housing, railroads, bridges, and public facilities were rebuilt astonished observers of the 1870s just as the swift postwar recovery of Germany and Poland has astonished observers of our day.

Infinitely worse were the biological losses—the radical hurts—inflicted by the Civil War. The killing of between 600,000 and 700,000 young men in a nation of 33,000,000 and the maiming or permanent debilitation of as many more had evil consequences projected into the far-distant future. We lost not only these men, but their children, and their children's children. Here, indeed, was a loss that proved highly cumulative. During the First World War, Lord Dunsany wrote a slender volume called *Tales of War*. One of his apologues showed the Kaiser, as the embodiment of German militarism, commanded by a spirit to come on a tour. They crossed the German plain to a neat garden. Look, said the spirit:

> The Kaiser looked; and saw a window shining and a neat room in a cottage; there was nothing dreadful there, thank the good German God for that; it was all right, after all. The Kaiser had had a fright, but it was all right, there was only a woman with a baby sitting before a fire, and two small children and a man. And it was quite a jolly room. And the man was a young soldier; and, why, he was a Prussian Guardsman—there was a helmet hanging on the wall—so everything was all right. They were jolly German children; that was well. How nice and homely the room was. . . . The firelight flickered, and the lamp shone on, and the children played on the floor, and the man was smoking out of a china pipe; he was strong and able and young, one of the wealth-winners of Germany.
> "Have you seen?" asked the phantom.
> "Yes," said the Kaiser. . . .
> At once the fire went out and the lamp faded away, the room fell

somberly into neglect and squalor, and the soldier and the children faded away with the room; all disappeared phantasmally, and nothing remained but the helmet in a kind of glow on the wall, and the woman sitting all by herself in the darkness.

"It has all gone," said the Kaiser.

"It has never been," said the phantom.

The Kaiser looked again. Yes, there was nothing there, it was just a vision. . . .

"It might have been," said the phantom.

Just so, we can say that the multitude of Civil War dead represent hundreds of thousands of homes, and hundreds of thousands of families, that might have been, and never were. They represent millions of people who might have been part of our population today and are not. We have lost the books they might have written, the scientific discoveries they might have made, the inventions they might have perfected. Such a loss defies measurement.

The only noteworthy attempt to measure the biological losses was made by David Starr Jordan and his son Harvey in a volume called *War's Aftermath* (1914). The authors circulated carefully drawn questionnaires in Spottsylvania and Rockbridge Counties in Virginia, and in Cobb County in Georgia, inquiring particularly into the eugenic effects of the conflict. One of their queries brought out evidence that by no means all casualties were among the men; numerous girls and women succumbed to the hardships and anxieties of the conflict in the South. Another question elicited unanimous agreement that "the flower of the people" went into the war at the beginning, and of these a large part died before the end. President Jordan, weighing all the responses, reached two conclusions: first, that the evidence "leaves a decided evidence in favor of grave racial hurt," and second, that "the war has seriously impoverished this country of its best human values."

Even the terrible loss of young, productive lives, the grave biological injury to the nation, however, did not constitute the worst side of the war. One aspect of the conflict was still more serious. It was the aspect to which Lowell referred in lines written a few years after Appomattox:

> *I looked to see an ampler atmosphere*
> *By that electric passion-gust blown clear*
> *I looked for this; consider what I hear. . . .*
> *Murmur of many voices in the air*
> *Denounces us degenerate,*
> *Unfaithful guardians of a noble fate. . . .*

The war, as Walt Whitman truly said, had grown out of defects in the American character; of American faults it cured few, accentuated a number, and gave some a violently dangerous trend. Far behind the lines, it added to the already discreditable total of violence in American life. Applying to industry a great forcing-draft, the bellows of huge wartime appropriations, it strengthened the materialistic forces in our civilization. Its state and federal contracts, its bounty system, its innumerable opportunities for battening on the nation's woes, made speculation fashionable, and corruption almost too common for comment. Its inflation bred extravagance and dissipation.

Every month heightened the intolerance of war; it began with mobs in New York threatening newspaper offices, a mob in Philadelphia trying to lynch Senator James A. Bayard, and mobs in the South flogging and exiling Union men; as it went on, freedom of speech almost disappeared over broad areas. The atmosphere of war fostered immorality; Richmond and Washington alike became filled with saloons, brothels, and gambling dens, and such occupied cities as Memphis and Nashville were sinks of iniquity. For every knightly martyr like James Wadsworth or Albert Sidney Johnston there arose two such coarse, aggressive, selfish careerists as Ben Butler and Dan Sickles. Wadsworth and Johnston died in battle, but Butler and Sickles remained to follow postwar political careers. Seen in perspective, the war was a gigantic engine for coarsening and lowering the American character even while it quickened certain of our energies.

Parson Brownlow, a Tennessee Unionist, went from city to city in the North in 1862 demanding "grape for the Rebel masses, and hemp for their leaders"; saying that he himself would tie the rope about the necks of some rebel generals; calling for the confiscation of all Southern property; proclaiming that he would be glad to arm every wolf, bear, catamount, and crocodile, every devil in hell, to defeat the South; and declaring he would put down the rebellion "if it exterminates from God's green earth every man, woman, and child south of Mason and Dixon's Line."

In the South two famous leaders, Robert Toombs and Howell Cobb, united that year in an address to their people just as vitriolic. "The foot of the oppressor is on the soil of Georgia," it began. "He comes with lust in his eye, poverty in his purse, and hell in his heart. How shall you meet him? . . . With death for him or for yourself!" Better the charnel house for every Southerner, they continued, than "loathsome vassalage to a nation already sunk below the contempt of the civilized world." Thaddeus Stevens nursed his hatred until he spoke of "exterminating" or driving into exile *all* Southerners, just as Sherman declared he would "slay millions" to assure the safety of the Mississippi. Women of the South meanwhile expressed the most vindictive detestation of all Yankees. "I hate them," wrote one Mississippi woman after a raid on their community, "more now than I did the evening I saw them sneaking off with all we cared for, and so it will be every day I live."

Hatred was seen in its most naked form in those communities divided against themselves and racked by guerrilla war; in Missouri, Arkansas, parts of Kentucky, and east Tennessee. Writes Charles D. Drake, a distinguished Missouri leader, of his state: "Falsehood, treachery, and perjury pervaded the whole social fabric." He went on: "Could there be written a full account of all the crimes of the rebels of Missouri, and the outrages and wrongs inflicted by them upon her loyal inhabitants, during the four years of the rebellion, the world would shrink aghast from a picture which has no parallel in the previous history of any portion of the Anglo-Saxon race." Confederate sympathizers in Missouri would have said the same of Union irregulars. One atrocity provoked another. These hatreds long survived the conflict, and indeed in some spots the embers still smoulder. Typifying the whole range of spiritual injuries wrought by the war, they justify the poet Blake's cry:

> *The soldier, armed with sword and gun,*
> *Palsied strikes the summer sun.*

The historian Mendelssohn Bartholdy, in his volume entitled *War and German Society*, written as part of the Carnegie Endowment's huge economic history of World War I, concluded that the moral effects of war are much worse than the material effects. He also concluded that they are radically bad, for they strike at the very heart of a country's character; "modern war, with its robot-like disregard of individual values, is bound to make the peculiar virtue of a nation an object of attack." As respects the Civil War, we can agree. If it was necessary for preserving the Union and extinguishing slavery, it was of course worth more than it cost; but should it have been necessary? Could not better leadership from 1830 to 1860 have averted it? This is a bootless question. But it is certain that the conflict, so much the greatest convulsion in our history, so tremendous in its impact on our national life, so fascinating in its drama, was in spite of all compensating elements, all the heroism, all the high example we find in Lee's character and Lincoln's wisdom, materially a disaster and morally a tragedy.

It is unfortunate that of the flood of books on the war ninety-nine in a hundred are on military topics and leaders, and that a great majority fasten attention on the floating banners, the high-ringing cheers, the humors of the camp, the ardors of the charge; the whole undeniable fascination and romance of the first true *volkskrieg* in history. It is right, within measure, to let them lift our hearts. But the long commemoration will pass essentially unimproved if it does not give us a deeper, sterner, more scientific study of the collision of two creeds and two ways of life as related to an examination of war in general.

We should probe more deeply into its roots, a process that will expose some of the weaknesses of our social fabric and governmental system. We should pay fuller attention to its darker aspects, and examine more honestly such misrepresentations as the statement it was distinguished by its generosity of spirit, the magnanimity with which the combatants treated each other; a statement absurd on its face, for no war which lasts four years and costs 600,000 lives leaves much magnanimity in its later phases. We should above all examine more closely the effects of the great and terrible war not on the nation's politics—we know that; not on its economy—we also know that; but on its character, the vital element of national life.

This examination will lead into unpleasant paths, and bring us to unhappy conclusions; but it will profit us far more than stirring battle canvases. All nations must be schooled in such studies if the world is ever to find an answer to a question uttered just after World War I by William E. Borah, a question that still rings in men's ears: "When shall we escape from war? When shall we loosen the grip of the monster?"

QUESTIONS TO CONSIDER

1. What outrageous conclusion does Nevins "logically" propose if the good in the Civil War outweighed the bad, as the literature seems to suggest?
2. What are two erroneous views of the Civil War that Nevins seeks to correct?
3. What is the point of the story about the German Kaiser?
4. What does Nevins claim is even more significant than the appalling maiming of men's bodies, and why?
5. What does Nevins call for in his conclusion?
6. What is your response to this article? Given the rise of television, have views of war changed since Nevins wrote it in 1961? In what way?

16

The New View
of Reconstruction*

Eric Foner

Eric Foner (1943–   ), both educated and educator at Columbia
University, is one of the fine scholars engaged in exploring the gaps
between perception and reality in the Civil War and Reconstruction era. He takes particular interest in blacks and radicalism. Two
of his books indicate his area of expertise: *Politics and Ideology in
the Age of the Civil War* (1981) and *Nothing but Freedom: Emancipation and Its Legacy* (1983). In 1988 he published a full-length
and well-received treatment of the subject of this article: *Reconstruction: America's Unfinished Revolution, 1863–1877.*

In this 1983 selection from *American Heritage,* Foner offers a
clear picture of the view of Reconstruction that prevailed from the
1870s through the 1950s and explains why it is no longer convincing. Reconstruction provides a good case study of historiography,
the history of history. As long as white racism was the social and historical norm, radical northern attempts to force black equality on
the South during Reconstruction appeared misguided, if not
downright malevolent. The civil rights movement in the 1950s and
1960s forced historians to reevaluate both their attitudes toward
current racial issues and their interpretations of the past. This new
look led to a shift in the roles of heroes and villains in Reconstruction. Now the Radical Republicans became the good guys and

*Reprinted by permission of *American Heritage* Magazine, a division of Forbes, Inc.
© Forbes, Inc., 1983.

President Andrew Johnson and southern obstructionists the obstacles to racial progress.

Foner suggests that a new, more radical, view has emerged: Reconstruction was simply not radical enough. The failure of the Radical Republicans to provide "forty acres and a mule" or any economic stake in the new postwar society left the freedmen at the mercy of their former masters—with the resultant economic gap lasting down to the present. Nevertheless, the door of hope was opened and blacks have been struggling through it ever since what W. E. B. DuBois termed the "splendid failure" of Reconstruction.

The American character is not static. Frederick Jackson Turner argued that the frontier was the most important factor forging it. Foner's article depicts human, political attempts to reshape it. The debate over Reconstruction is in part a debate over whether the Radical Republicans, promoting greater racial equality, or the Southern Redeemers, seeking continued racial supremacy, were truer to what the American character has been—or could be.

In the past twenty years, no period of American history has been the subject of a more thoroughgoing reevaluation than Reconstruction—the violent, dramatic, and still controversial era following the Civil War. Race relations, politics, social life, and economic change during Reconstruction have all been reinterpreted in the light of changed attitudes toward the place of blacks within American society. If historians have not yet forged a fully satisfying portrait of Reconstruction as a whole, the traditional interpretation that dominated historical writing for much of this century has irrevocably been laid to rest.

Anyone who attended high school before 1960 learned that Reconstruction was an era of unrelieved sordidness in American political and social life. The martyred Lincoln, according to this view, had planned a quick and painless readmission of the Southern states as equal members of the national family. President Andrew Johnson, his successor, attempted to carry out Lincoln's policies but was foiled by the Radical Republicans (also known as Vindictives or Jacobins). Motivated by an irrational hatred of Rebels or by ties with Northern capitalists out to plunder the South, the Radicals swept aside Johnson's lenient program and fastened black supremacy upon the defeated Confederacy. An orgy of corruption followed, presided over by unscrupulous carpetbaggers (Northerners who ventured south to reap the spoils of office), traitorous scalawags (Southern whites who cooperated with the new governments for personal gain), and the ignorant and childlike freedmen, who were incapable of properly exercising the political power that had been thrust upon them. After much needless suffering, the white community of the South banded together to overthrow these "black" governments and restore home rule (their euphemism for white supremacy). All told, Reconstruction was just about the darkest page in the American saga.

Originating in anti-Reconstruction propaganda of Southern Democrats during the 1870s, this traditional interpretation achieved scholarly legitimacy around the turn of the century through the work of William Dunning and his students at Columbia University. It reached the larger public through films like *Birth of a Nation* and *Gone With the Wind* and that best-selling work of myth-making masquerading as history, *The Tragic Era,* by Claude G. Bowers. In language as exaggerated as it was colorful, Bowers told how Andrew Johnson "fought the bravest battle for constitutional liberty and for the preservation of our institutions ever waged by an Executive" but was overwhelmed by the "poisonous propaganda" of the Radicals. Southern whites, as a result, "literally were put to the torture" by "emissaries of hate" who manipulated the "simple-minded" freedmen, "inflaming the negroes' egotism" and even inspiring "lustful assaults" by blacks upon white womanhood.

In a discipline that sometimes seems to pride itself on the rapid rise and fall of historical interpretations, this traditional portrait of Reconstruction enjoyed remarkable staying power. The long reign of the old interpretation is not difficult to explain. It presented a set of easily identifiable heroes and villains. It enjoyed the imprimatur of the nation's leading scholars. And it accorded with the political and social realities of the first half of this century. This image of Reconstruction helped freeze the mind of the white South in unalterable opposition to any movement for breaching the ascendancy of the Democratic party, eliminating segregation, or readmitting disfranchised blacks to the vote.

Nevertheless, the demise of the traditional interpretation was inevitable, for it ignored the testimony of the central participant in the drama of Reconstruction—the black freedman. Furthermore, it was grounded in the conviction that blacks were unfit to share in political power. As Dunning's Columbia colleague John W. Burgess put it, "A black skin means membership in a race of men which has never of itself succeeded in subjecting passion to reason, has never, therefore, created any civilization of any kind." Once objective scholarship and modern experience rendered that assumption untenable, the entire edifice was bound to fall.

The work of "revising" the history of Reconstruction began with the writings of a handful of survivors of the era, such as John R. Lynch, who had served as a black congressman from Mississippi after the Civil War. In the 1930s white scholars like Francis Simkins and Robert Woody carried the task forward. Then, in 1935, the black historian and activist W. E. B. DuBois produced *Black Reconstruction in America,* a monumental reevaluation that closed with an irrefutable indictment of a historical profession that had sacrificed scholarly objectivity on the altar of racial bias. "One fact and one alone," he wrote, "explains the attitude of most recent writers toward Reconstruction; they cannot conceive of Negroes as men." DuBois's work, however, was ignored by most historians.

It was not until the 1960s that the full force of the revisionist wave broke over the field. Then, in rapid succession, virtually every assumption of the traditional viewpoint was systematically dismantled. A drastically different portrait emerged to take its place. President Lincoln did not have a coherent "plan" for Reconstruction, but at the time of his assassination he had been cautiously contemplating black suffrage. Andrew Johnson was a stubborn, racist politician who lacked the ability to compromise. By isolating himself from the broad currents of public opinion that had nourished Lincoln's career, Johnson created an impasse with Congress that Lincoln would certainly have avoided, thus throwing away his political power and destroying his own plans for reconstructing the South.

The Radicals in Congress were acquitted of both vindictive motives and the charge of serving as the stalking-horses of Northern capitalism. They emerged instead as idealists in the best nineteenth-century reform tradition. Radical leaders like Charles Sumner and Thaddeus Stevens had worked for the rights of blacks long before any conceivable political advantage flowed from such a commitment. Stevens refused to sign the Pennsylvania Constitution of 1838 because it disfranchised the state's black citizens; Sumner led a fight in the 1850s to integrate Boston's public schools. Their Reconstruction policies were based on principle, not petty political advantage, for the central issue dividing Johnson and these Radical Republicans was the civil rights of freedmen. Studies of congressional policy-making, such as Eric L. McKitrick's *Andrew Johnson and Reconstruction*, also revealed that Reconstruction legislation, ranging from the Civil Rights Act of 1866 to the Fourteenth and Fifteenth Amendments, enjoyed broad support from moderate and conservative Republicans. It was not simply the work of a narrow radical faction.

Even more startling was the revised portrait of Reconstruction in the South itself. Imbued with the spirit of the civil rights movement and rejecting entirely the racial assumptions that had underpinned the traditional interpretation, these historians evaluated Reconstruction from the black point of view. Works like Joel Williamson's *After Slavery* portrayed the period as a time of extraordinary political, social, and economic progress for blacks. The establishment of public school systems, the granting of equal citizenship to blacks, the effort to restore the devastated Southern economy, the attempt to construct an interracial political democracy from the ashes of slavery, all these were commendable achievements, not the elements of Bowers's "tragic era."

Unlike earlier writers, the revisionists stressed the active role of the freedmen in shaping Reconstruction. Black initiative established as many schools as did Northern religious societies and the Freedmen's Bureau. The right to vote was not simply thrust upon them by meddling outsiders, since blacks began agitating for the suffrage as soon as they were freed. In 1865 black conventions throughout the South issued eloquent, though unheeded, appeals for equal civil and political rights.

With the advent of Radical Reconstruction in 1867, the freedmen did enjoy a real measure of political power. But black supremacy never existed. In most states blacks held only a small fraction of political offices, and even in South Carolina, where they comprised a majority of the state legislature's lower house, effective power remained in white hands. As for corruption, moral standards in both government and private enterprise were at low ebb throughout the nation in the postwar years—the era of Boss Tweed, the Credit Mobilier scandal, and the Whiskey Ring. Southern corruption could hardly be blamed on former slaves.

Other actors in the Reconstruction drama also came in for reevaluation. Most carpetbaggers were former Union soldiers seeking economic opportunity in the postwar South, not unscrupulous adventurers. Their motives, a typically American amalgam of humanitarianism and the pursuit of profit, were no more insidious than those of Western pioneers. Scalawags, previously seen as traitors to the white race, now emerged as "Old Line" Whig Unionists who had opposed secession in the first place or as poor whites who had long resented planters' domination of Southern life and who saw in Reconstruction a chance to recast Southern society along more democratic lines. Strongholds of Southern white Republicanism like east Tennessee and western North Carolina had been the scene of resistance to Confederate rule throughout the Civil War; now, as one scalawag newspaper put it, the choice was "between salvation at the hand of the Negro or destruction at the hand of the rebels."

At the same time, the Ku Klux Klan and kindred groups, whose campaign of violence against black and white Republicans had been minimized or excused in older writings, were portrayed as they really were. Earlier scholars had conveyed the impression that the Klan intimidated blacks mainly by dressing as ghosts and playing on the freedmen's superstitions. In fact, black fears were all too real: the Klan was a terrorist organization that beat and killed its political opponents to deprive blacks of their newly won rights. The complicity of the Democratic party and the silence of prominent whites in the face of such outrages stood as a indictment of the moral code the South had inherited from the days of slavery.

By the end of the 1960s, then, the old interpretation had been completely reversed. Southern freedmen were the heroes, the "Redeemers" who overthrew Reconstruction were the villains, and if the era was "tragic," it was because change did not go far enough. Reconstruction had been a time of real progress and its failure a lost opportunity for the South and the nation. But the legacy of Reconstruction—the Fourteenth and Fifteenth Amendments—endured to inspire future efforts for civil rights. As Kenneth Stampp wrote in *The Era of Reconstruction*, a superb summary of revisionist findings published in 1965, "If it was worth four years of civil war to save the Union, it was worth a few years of radical reconstruction to give the American Negro the ultimate promise of equal civil and political rights."

As Stampp's statement suggests, the reevaluation of the first Reconstruction was inspired in large measure by the impact of the second—the modern civil rights movement. And with the waning of that movement in recent years, writing on Reconstruction has undergone still another transformation. Instead of seeing the Civil War and its aftermath as a second American Revolution (as Charles Beard had), a regression into barbarism (as Bowers argued), or a golden opportunity squandered (as the revisionists saw it), recent writers argue that Radical Reconstruction was not really very radical. Since land was not distributed to the former slaves, they remained economically dependent upon their former owners. The planter class survived both the war and Reconstruction with its property (apart from slaves) and prestige more or less intact.

Not only changing times but also the changing concerns of historians have contributed to this latest reassessment of Reconstruction. The hallmark of the past decade's historical writing has been an emphasis upon "social history"—the evocation of the past lives of ordinary Americans—and the downplaying of strictly political events. When applied to Reconstruction, this concern with the "social" suggested that black suffrage and officeholding, once seen as the most radical departures of the Reconstruction era, were relatively insignificant.

Recent historians have focused their investigations not upon the politics of Reconstruction but upon the social and economic aspects of the transition from slavery to freedom. Herbert Gutman's influential study of the black family during and after slavery found little change in family structure or relations between men and women resulting from emancipation. Under slavery most blacks had lived in nuclear family units, although they faced the constant threat of separation from loved ones by sale. Reconstruction provided the opportunity for blacks to solidify their preexisting family ties. Conflicts over whether black women should work in the cotton fields (planters said yes, many black families said no) and over white attempts to "apprentice" black children revealed that the autonomy of family life was a major preoccupation of the freedmen. Indeed, whether manifested in their withdrawal from churches controlled by whites, in the blossoming of black fraternal, benevolent, and self-improvement organizations, or in the demise of the slave quarters and their replacement by small tenant farms occupied by individual families, the quest for independence from white authority and control over their own day-to-day lives shaped the black response to emancipation.

In the post–Civil War South the surest guarantee of economic autonomy, blacks believed, was land. To the freedmen the justice of a claim to land based on their years of unrequited labor appeared self-evident. As an Alabama black convention put it, "The property which they [the planters] hold was nearly all earned by the sweat of *our* brows." As Leon Litwack showed in *Been in the Storm So Long,* a Pulitzer Prize-winning account of the black response to emancipation, many freedmen in 1865 and 1866 refused to sign labor contracts, expecting the federal government to give them land. In some localities, as one Alabama overseer reported, they "set up claims to the plantation and all on it."

In the end, of course, the vast majority of Southern blacks remained propertyless and poor. But exactly why the South, and especially its black population, suffered from dire poverty and economic retardation in the decades following the Civil War is a matter of much dispute. In *One Kind of Freedom,* economists Roger Ransom and Richard Sutch indicted country merchants for monopolizing credit and charging usurious interest rates, forcing black tenants into debt and locking the South into a dependence on cotton production that impoverished the entire region. But Jonathan Wiener, in his study of postwar Alabama, argued that planters used their political power to compel blacks to remain on the plantations. Planters succeeded in stabilizing the plantation system, but only by blocking the growth of alternative enterprises, like factories, that might draw off black laborers, thus locking the region into a pattern of economic backwardness.

If the thrust of recent writing has emphasized the social and economic aspects of Reconstruction, politics has not been entirely neglected. But political studies have also reflected the postrevisionist mood summarized by C. Vann Woodward when he observed "how essentially nonrevolutionary and conservative Reconstruction really was." Recent writers, unlike their revisionist predecessors, have found little to praise in federal policy toward the emancipated blacks.

A new sensitivity to the strength of prejudice and laissez-faire ideas in the nineteenth-century North has led many historians to doubt whether the Republican party ever made a genuine commitment to racial justice in the South. The granting of black suffrage was an alternative to a long-term federal responsibility for protecting the rights of the former slaves. Once enfranchised, blacks could be left to fend for themselves. With the exception of a few Radicals like Thaddeus Stevens, nearly all Northern policy-makers and educators are criticized today for assuming that, so long as the unfettered operations of the marketplace afforded blacks the opportunity to advance through diligent labor, federal efforts to assist them in acquiring land were unnecessary.

Probably the most innovative recent writing on Reconstruction politics has centered on a broad reassessment of black Republicanism, largely undertaken by a new generation of black historians. Scholars like Thomas Holt and Nell Painter insist that Reconstruction was not simply a matter of black and white. Conflicts within the black community, no less than divisions among whites, shaped Reconstruction politics. Where revisionist scholars, both black and white, had celebrated the accomplishments of black political leaders, Holt, Painter, and others charge that they failed to address the economic plight of the black masses. Painter criticized "representative colored men," as national black leaders were called, for failing to provide ordinary freedmen with effective political leadership. Holt found that black officeholders in South Carolina mostly emerged from the old free mulatto class of Charleston, which shared many assumptions with prominent whites. "Basically bourgeois in their origins and orientation," he wrote, they "failed to act in the interest of black peasants."

In emphasizing the persistence from slavery of divisions between free blacks and slaves, these writers reflect the increasing concern with continuity and conservatism in Reconstruction. Their work reflects a startling extension of revisionist premises. If, as has been argued for the past twenty years, blacks were active agents rather than mere victims of manipulation, then they could not be absolved of blame for the ultimate failure of Reconstruction.

Despite the excellence of recent writing and the continual expansion of our knowledge of the period, historians of Reconstruction today face a unique dilemma. An old interpretation has been overthrown, but a coherent new synthesis has yet to take its place. The revisionists of the 1960s effectively established a series of negative points: the Reconstruction governments were not as bad as had been portrayed, black supremacy was a myth, the Radicals were not cynical manipulators of the freedmen. Yet no convincing overall portrait of the quality of political and social life emerged from their writings. More recent historians have rightly pointed to elements of continuity that spanned the nineteenth-century Southern experience, especially the survival, in modified form, of the plantation system. Nevertheless, by denying the real changes that did occur, they have failed to provide a convincing portrait of an era characterized above all by drama, turmoil, and social change.

Building upon the findings of the past twenty years of scholarship, a new portrait of Reconstruction ought to begin by viewing it not as a specific time period, bounded by the years 1865 and 1877, but as an episode in a prolonged historical process—American society's adjustment to the consequences of the Civil War and emancipation. The Civil War, of course, raised the decisive questions of America's national existence: the relations between local and national authority, the definition of citizenship, the balance between force and consent in generating obedience to authority. The war and Reconstruction, as Allan Nevins observed over fifty years ago, marked the "emergence of modern America." This was the era of the completion of the national railroad network, the creation of the modern steel industry, the conquest of the West and final subduing of the Indians, and the expansion of the mining frontier. Lincoln's America—the world of the small farm and artisan shop—gave way to a rapidly industrializing economy. The issues that galvanized postwar Northern politics—from the question of the greenback currency to the mode of paying holders of the national debt—arose from the economic changes unleashed by the Civil War.

Above all, the war irrevocably abolished slavery. Since 1619, when "twenty negars" disembarked from a Dutch ship in Virginia, racial injustice had haunted American life, mocking its professed ideals even as tobacco and cotton, the products of slave labor, helped finance the nation's economic development. Now the implications of the black presence could no longer be ignored. The Civil War resolved the problem of slavery but, as the Philadelphia diarist Sydney George Fisher observed in June 1865, it opened an even more intractable problem: "What shall we do with the Negro?" Indeed, he went on, this was a problem "*incapable* of any solution that will satisfy both North and South."

As Fisher realized, the focal point of Reconstruction was the social revolution known as emancipation. Plantation slavery was simultaneously a system of labor, a form of racial domination, and the foundation upon which arose a distinctive ruling class within the South. Its demise threw open the most fundamental questions of economy, society, and politics. A new system of labor, social, racial, and political relations had to be created to replace slavery.

The United States was not the only nation to experience emancipation in the nineteenth century. Neither plantation slavery nor abolition were unique to the United States. But Reconstruction was. In a comparative perspective Radical Reconstruction stands as a remarkable experiment, the only effort of a society experiencing abolition to bring the former slaves within the umbrella of equal citizenship. Because the Radicals did not achieve everything they wanted, historians have lately tended to play down the stunning departure represented by black suffrage and officeholding. Former slaves, most fewer than two years removed from bondage, debated the fundamental questions of the polity: What is a republican form of government? Should the state provide equal education for all? How could political equality be reconciled with a society in which property was so unequally distributed? There was something inspiring in the way such men met the challenge of Reconstruction. "I knew nothing more than to obey my master," James K. Greene, an Alabama black politician later recalled. "But the tocsin of freedom sounded and knocked at the door and we walked out like free men and we met the exigencies as they grew up, and shouldered the responsibilities."

"You never saw a people more excited on the subject of politics than are the negroes of the south," one planter observed in 1867. And there were more than a few Southern whites as well who in these years shook off the prejudices of the past to embrace the vision of a new South dedicated to the principles of equal citizenship and social justice. One ordinary South Carolinian expressed the new sense of possibility in 1868 to the Republican governor of the state: "I am sorry that I cannot write an elegant stiled letter to your excellency. But I rejoice to think that God almighty has given to the poor of S. C. a Gov. to hear to feel to protect the humble poor without distinction to race or color. . . . I am a native borned S. C. a poor man never owned a Negro in my life nor my father before me. . . . Remember the true and loyal are the poor of the whites and blacks, outside of these you can find none loyal."

Few modern scholars believe the Reconstruction governments established in the South in 1867 and 1868 fulfilled the aspirations of their humble constituents. While their achievements in such realms as education, civil rights, and the economic rebuilding of the South are now widely appreciated, historians today believe they failed to affect either the economic plight of the emancipated slave or the ongoing transformation of independent white farmers into cotton tenants. Yet their opponents did perceive the Reconstruction governments in precisely this way—as representatives of a revolution that had put the bottom rail, both racial and economic, on top. This perception helps explain the ferocity of the attacks leveled against them and the pervasiveness of violence in the postemancipation South.

The spectacle of black men voting and holding office was anathema to large numbers of Southern whites. Even more disturbing, at least in the view of those who still controlled the plantation regions of the South, was the emergence of local officials, black and white, who sympathized with the plight of the black laborer. Alabama's vagrancy law was a "dead letter" in 1870, "because those who are charged with its enforcement are indebted to the vagrant vote for their offices and emoluments." Political debates over the level and incidence of taxation, the control of crops, and the resolution of contract disputes revealed that a primary issue of Reconstruction was the role of government in a plantation society. During presidential Reconstruction, and after "Redemption," with planters and their allies in control of politics, the law emerged as a means of stabilizing and promoting the plantation system. If Radical Reconstruction failed to redistribute the land of the South, the ouster of the planter class from control of politics at least ensured that the sanctions of the criminal law would not be employed to discipline the black labor force.

An understanding of this fundamental conflict over the relation between government and society helps explain the pervasive complaints concerning corruption and "extravagance" during Radical Reconstruction. Corruption there was a plenty; tax rates did rise sharply. More significant than the rate of taxation, however, was the change in its incidence. For the first time, planters and white farmers had to pay a significant portion of their income to the government, while propertyless blacks often escaped scot-free. Several states, moreover, enacted heavy taxes on uncultivated land to discourage land speculation and force land onto the market, benefiting, it was hoped, the freedmen.

As time passed, complaints about the "extravagance" and corruption of Southern governments found a sympathetic audience among influential Northerners. The Democratic charge that universal suffrage in the South was responsible for high taxes and governmental extravagance coincided with a rising conviction among the urban middle classes of the North that city government had to be taken out of the hands of the immigrant poor and returned to the "best men"—the educated, professional, financially independent citizens unable to exert much political influence at a time of mass parties and machine politics. Increasingly the "respectable" middle classes began to retreat from the very notion of universal suffrage. The poor were no longer perceived as honest producers, the backbone of the social order; now they became the "dangerous classes," the "mob." As the historian Francis Parkman put it, too much power rested with "masses of imported ignorance and hereditary ineptitude." To Parkman the Irish of the Northern cities and the blacks of the South were equally incapable of utilizing the ballot: "Witness the municipal corruptions of New York, and the monstrosities of negro rule in South Carolina." Such attitudes helped to justify Northern inaction as, one by one, the Reconstruction regimes of the South were overthrown by political violence.

In the end, then, neither the abolition of slavery nor Reconstruction succeeded in resolving the debate over the meaning of freedom in American life. Twenty years before the American Civil War, writing about the prospect of abolition in France's colonies, Alexis de Tocqueville had written, "If the Negroes have the right to become free, the [planters] have the incontestable right not to be ruined by the Negroes' freedom." And in the United States, as in nearly every plantation society that experienced the end of slavery, a rigid social and political dichotomy between former master and former slave, an ideology of racism, and a dependent labor force with limited economic opportunities all survived abolition. Unless one means by freedom the simple fact of not being a slave, emancipation thrust blacks into a kind of no-man's land, a partial freedom that made a mockery of the American ideal of equal citizenship.

Yet by the same token the ultimate outcome underscores the uniqueness of Reconstruction itself. Alone among the societies that abolished slavery in the nineteenth century, the United States, for a moment, offered the freedmen a measure of political control over their own destinies. However brief its sway, Reconstruction allowed scope for a remarkable political and social mobilization of the black community. It opened doors of opportunity that could never be completely closed. Reconstruction transformed the lives of Southern blacks in ways unmeasurable by statistics and unreachable by law. It raised their expectations and aspirations, redefined their status in relation to the larger society, and allowed space for the creation of institutions that enabled them to survive the repression that followed. And it established constitutional principles of civil and political equality that, while flagrantly violated after Redemption, planted the seeds of future struggle.

Certainly, in terms of the sense of possibility with which it opened, Reconstruction failed. But as DuBois observed, it was a "splendid failure." For its animating vision—a society in which social advancement would be open to all on the basis of individual merit, not inherited caste distinctions—is as old as America itself and remains relevant to a nation still grappling with the unresolved legacy of emancipation.

QUESTIONS TO CONSIDER

1. Prior to 1960, who did historians describe as the "good guys" and "bad guys" of Reconstruction? Why?
2. What caused that long-lived interpretation to crumble?
3. What was the focal point of Reconstruction, according to Foner and Sydney George Fisher?

4. In the long run, how did Reconstruction most fail the freedmen? Why did it happen and why was it critical?

5. Does Foner conclude the Reconstruction was a success or a failure? What do *you* conclude?